CARBON CAPITAL

Carbon Capital

Climate Change and the Ethics of Oil Investing

Sean Field

NEW YORK UNIVERSITY PRESS
New York

NEW YORK UNIVERSITY PRESS
New York
www.nyupress.org

© 2025 by New York University
All rights reserved

Library of Congress Cataloging-in-Publication Data

Names: Field, Sean (Energy policy analyst), author.
Title: Carbon capital : climate change and the ethics of oil investing / Sean Field.
Description: New York : New York University Press, [2025] | Includes bibliographical references and index.
Identifiers: LCCN 2024041478 (print) | LCCN 2024041479 (ebook) | ISBN 9781479831692 (hardback ; alk. paper) | ISBN 9781479831708 (paperback ; alk. paper) | ISBN 9781479831715 (ebook) | ISBN 9781479831722 (ebook other)
Subjects: LCSH: Petroleum industry and trade—United States—Finance. | Gas industry—United States—Finance. | Energy industries—Moral and ethical aspects—United States. | Climatic changes.
Classification: LCC HD9565 .F54 2025 (print) | LCC HD9565 (ebook) | DDC 338.2/72820973—dc23/eng/20250212
LC record available at https://lccn.loc.gov/2024041478
LC ebook record available at https://lccn.loc.gov/2024041479

This book is printed on acid-free paper, and its binding materials are chosen for strength and durability. We strive to use environmentally responsible suppliers and materials to the greatest extent possible in publishing our books.

The manufacturer's authorized representative in the EU for product safety is Mare Nostrum Group B.V., Mauritskade 21D, 1091 GC Amsterdam, The Netherlands.
Email: gpsr@mare-nostrum.co.uk.

Manufactured in the United States of America

10 9 8 7 6 5 4 3 2 1

Also available as an ebook

For Rilke, Esban, Fyfe, Quinn, Meagan, Noah, and Ethan

CONTENTS

Introduction	1
1. The Lone Star State	35
2. Financing the US Shale Revolution	57
3. Ethical Calculations	86
4. Not a Dichotomy: Climate Change and Hydrocarbons	106
5. "What the Hell Is ESG?" and the Moral Case for Oil	131
Conclusion	159
Acknowledgments	169
Notes	171
References	179
Index	197
About the Author	207

Introduction

"You don't care, you're dirty, you're old-fashioned, and just need to go away," Tony said, paraphrasing the criticism directed at the US oil and gas industry. Then, after a moment of pause and with a note of contemplation in his voice, he reflected on this criticism, on *his* place in the industry, and *this* industry's place in the world. "Are they right? Are they right to some degree? Where do I fit in? What good do I do for society? ... Are we a force for good or not?"

I first met Tony in early 2019, shortly after I had arrived in Houston, Texas. One of my interlocutors had introduced us over email, and Tony suggested that we meet at the luxurious street-level bar and restaurant of the JW Marriot in downtown Houston, across the street from his work. It was a balmy Houston afternoon and downtown was coming alive as people began to depart from their office-tower enclaves on their way home, on their way for a drink with colleagues, or on their way to the gym with gym bag in hand. I arrived early and was scanning the sparsely populated bar, tables, and lush brown leather couches for Tony at this transitional hour before the dinner and after-work rush, when he messaged me: "On my way ... orange tie." Arriving a few minutes later, Tony sported a suave crisp grey suit, white shirt, the tie, and neatly parted hair. He immediately reminded me of Don Draper from the American television series *Mad Men*, with whom he shares a striking likeness. We found seats near one of the large windows looking out onto bustling Main Street, and began to chat. He told me that he liked to help "cowboy" oil entrepreneurs who need $50–$500 million in financing to get their exploration and production projects going—"small range" private equity, debt, venture capital, as he put it. A veteran of oil and gas finance, Tony leads his own Houston-based firm, which specializes in channeling private investment capital into oil and gas assets and companies. From the midwestern United States, he came to Houston to start an MBA in finance and never left. He explained, "I came to this industry with the viewpoint that it's not very exciting, not very smart, not very clean, because Exxon Valdez had happened just a few years before. That was the most of what I knew about the industry. It was, you know, *bad*. And we weren't talking about global warming at that time."

He does not think that anymore. He joked that people outside of the industry think that oil and gas is about "killing babies"; but in his view, the wealth that the oil and gas industry has generated has helped reduce global poverty and infant mortality. He explained, "There's a huge correlation with energy and the eradication of poverty." He continued, "It's okay to say that 'hey I'm worried about CO_2 that it might affect the climate, is affecting the climate, or has affected the climate.' Okay. But energy plays a huge role in the economy, much of it is positive. And to add up the positives and negatives, with any decision, I think is an important basic framework.

Nobody wants to work in an industry that is 'killing people,' but to actually live in a society with . . . no power, it's really kind of interesting," he said skeptically. By "power" he meant electricity and the fuel that feeds combustion engines big and small, implying the centrality of hydrocarbons to enabling fulfilling lives and lifestyles. Moreover, he argued, the oil and gas that he helps produce are the basis for "freedom." He illustrated his point with an example, explaining that "public transit is great" but "what are your options on the train? Sixteen to twenty stops? With a car, you can go anywhere." The American oil and gas industry, he told me, provides low-cost forms of energy that heat homes, keep the lights on, power air conditioning, charge devices, and fuel vehicles, and "cheap transportation is freedom on steroids." He is not against electric cars or renewable energy, and he is concerned about anthropogenic climate change, but he is *for* the hydrocarbon industry because, for Tony, the benefits of hydrocarbons outweigh the risks. Tony is not alone.

Far from black-and-white, and marked with nuance and idiosyncrasies, Tony's sentiments are shared by many I came to know in the US oil and gas finance industries. Tony evaluates oil and gas with a libertarian sensibility that embraces American capitalism in all its diversity. He is also a man of strong Christian faith who values family and community, and these values animate his sensibilities toward oil and gas. The hydrocarbon exploration and production activities that he and others help finance generate financial benefits for an array of investors, including universities, hospitals, and pension funds, as well as materially provisioning the energy needed for our ways of living, our lifestyles, and our livelihoods.[1] How he and others in the industry ethically evaluate energy is of consequence. Since the mid-2000s, financiers like Tony have helped turn the US hydrocarbon sector from a sunset industry into the largest producer of oil and gas in the world, to the cheers of industry insiders and the protest of climate change activists.

This book is about the people who finance the US oil and gas industry. It is about how they ethically value hydrocarbon extraction in the face of climate change, the factors that influence the ethical frameworks by which they navigate the world, the futures they imagine and are working to create, and how they draw on these factors and imaginaries to weave future-gazing allegorical narratives. It is about what they judge to be right and good and why. The goal of this book is to show that energy financiers are moral agents who apply ethical frameworks to evaluate what energy projects, companies, and, indeed, worldly *futures* should be materialized or even imagined.

To make this case, I draw on ethnographic field research that I have conducted with oil and gas financiers in Houston, Texas. My interlocutors include private equity partners, managing directors, bankers, lawyers, accountants, consultants, geologists, and engineers engaged in the practice of energy investing and lending. Many of my interlocutors hold senior and leadership positions. They have let me into their offices, their homes, and their lives, enabling me to carry out interviews, participate in private industry events, "hang out" with them socially over dinner at home and at the pool, and observe the oil finance sector from inside its close-knit social circles, which cut across firms. In a world faced with anthropogenic climate change and rising energy demand and tumultuous energy markets, the kinds of futures that are materialized will in part be shaped by the ethical sensibilities of these financiers. These sensibilities influence the sorts of futures that they deem to be "right" and "good" and are guided by the way they reconcile calculations of economic value with their broader social values.

The title *Carbon Capital* is influenced by Timothy Mitchell's (2011) *Carbon Democracy* and recent calls for the decarbonization of capital.[2] In his concluding chapter, Mitchell argues that the uncertainty caused by the combination of rising energy demand, the end of "cheap" hydrocarbon energy, and anthropogenic climate change is creating the circumstances by which economic calculation is displacing democratic debate. At the same time, Paul Langley and colleagues have observed that while "private investment capital is now widely held to be strategically significant to the governance of climate change," the ethical evaluation of low- and high-carbon investments still rests on future financial "risk and return" calculations by financial professionals, their shareholders, and their investors (Langley et al. 2021: 495, 511). Without critically and empathetically understanding the diversity of investor and financial practitioner perspectives, as well as the social-ethical dynamics that drive them, scholars, publics, and policymakers may be lying to themselves about possibilities for achieving net-zero and curbing climate change. They may, for example, find themselves in an echo chamber of calls for fossil fuel divestment, new net-zero announcements, and celebratory statements about Environmental, Social, and Governance (ESG) frameworks and the growth of the sustainable bond market, while ignoring real investor sentiments and trends in energy capital, exploration, and production. Moreover, by not seizing this critical moment for research at the intersection of business, investing, ethics, and climate change, they may miss an opportunity to forge new understandings that incite meaningful interventions where previous interventions have failed.

By contrast with assertions that those who work in the hydrocarbon industry are "immoral" (Hughes 2017: 148) and should be cast to the wastebin of time, I argue that the people I came to know are highly moral, but that the ethical frameworks by which they evaluate hydrocarbons, energy, and climate change lead them to different conclusions from those who oppose the industry. These ethical frameworks are informed by the historical context in which they operate, their Christian cosmologies, their own political-economic projects, and the broader capitalist system in which they are operating, all of which come together to shape their moral understandings about what a good energy future looks like. My interlocutors point to the wealth that the oil and gas industry has generated and how it has helped to reduce global poverty and infant mortality, and the outsize role, much of it positive, that energy plays in the economy. They may not be against electric cars or renewable energy, and they may be concerned about climate change, but they are still supporters of the hydrocarbon industry because, in their eyes, as with Tony, the benefits of hydrocarbons outweigh the risks. Thus, as will become clear, we cannot adopt a stark black-and-white view that those involved in financing fossil fuel development simply do not care about the ethics of their choices. The reality is much more nuanced. While their ethical worldview may not align with our own, given their importance in shaping environmental approaches, it is crucial that we understand what drives their ethical sensibilities.

I use the term "hydrocarbons" in this book to refer to oil and gas because this is the way my interlocutors use the term. In scientific terms, hydrocarbons are a class of organic compounds composed of hydrogen (H) and carbon (C). These compounds include oil and gas but also coal. Where I refer to hydrocarbons in this book, I refer to oil and gas unless otherwise specified. The overarching argument I make in this book is that by understanding how energy financiers ethically and financially value energy, oil and gas in particular, we can understand how capital shapes the energy worlds we find ourselves in and the future energy worlds that are being created on our collective behalf. In making this argument, I adopt what Mette High and Jessica Smith describe as an energy ethics approach. Smith and High (2017: 1) coin the term "energy ethics" to "capture the ways in which people understand and ethically evaluate energy" in ways that contribute to or imperil "the kinds of lives, societies, and futures that they deem to be good and valuable." Rather than apply predefined notions of ethics by which to judge the rightness or wrongness of my interviewees' perceptions or actions or impose what I deem to be valuable or "right" on their actions and beliefs, this approach takes seriously my interlocutors' own ethical persuasions, motivations, and yearnings, without endorsing their ethical viewpoints or worlds.

This approach broadly follows an anthropological view on ethics. James Laidlaw (2014: 3) explains that the anthropology of ethics "rests not on the evaluative claim that people are good" but rather on the "descriptive claim that they are evaluative"—that is, that people are moral agents who are constantly making sense of what they deem to be "right" and "good" in the world in ways that are complex and perhaps diverge from our own ethical sensibilities and moral judgments. This approach does not necessitate that we endorse the standpoints of my interlocutors, their ethical worlds, or the contradictions therein; nor does it necessitate that we defend or contest their ethical worlds. Rather, an anthropology-of-ethics approach encourages us to better understand my interviewees "on their own terms," to unsettle taken-for-granted assumptions, and to contribute plurality, complexity, and idiosyncrasy to academic and popular debates in order to more effectively engage and respond to them (High and Smith 2019: 20). Such an approach follows what Michael Lambek (2010: 1) describes as an "ordinary ethics," which he contends is intrinsic to "speaking and acting with ethical consequences, evaluating our actions and those of others, acknowledging and refusing to acknowledge, caring and taking care, but also being aware of our failure to do so consistently." This sort of ethical approach diverges from common and historically situated notions of ethics that are associated with religion and codes of conduct that delineate right from wrong and how one ought to behave (Lambek 2010). As a branch of philosophy, ethics "concerns one's actions, choices, decisions and moral preferences," and etymologically the word stems from the Greek terms "*ethikos*" and "*ethos*," describing "ethical" and "moral character" (Frigo 2017: 9).[3] An ordinary energy ethics calls attention to the everyday performances of ethics that are tacit, idiosyncratic, and socially negotiated over time by people (Lambek 2010). In this regard, this book endeavors to shed light on the people inside an industry that is largely opaque to outsiders by examining the practices, perspectives, motivations, and worldviews of experts and executives who play a decisive role in shaping it.

An energy-ethics approach to energy and energy finance does not render issues of energy and finance as apolitical. By contrast, both energy and finance are *extremely* political. At a time of increased calls to take action to mitigate anthropogenic climate change, to transition away from fossil fuels, to leave hydrocarbons in the ground, and to decarbonize capital in favor of "green" and "sustainable" forms of investment, issues of energy could hardly be *more* political (High and Smith 2019; Langley et al. 2021; Smith and High 2017). Add to this perennial oil spills and hydrocarbon disasters that contaminate local environments, threaten wildlife, and jeopardize livelihoods; ongoing local and indigenous protests over land and water rights where hydrocarbon infrastructure is being (or is proposed to be) built; geopolitical struggles to control energy resources and infrastructures; rising energy costs and regional energy shortages that exacerbate poverty and stoke civil unrest;

and, extraction and waste practices that have poisoned local populations and aggravated settler-colonial injustices against indigenous peoples (Appel 2019; Field 2021a; Fiske 2017; O'Brien 2023; Powell 2017; Sawyer 2015). There may be few issues that are more political than the way we find, extract, move, process, use, and dispose of energy resources and infrastructures.

Finance, meanwhile, has long been recognized as political. The financial industry has historically provided the credit facilities required to expand industries and mend crises of liquidity for corporations and governments (not to mention households)—playing a central role in reproducing the prevailing political economies and the inherent inequalities therein (Arrighi 1994; Braudel 1992; Graeber 2012; Harvey 2006 [1982]). Since the early 2000s, scholars working across the disciplines of anthropology, geography, and sociology have turned their analytical attention to the finance sector. Karen Ho's (2009) ethnographic exposition of New York investment banks revealed, for example, how the internal politics of investment banking exacerbated gendered and racial divisions of labor within banks, while banks externally worked to deepen socioeconomic inequalities through merging, downsizing, and reorganizing workforces, which disproportionately affected the poorest. Daniel Souleles (2019) makes a similar argument in his ethnography of US private equity firms. Documenting the influential rise of these firms in the last quarter of the twentieth century, he argues that private equity firms circumvent democratic political processes in the restructuring of industries, the laying off of workforces, and the shaping of the US economic system in the name of meritocracy and shareholder value, echoing Ho (2009). Horacio Ortiz too makes this point. Drawing on his ethnography with a French multinational financial firm, he argues that when financial analysts determine the financial value of something, they are "partaking in a political project of social distribution that extends to the world" by imposing on it, and integrating it into, a social hierarchy that implies a "morally and politically just" appraisal of its value (Ortiz 2013: 65, 76; Ortiz 2021a, 2021b).

I build on and engage with these and other authors to suggest that it is possible to acknowledge that energy and finance are deeply imbued with politics and ethics, while making ethnographic space to investigate how my interlocutors, who work at the intersection of energy and finance, make sense of the world. As they are gatekeepers of capital, purveyors of potential energy futures, and financial conduits that connect investors from around the world to hydrocarbon activities in the United States, this line of ethnographic inquiry is extremely important if we wish to understand the ethical sensibilities of people who shape the energy worlds that we find ourselves in. This approach is distinct from but complementary to energy justice approaches. These approaches often advocate for a recognition of energy injustices, a "fair" reorganization of economies, a redistribution of the economic and social benefits of energy infrastructures, and a consideration of the procedures and policies that generate these injustices (Jenkins et al. 2016, 2019; Smith and High 2017; Sovacool 2013; Sovacool and Dworkin 2014; Sovacool et al. 2016). The problem with justice approaches, however, is that what constitutes "justice" resides in the eyes of the beholder. While there may be broad coalitions working to curb climate change and to end energy poverty, for example, the way these efforts should be accomplished, why, and to what end are far from unanimously agreed upon. It is this diversity among moral positions, and the ethical frameworks that determine these positions, that are ripe for empirical inquiry. It is in this space that ethics approaches seek to shed novel and nuanced light on the people and factors that shape our present energy worlds and the energy worlds they are working to bring to fruition.

Although this approach may, for some readers, be akin to a kind of moral relativism, it is instead, I suggest, an empirical approach to understanding morals and ethics. It is what philosophers call a "descriptive" analytical approach to ethics rather than a normative analytical approach (Hämäläinen 2016; Widdershoven and van der Scheer 2008). It examines how and why people come to define climate justice—including areas of divergence and convergence—rather than defining climate justice and suggesting how this might be achieved. Both approaches are important and complementary, yet distinct. In taking its descriptive approach, this book aims to contribute to existentially important debates in which energy, finance, ethics, and the diverse futures we are working to create intersect. It engages energy issues that cut across disciplines and aims to engage scholars across the social sciences, from anthropology to economics and business, and from environmental science to geography and science and technology studies.

An Unconventional Time in the US Oil Capital

The explosive growth in unconventional oil and gas extraction in the United States (colloquially known as "fracking") is both the context and the impetus for the research on which this book is based. I chose Houston as the field site for this project because it was, and continues to be, the center for US oil and gas finance. Texas cemented its reputation as the center of the United States' oil and gas sector throughout the twentieth century, beginning with the Spindletop gusher, just east of Houston, followed by massive exploration and production activities in the state's southeast, north, and west hydrocarbon basins. As energy lawyer and industry expert Bernard Clark (2016: ii) documents, financiers and financial infrastructures have been vital to these exploration and production activities since the beginning because "capital has always been a critical tool in the exploration for and development of oil and gas." Houston's reputation as the focal point of the United States' oil and gas finance sector, however, came in the late 1990s and early 2000s, at the expense of its two US metropolitan rivals, Dallas and New Orleans. Dallas was the historical center of US oil finance and known for dynastic oil families dating back to Texas's early oil days. As oil and gas firms and infrastructures were increasingly located in Texas's southern regions beginning in the early 2000s, however, so too were oil and gas financiers, my interlocutors told me. New Orleans, by contrast, was known as the financial and operational hub for off-shore Gulf of Mexico oil and gas operations. But this status was undermined as US onshore production was revitalized by unconventional extraction and, as many attested, by the disastrous flooding caused by Hurricane Katrina in 2005, which forced businesses and families to migrate, with many moving to Houston. As one interviewee who migrated from New Orleans to Houston explained,

> When Katrina hit, the schools closed. So, everybody with school-age children needed to enroll their kids in another school or they were going to miss a semester to a year of school. In the first days after Katrina, everybody thought it was a temporary issue and they would all return to their homes. But then the levees broke, and New Orleans flooded, and then people realized this was going to be a very long-term, possibly permanent

change. . . . In the multiyear period prior to Katrina there was already a shift from New Orleans to Houston, but overnight it accelerated that process.

In the lead-up to the 2000s, Houston was headquarters to Enron, whose twin towers still dominate the city's landscape (see figure 1.1). Prior to its spectacular collapse in 2001, Enron helped usher in a new era of energy financialization and attracted financiers to the city (McLean and Elkind 2004). This same interviewee explained, "The whole Enron era really transformed the energy industry and so that made Houston extremely unique. No other city had the trading shops and the infrastructure to handle deregulated energy like Houston did. And so, once it had that, it really created a competitive advantage for itself. . . . It's an industry that's hard to replicate. Chicago has repeatedly tried to." Another person similarly remarked, "Enron Capital was very smart and attracted a lot of really smart guys. . . . You know, for all the bad things about Enron, they knew how to make money."

The collapse of Enron did not dissipate Houston's growing reputation as the center for US energy and hydrocarbon finance. Enron's financial talent was absorbed by other Houston firms, with some going on to found their own private equity and consultancy firms. During my fieldwork I was surprised by the number of people who had worked for Enron. Even those who did not work for Enron had some direct connection or dealing linked to the failed giant.

Houston's fortunes were further solidified by the US "shale revolution." The "revolution" started in earnest in 1994, when Occidental Petroleum drilled a successful horizontal well, showing that it was possible to access a layer of source rock from which to potentially extract hydrocarbons (McLean 2018). A few years later, Houston-based Mitchell Energy successfully combined horizontal drilling with hydraulic fracturing in the Barnett Shale, a geological formation of hydrocarbon containing sedimentary rock, not far from Dallas. Devon Energy bought Mitchell Energy in 2001 and began expanding the use of unconventional extraction technology. Within a few years, big oil and gas companies wanted "proven but undeveloped" drilling prospects (PUDs) to expand their unconventional extraction operations. There was a fever for this new technology and the renaissance it promised for the US onshore oil and

Figure 1.1: One of two iconic former Enron towers that defines Houston's cityscape.
Source: Author.

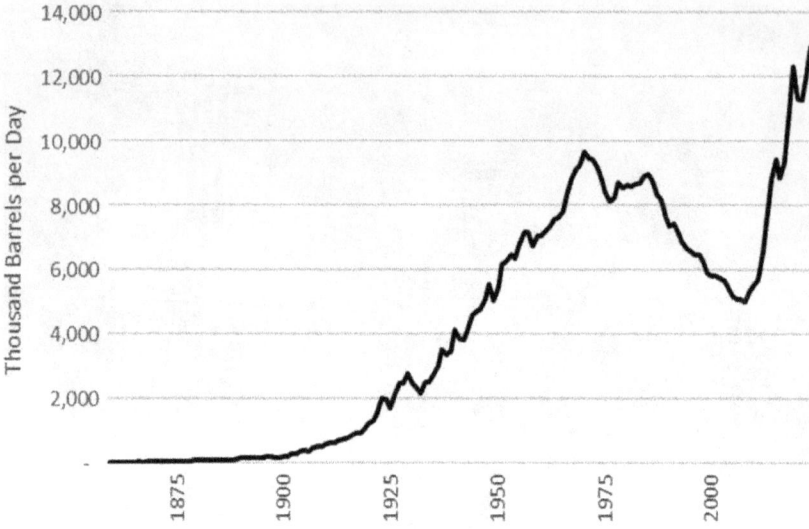

Figure I.2: US field production of crude oil, 1859–2023. Data source: USEIA (2024).

gas industry. Start-ups and financiers rushed in to claim a piece of the first, and perhaps the last, oil and gas boom of this century. This flurry of new oil and gas exploration activity turned legacy onshore US oil fields, depleted from decades of conventional extraction, into hives of productivity (USEIA 2021a, 2021b, 2021c, 2024; see figure I.2). Between the early 1970s and the early 2000s, the United States was a declining producer and a net importer of oil. Since then, the United States has become the world's largest producer of oil and natural gas, followed by Saudi Arabia and Russia, respectively, as well as a net exporter of oil and gas (USEIA 2016, 2018, 2021b, 2021c, 2022a, 2024). Unconventional extraction ("fracking") is credited with this previously unthinkable boom in hydrocarbon production. Houston was the "place to be" as the shale revolution unfolded because it had what economic geographers would describe as the "right" agglomeration of skilled labor, financiers, infrastructures, and firms. Nearly every US oil and gas firm—from supermajors to small independents—as well as every oil and gas financier had an office in Houston because, as one of my interlocutors explained to me, "Houston . . . [was] the center of the whole thing."

Transitional Times

The United States' resurgent place in the world of oil and gas production,[4] which has occurred amid increasing concern about anthropogenic climate change and calls to divest from fossil fuel extraction, marks a transitional time that, in the last decade, has generated a surge of new energy research. This book contributes to this new wave of energy and hydrocarbon scholarship by shedding light on the performance of financial expertise and corporate financial practices that underwrite the calculations of risk and the valuation of oil and gas and extractive energy technologies in the United States. I say "new wave" because the current surge in hydrocarbon scholarship builds on, and is situated in, a long history of analytical inquiry into energy as vital to social and economic life. Writing some 250 years ago, for example, Adam Smith was acutely aware of the centrality of hydrocarbons (coal specifically) to not only the everyday lives of people and work but also the location of industries and infrastructure in a rapidly industrializing UK.

Smith was writing at a transitional time in the history of energy because Britain was entering the first phase of its industrial revolution and was a geopolitical imperial superpower struggling to maintain control of its North American colonies. The transition into industrialization brought new energy demands, and coal became increasingly important as the fuel source on which lives and industry turned.[5] In this context, he remarked in *The Wealth of Nations*,

> In a country where the winters are so cold as in Great Britain, fuel is, during that season, in the strictest sense of the word, a necessary of life, not only for the purpose of dressing victuals, but for the comfortable subsistence of many different sorts of workmen who work within doors; and coals are the cheapest of all fuel. The price of fuel is so important an influence upon that of labour that all over Great Britain manufactures have confined themselves principally to the coal countries. . . . In some manufactures, besides, coal is a necessary instrument of trade, as in those of glass, iron, and other metals. (Smith 1999a [1776]: 469–70)

Max Weber was also acutely aware of how closely enmeshed sociocultural and economic life was with hydrocarbons. Writing 125 years after

Smith, at the precipice of an industrial transition from coal to oil, he predicted that the entanglement of Puritan asceticism with industrial capitalism would likely persist "until the last ton of fossilized coal is burnt" (Weber 1958 [1905]: 181).[6]

It was Leslie White, however, who defined the first generation of anthropologists to study energy (Boyer 2014; Rogers 2015a). Writing at the dawn of a new nuclear era, he sought to link energy with the "evolution of culture." White (1943: 335) boldly claimed that "everything in the universe may be described in terms of energy.... The civilizations or cultures of mankind, also, may be regarded as a form or organization of energy." He, too, was writing at a transitional time because he and others believed that available reserves of oil and coal were quickly running out, unaware of the vast hydrocarbon reserves yet to be discovered. "The key to the future," he argued, "lies in the energy situation.... Wind, water, waves, tides, solar boilers, photochemical reactions, atomic energy, etc. are sources which might be tapped or further exploited" (White 1943: 350). In an age of perceived hydrocarbon scarcity, for White, atomic energy provided a promising transitional potential to a prosperous energy-rich future. Dominic Boyer (2014: 311) notes that while White was unsuccessful in forging an anthropology of energy in his time, he sowed "the seeds of an idea that had great, but mostly undeveloped, critical potential: the notion that modern capitalist society was a fuel society to its core." This idea remains relevant today and is echoed in oil-oriented concepts such as "petrocultures," "petrofutures," and "petrocapitalism" (Canavan 2014; Johnson 2019; Wilson et al. 2017).[7] Following White, a second generation of energy-oriented anthropologists emerged in the 1970s and 1980s, focused on the impact of energy practices on indigenous communities and the environment (Kruse et al. 1982; Nordstrom et al. 1977; Robbins 1980, 1984).

For my analysis in this book, the work of Laura Nader that emerged during this time is foundational. Nader studied not only energy but how the expertise of nuclear scientists and policy makers became entangled with their worldviews and prescriptions about what energy futures should be materialized (Nader 1980; Nader and Beckerman 1978). Diverging from other anthropologists and social science scholars studying energy at the time, her line of ethnographic inquiry advanced her call for "studying up" by researching those empowered to make decisions that affected society at the regional, national, and global scales (Nader 1964, 1972). Nader's call to "study up" was not just methodological but ethical—she argued that anthropologists and social scientists had, at that time, neglected to turn their analytical lens to those empowered to make decisions on our collective behalf,[8] especially in the United States and Europe. Like White, this generation of energy anthropologists was writing and engaging with energy at a transitional time in predominant energy regimes in the United States and western Europe, defined by what Douglas Rogers (2015b) argues was, again, a pervasive collective sense of hydrocarbon scarcity. For this second generation, scarcity emerged not from an acute sense of dwindling geological deposits, as in the case of White, but from the erosion of American oil hegemony in the wake of OPEC's formation, which undermined US influence over global oil reserves and threatened to restrict access to the "lifeblood" on which the US economy turned (Clark 2016; Huber 2013; Rogers 2015a).

A new wave of energy research has emerged since the mid-2000s, prompted by a new transitional time. By contrast with previous generations, the present wave of social science research has not been prompted by hydrocarbon scarcity, "peak oil" narratives, nor the geopolitical scramble to control what exploitable oil and gas reserves are left, which prevailed from the 1970s through to the early 2000s. Instead, it has been prompted by an *abundance of hydrocarbons* unlocked by new forms of unconventional extraction and the discovery of new deep-water oil and gas reserves, combined with a growing consensus about the *scarcity of time* by which we must collectively transition away from hydrocarbons to avert the catastrophic effects of anthropogenic climate change. Reflecting on this wave of research and the transitional time it is situated in, Sheena Wilson, Adam Carlson, and Imre Szeman (2017: 3–4) have remarked that in just the last decade, "researchers in the arts, humanities and social sciences have turned their critical attention toward oil and energy as never before" because it is the fulcrum on which "today's most pressing social, economic and political issues" turn. Research in this current wave is more diverse and geographically expansive than previous waves of scholarship. Characterized by a truly global array of settings, ranging from offshore and rural enclaves to corporate offices, and from other-than-human entities to corporate managers, this current wave has yielded new and nuanced insights into the challenges and opportunities in addressing the global existential energy dilemma of meeting growing energy demand while reducing the anthropogenic effects of our energy practices (Appel et al. 2015; Cross 2020; Howe 2019; Jalbert et al. 2017; Sawyer 2022; Strauss et al. 2016; Wilson et al. 2017).

Attention to the role that experts play in the industry has been a key contribution of this new wave. This book builds on and advances a growing pool of work in this area, in which Arthur Mason's work has been foundational in showing how economic experts and financial expertise have shaped the US energy landscape. Following in the footsteps of Nader and drawing on his time as the energy coordinator for the Alaska governor, Mason reveals how economic expertise came to shape US energy infrastructures. He shows how forecasting the future and calculating future price risks became increasingly important following the oil price shocks of the 1970s and the progressive deregulation of energy markets in the 1980s (Mason 2007, 2019). Combining technical predictions with suave communicative exchanges at closed-door industry and policy forums, these economic and financial experts create visions and knowledges of the future that socially circulate within industry and governmental circles (Mason 2007). In the process of forecasting, he argues, experts draw the future into the present, making it almost knowable, assigning it economic values, and weighing its financial risks.[9] Working in a similar vein, Caura Wood's (2016, 2019) ethnography of an independent oil and gas company demonstrates how financial expertise and geological expertise are combined in the forecasting of the future and expectations of financial value creation. Complementing Mason, Wood (2016: 44, 53) provides unique insights into "the specific corporate and geoscientific practices" through which oil, finance, and infrastructures are connected, positing that it is through finance that "hydrocarbon value is formatted into a temporal rate of return" and that such valuations "privilege the time value of money over questions of long-term energy sustainability." This evaluative work, Wood (2019) shows, has complex ethical dimensions, related not only to financial valuation practices on which the importance of oil and gas is given quantitative monetary measures but also to durational moral commitments of responsibility to yield envisioned outcomes in the face of dismal personal financial prospects and loss.[10]

The work of these and other authors is foundational for my analysis in this book. From hydrocarbon exploration and production to the marketing of refined oil and gas products, leagues of experts are involved in the process, deriving a piece of the financial value that hydrocarbons generate in the form of compensation, fees, interest, and profit sharing. Even before hydrocarbons are extracted from deep underground, these oil and gas deposits are commodified into units *to be* extracted and are sold for a portion of their future expected financial value, based on the projections of experts. Once produced, oil and gas enter a world of pipelines, pumping stations, storage tanks, and refineries before reaching their point of consumption in the form of petrochemical products, fuels, and lubricants (Simpson 2019; Field 2024; High and Field 2020). Experts are vital to every step of this process. From exploration to retailing, experts' price forecasts, profitability projections, and risk assessments are integral to the US hydrocarbon industry. Only a handful of interlocutors in my research are independent "oilmen," carving careers and identities from personally financing and directing their own exploration and production companies. The majority are financial, legal, and technological specialists who use their expertise to "chase oil," as one interlocutor put it. Working with oil and gas companies as employees, contractors, consultants, and financial partners, they make and steer managerial decisions, craft imaginaries of the future, help decide whether wells are drilled, and act as gatekeepers of capital in deciding whether money will be loaned or invested. Hydrocarbon exploration and production and finance require investors, lenders, and entrepreneurs to envision and evaluate a whole range of things that have not yet happened. These include how much oil and gas are potentially underground, commodity prices, relationships, demand, costs, profits, technological changes, how much money is to be made, the likelihood of being paid back, and accidents. While it is not possible to know these things before they happen or are confirmed, they can be imagined. These imaginaries are not inert navel-gazing exercises. Instead, they are entangled with allegorical narratives that my interlocutors tell about themselves, the industry, the future, and their place in these futures.

Allegories convey not just a descriptive narrative but also a set of ethical sensibilities and moral conclusions that are conveyed via storylines and images that instruct and orient orators and audiences (Holmes 2014;

Donald McCloskey 1995; Deirdre McCloskey 1998). Understanding narratives as allegories draws attention not just to the persuasive labor of these narratives but to their moral message(s). Allegories are powerful vehicles for orienting people toward shared understandings of what is important, what time frames are worth considering, how and why risks should be defined, and to whom responsibility should be assigned. The people quoted in this book draw on imaginaries and weave allegories that are tied to four main concepts—value, time, risk, and responsibility.

Value, Time, Risk, and Responsibility

The people I got to know in Houston's oil industry orient their hydrocarbon expertise and practices around financial "value creation," often talk in terms of "value," and are informed by a wider set of social priorities and virtue aspirations that might be described as "values." They talk about and describe oil and gas in terms of what they call "value" (measured in money), assess the worthiness of projects and companies according to metrics of "value" (also measured in money), and evaluate themselves within a world in which "value creation" is important to their professional and their personal senses of self-worth. As one of my interlocutors explained to me, value measured in terms of money is a way of keeping score of how "good" someone is. These notions of value, however, are connected to a constellation of other various and idiosyncratic social values that inform the importance of money as a unit of analysis and a measure of worthiness.

Value has long been considered by philosophers, anthropologists, economists, and social scientists alike—making it a fundamental concept in both thought and everyday practice (Field 2023). It was Adam Smith (1999a [1776], 1999b [1776]) who came to define contemporary notions of value in *The Wealth of Nations* (Frondizi 1971; Schnädelbach 1984).[11] Articulating the concept famously in relation to commodities in his foundational labor theory of value, Smith wrote, "The value of any commodity, therefore, to the person who possesses it, and who means not to use or consume it himself, but to exchange it for other commodities, is equal to the quantity of labour which it enables him to purchase or command" (Smith 1999b [1776]: 133). Nuanced in his formulation, value as he describes it is something that can be relativized in exchange and, at the same time, is something that is idiosyncratically evaluated by people.

Smith's articulation became central to scholarly and popular understandings of value thereafter, including in political economy, economics, philosophy, and anthropology (Frondizi 1971; Robbins 2015a; Schnädelbach 1984). These understandings, however, evolved in distinct ways. Philosopher Hermann Lotze (1841) made value a key element of his philosophical theory and put it at the center of German philosophical debate, locating his theory of value in subjective processes of valuation, upon which cognition and matters of the "soul" were brought to bear (Frondizi 1971; Schnädelbach 1984: 179). In economics, David Ricardo (2004 [1817]) used Smith's notion of exchange value to formulate his theory of trade, and this notion came to be merged with theories of utility, shaping objectivist notions of value in economics in the centuries that followed. Karl Marx (1990 [1867]), meanwhile, developed the notions of use-value and exchange-value in his incisive analysis of capitalism, where surplus value is foundational for understanding the unequal accumulation of wealth and labor exploitation. In the early twentieth century, however, Joel Robbins (2015: 19) observes, popular and scholarly debates about value "largely fade from the scene outside of their original home in economics," leaving neoclassical economists to take an influential position in formulating contemporary understandings of the concept. This is why anthropologists such as David Graeber (2001, 2013) and Michael Lambek (2008, 2013) have observed that when popular and scholarly debates evoke the term "value," they often refer to meanings rooted in economics. Key to understanding these contemporary notions of economic value is situating them in the "scientific-materialist worldview" from which they emerged, where economics formulated "value" as a tangible "is" rather than an evaluative "ought" (Robbins 2015: 19). This formulation is vitally important because it vacated value's philosophical moral meanings and supplemented it with a positive normativity associated with capitalist production.

Anthropologists have long rejected this dichotomy and have documented how economic notions of value have percolated into calculative and moral practices of business and finance (Ho 2009; Leins 2018; Miyazaki 2013; Ortiz 2021a; Zaloom 2006). Bronislaw Malinowski took up the question of value(s) in his foundational anthropological ethnography of villagers in what is now Papua New Guinea. Arguing that these notions are entangled, he notes that food has "value" not only as something to be consumed and stored as a symbol of wealth but also as something that is socially "valued" as a product of "good" gardening, as the object of ceremonial handling, and for its ability to satisfy human needs—making it "capable of evoking emotions" (Malinowski 2010 [1922]: 60, 170–72).[12] Recent and important contributions to the way we might think about value and values come from David Graeber. Graeber (2001: 47) argues that value may be thought of as "the way people represent the importance of their own actions to themselves, as reflected in one or another socially recognized form"—in money, prestige, family size, or food stocks, for example. Reflecting on the "value/values problem," Graeber observes, "The entire field of anthropological value theory since the 1980s has been founded on a single intuition: the fact that we use the same word to describe the benefits and virtues of a commodity for sale on the market (the 'value' of a haircut or curtain rod) and our ideas about what is ultimately important in life ('values' such as truth, beauty, justice), is not a coincidence. There is some hidden level where both come down to the same thing" (Graeber 2013: 224). Graeber's (2013) value-values assertion bears some resemblance to the recent assertion of former Goldman Sachs managing director and former head of the Bank of England, Mark Carney, who argued, "In the most general terms, values represent the principles or standards of behaviour; they are judgements of what is important in life. Examples include integrity, fairness, kindness, excellence, sustainability, passions and reason. Value is the regard that something is held to deserve—the importance, worth, or usefulness of something. Both value and values are judgements" (Carney 2021: 4). Graeber and Carney are not making the same argument, nor are they theoretically aligned, but both recognize that the concepts of value and values are connected. Theoretically, Graeber's call is to bridge the theoretical disjunction between value and values first opened by Smith and early economists and to "understand human beings as projects of mutual creation" and "value as the way such projects become meaningful" to other people and the worlds we create (Graeber 2013: 238).

Anthropologists of finance have also engaged with the concept of value. In his ethnography of private equity firms, for example, Daniel

Souleles (2019) shows not only that the concept of value is central to financial practices but also that it carries a double meaning as both a notion of capitalistic account and a moral aspiration. He argues, "Value always needs to circulate from the realm of the noble and the aspirational to the realm of price—that is, after all, how you keep score. . . . For investors there must always be an equivalence between value and values" (Souleles 2019: 120). Drawing analytical attention to the ways in which the concept of "value" is used and circulated in finance, Horacio Ortiz (2013, 2021a) urges us not to adopt it as an analytical concept but, instead, to examine the ways it is deployed and its connotations. By giving it critical attention rather than taking it for granted as an economic-financial concept, he suggests, anthropologists should decipher its multiple meanings and its ethical significance in shaping day-to-day practices and our material worlds. He shows, for example, how financiers work with interdependent notions of value that share a normative orientation that places investors at the center of financiers' calculus, in ways that assert that this orientation is a politically and morally just way of organizing society.

A key contribution of this book to anthropological and social science scholarship is that it sheds light on how hydrocarbon financiers define and engage with notions of value in ways that involve financial calculation but also broader notions of values. In line with Souleles and Graeber, I assert the connection between value and values, as well as investigate how my interlocutors themselves work with interdependent notions of value. For clarity, I use the term "value" hereafter to discuss how worldly things are valuated in terms of money, and I use the term "ethics" to discuss broader notions of what people considered to be important. Ethics allows us to locate assessments of what is important and worthy not in the action of *valuation* (assigning something a "value") but in the process of *evaluation*, on which valuation depends. Ethics is a way to talk about what otherwise may be described as "social values" in a way that acknowledges the importance of the evaluative process of assessing what we individually and collectively deem to be important in our worlds, while recognizing the diversity of internal and external factors that come to bear on this process. The significance of notions of value, meanwhile, is not how value is measured in dollars, pounds, or yen per se but instead how it indexes people toward shared capitalistic orientations of *what* has worth and how that worth *should* be measured—especially when notions of value are woven into allegories. In making this analytical move, I bridge the Smithian divide between value and values and illustrate how value claims are moral claims that are built on the evaluative scaffolding of ethics. I show that "value claims" are not just limited to the calculative methods that define value numerically but draw on historical and future-oriented imaginaries that are entangled with these calculations and the allegories woven with them (Leins and Yonte-André in-press). While I take seriously Ortiz's (2013, 2021a) argument that it is important to investigate value as an object of analytical inquiry rather than as an assumed concept, I argue that when it is invoked by my interlocutors (in competing but overlapping ways), it is suggestive of a shared, indeed hypernormalized, way of evaluating the worth of worldly things. It is indicative of an ethics. This ethical orientation is not unique to hydrocarbon financiers or the hydrocarbon industry, and may instead be understood as part of a broader process of financialization. In the context of this book, it is vital to pay analytical attention to the ways in which value orientations shape evaluations of energy and the climate, as well as the time frames and stakeholders worth considering.

In this vein, time has long been shown to be integral to conceptions of value. Through practices of credit, value in the past, present, and future is linked through social relations of debt that connect people in webs of repayment obligations (Graeber 2012; Harvey 2006 [1982]). Lending and investment practices, in which the interlocutors who feature in my analysis are engaged, for example, depend on their assessments of borrowers' history of repayment, the value of their accumulated collateral assets, and their perceived likelihood to meet their repayment obligations in the future. Entrepreneurs seeking investors face similar scrutiny, which collectively assesses how they have managed loans and investments in the past and present, and how likely they are to return capital to lenders and investors in the future. Capital is classically defined as value in motion over time—that is, value (often in monetary form) that is loaned or invested for the purpose of obtaining this value plus more back at a future anticipated date (Harvey 2006 [1982]). Ethnographers of finance have shown that financial practices such as lending, investing, and arbitrage turn on projections of future monetary value, future price forecasts, and imaginaries of future material production (Zaloom 2004; Miyazaki 2013). Caura Wood (2019) and Fabian Muniesa (2017) show, for example, that investment and lending practices depend on fostering shared imaginations of future "value creation" and a future-oriented "moral horizon" shared among investors, lenders, and entrepreneurs (Wood 2019: 68). Time figures into my interlocutors' sense of themselves, their career trajectories, which they shared with me, and their broader projects of being in ways that intersect with, but are also distinct from, processes of capital value creation (Field 2021b). In this book, I utilize the concept of time to pay attention to the ways in which my interlocutors draw on the past, present, and future in weaving allegorical narratives, and to examine how valuation practices used in these allegories have specific time horizons that lean toward the near-present.

Future-oriented practices involve engaging with risk—exposing oneself and others to the possibility of harm or loss—because future-oriented endeavors necessarily mean engaging with that which is not yet known and outcomes that are uncertain. Hunting boars, jumping into a murky body of water, investing time into inventing a new technology, lending money to a colleague, and founding a start-up company all share a future orientation that engages with risk. Variously defined, risk may include exposure to bodily harm, the loss of property, injury to relationships and reputations, cost to financial wealth and security, and damage to one or more future possibilities of meeting one's goals or leading a happy life, for example. Like value, risk (and the cognate concept of uncertainty) may be thought of as a fundamental concept integral to the human condition as we move from what is now to what is next.[13] For the people described in this book, the risks they are engaged with are primarily financial risks, the risk of losing their and their investor's money or of a loan defaulting, but these are enmeshed with a complexity of other risks. Socially, these financial risks (and the successes and failures associated with them) are tied to my interlocutors' place in the ever-shifting social and corporate hierarchies in the US hydrocarbon finance sector (Field 2021a, 2021b). More broadly, critics of the industry tie hydrocarbon exploration and production to the risk of exacerbating anthropogenic climate change (Hughes 2017). While there is not yet an anthropology of risk,[14] the concept of risk has run through anthropological scholarship since the discipline's earliest days. Recently, it has found new attention in economic anthropology as a growing pool of anthropological work on finance has shown how financial risk taking is a formative part of financial practices and expertise (Miyazaki 2013; Ortiz 2013; Tripathy 2017; Zaloom 2004). Caitlin Zaloom (2004, 2006) has shown, for example, how commodity traders have routinized financial risk taking in the buying and selling of futures contracts in hopes that future price movements in these contracts will generate profits. Hirokazu Miyazaki (2007, 2013) has similarly shown how Japanese arbitrageurs actively engage with financial risk by buying and selling identical (or similar) securities in two different markets, hoping to profit off the price differential. What these and other anthropologists of finance have shown is that financiers do not heed caution in the face of financial risk but actively engage with it in calculated ways "in order to exploit it" for financial gain (Appadurai 2016: 47). This book shows not only how hydrocarbon financiers engage with risk in ways akin to the ways risk is engaged in other forms of finance—because of shared methods, schools of financial thought, and elite MBA training—but also how these engagements are applied to exploration and production in the midst of growing public and policy anxiety about climate change.

Connecting what Rebecca Bryant and Daniel Knight (2019: 8) call the "temporal triangle" of the past, present, and future, responsibility is what holds us to account for what has been done and bounds us to commitments to yield future envisioned outcomes for ourselves and others. Long associated with liability for wrongdoing and retributive attributions of witchcraft, responsibility has long been considered by anthropologists and social science scholars (Gluckman 1972). Since the early 2000s, responsibility has often been framed in economic and corporate studies in terms of corporate social responsibility, whereby corporations commit to mitigate the environmental and social impact of their operations on the communities in which they are situated (Cross 2014; Rajak 2011). Notions of responsibility can also be understood to be future gazing and captured in the cognate notions of Kantian-like duty and legal obligation, whereby it is the responsibility of people to behave in particular morally defined ways and to carry out particular actions. The fiduciary duty of corporate officers to maximize shareholder value is an example of such an obligation in the area of finance, economics, and corporate studies. Laidlaw (2014) has shown, however, that responsibility is a far more complex concept than is communicated by notions of liability, duty, and obligation, which tend to emphasize causes and effects. Attributions of responsibility that transverse the past, present, and future depend on diverse perceptions of causes, intentions, circumstances, and the necessity of responsive action. In the area of finance, Zaloom shows, for example, that commodity traders personally see it as "their responsibility" to voluntarily and actively "engage with risk" to produce profit, not simply heed caution in the face of potential financial losses and personal financial ruin (Zaloom 2004: 366, 383). Wood (2019: 83), meanwhile, has shown how the moral horizons between investors and managers are shaped as much by hopes of future profits as by financial managers' feelings of "commitment, responsibility and perseverance" to be good stewards of capital in the face of financial risks and uncertain economic outcomes. Thus, interlaced notions of value, time, risk, and responsibility have been central to economic anthropology for decades.

For the analysis in this book, these concepts are vital for interpreting what my interlocutors consider to be important and why; who and what they feel obliged to and when; and what they understand to be at stake in their lives and through their actions. While these are classic concepts in the study of markets and finance, they take on new significance in the context of hydrocarbon extraction and anthropogenic climate change. Climate change has, in many ways, called into question how and why these classic economic-financial concepts should be utilized and interpreted, and by whom. Should interlocutors incorporate climate risk concerns into their valuation practices and into the temporal horizons on which valuation practices turn? Should their responsibilities extend beyond their fiduciary duties? If responsibility for anthropogenic climate change should be attributed, how should this attribution happen? While seemingly benign, the utilization and interpretation of these concepts are central to the performance of financial expertise, future-gazing allegories, and how the hydrocarbon industry is being challenged by investors, activists, and policy makers alike. The performance of financial expertise and future-gazing allegories, moreover, do not just happen in a silo; they underpin entire ways of life—American ways of life—and an entire political economy structured on hydrocarbon capitalism. Thus, while this book contributes to the social science literatures on finance and energy, the analysis and ethnographic data in the chapters that follow document a transitional time in the hydrocarbon industry, in energy finance, and in the United States at large.

About This Book

This book is based on ethnographic research that began in late 2018. My research began slowly, as most ethnographic research projects do, starting with half a dozen interviews with interlocutors whom I was introduced to through the principal investigator of the project from which this book stems, Mette High. These early interlocutors became central to my research, as they kindly shared their time, thoughts, and lives with me over the many months after our first encounters, as well as introduced me to some of their colleagues. Early weeks of field research were spent wandering downtown Houston, where many of my interlocutors work, making field notes and proactively researching people and firms in Houston's oil and gas finance sector. An early break in my research came when Tony, whom we met at the start of this chapter, recommended that I attend a one-day oil and gas finance conference in early 2019. Hosted at a hotel in the city's Galleria district, southwest of downtown, it was a who's who of the city's hydrocarbon finance sector. In the days leading up to the conference, I emailed the organizers and begged them to let me attend at a discounted "student" rate, to which they thankfully agreed. With a mixture of excitement and anxiety that is common in the early days of fieldwork, I drove to the conference hotel on a clear, crisp morning in late January. Tensely toggling my attention between the driving instructions on my phone and the heavy rush-hour traffic in an unfamiliar city, I found my way to the conference. As my phone alerted me "you have arrived at your destination," I abruptly careened across two lanes of traffic and into the lineup of luxury vehicles on Westheimer Road queuing to enter the hotel driveway, waiting to be attended to by parking staff. Relieved that I had arrived in one piece and on time, I then realized that I appeared out of place. Arriving in our beat-up family Dodge Caravan with car seats, interior smeared with kid mess, a spare tire in the back, and smelling like wet dog from our drive from Toronto to Houston days earlier, I found myself in a long queue of sports cars, sedans, and SUVs—Mercedeses, BMWs, Land Rovers, Lexuses, Cadillacs, Porsches, Ferraris, Maseratis, and Jaguars. While this was perhaps not the smoothest introduction to prospective interlocutors, it was at this conference that I came to meet many people who became vital to my research.

To some of the people I met there and came to know well, I owe particular thanks. A few in particular graciously gave me their time, put me in touch with senior colleagues across Houston's oil and gas sector, and granted me extraordinary access to the industry's inner circles. I am deeply thankful to them and others who so graciously shared their life stories with me, replied to my emails, connected me to their networks, and met with me over coffee, lunch, and dinner. For research ethics reasons I cannot thank them by name, but this project could not have happened without their help, and I am extremely grateful to them. These industry network connections meant that I was able to participate in and observe conversations between interfirm colleagues, some of whom had previously worked together and had known each other for years. Being invited to participate in these networks meant occupying the liminal space between insider and outsider, which I believe yielded many advantages as an ethnographer. In this liminal space, my perception was that I was not deemed a threat to interlocutors competing with their interfirm colleagues to attract investors and clients; moreover, because research ethics demanded that I keep confidential any information that might identify them, their clients, or their places of work, most people seemed comfortable sharing information, thoughts, and perspectives with me. Being a man from an elite British university and having a postgraduate degree in economics helped. In a politically polarizing era in many ways defined by President Trump, my not being from Texas meant that many people did not expect me to have a position on US politics (although some did ask what I thought), which could have affected my ethnographic access and the trajectory of my research. My having a postgraduate degree in economics, meanwhile, was an instant source of rapport between my interlocutors and me. When they inquired who I was, how I came to study oil and gas in Houston, and what sort of education I had, my response that I am a social anthropologist was often met with blank stares and curious looks. When I followed that I had a master's in economics and a background in business, many looked visibly relieved or at least looked as if I had said something that sounded familiar to them. They looked further relieved when I told them that my cousin had worked as a geologist for Exxon in Houston and my uncle had worked as a geologist for the oil industry in Canada many years earlier. It did not make me an "insider," but it did give us some things in common. Many had degrees in business or MBAs, and my own biography invited them to *start* talking with me about what they thought I should know in terms of "markets," supply-and-demand fundamentals, and price volatility. By the time I began to write this book, this research culminated in over two hundred informal interviews, hundreds of pages of notes, over seventy in-depth recorded interviews, participation in many insider industry events, and collection of dozens of historical and industry documents.

Most of my interlocutors were white men, not unlike myself. In one of the most racially diverse cities in the United States, nonwhite workers are estimated to comprise only 12 percent of the gas and oil industry's workforce, and African Americans only 7 percent (Greater Houston Partnership 2020; Osborne 2020a). Women, meanwhile, account for 10–15 percent of the workforce, and very few hold executive and managerial positions (Yanosek et al. 2019). My observations roughly confirm these statistics. The majority of nonwhite people in the corporate spaces where my fieldwork took place were security guards, servers, and maintenance staff. The majority of women whom I encountered in corporate offices were receptionists. Only a couple of my interlocutors were women, and only a few were nonwhite. When I asked about this lack of diversity, many said that the hierarchies within the industry are built on networks of trust, which can raise barriers to newcomers. My subjects are making and managing investments and loans worth billions of dollars, they told me, and they want to work with people they know and are familiar with—implying that informal social networks are an artefact of past capital practices and the basis for new capital arrangements. Many, including those few nonwhite and nonmale people with whom I spoke, told me that the industry had changed and continued to change to diversify, but that change was slow. For me, this racial and gender division of labor was omnipresent throughout my research. Indeed, embodied white, masculine, heteronormative performances were a key aspect of hydrocarbon finance expertise that I observed throughout my research.[15]

Things did not always go well over the course of my fieldwork. Dozens of my emails went unanswered. Some people whom I met with for an informal interview then declined to meet with me again. Others simply canceled and stopped responding to my emails. One well-known energy financier who stopped responding, for example, explained to me that he was apprehensive about doing a recorded interview because of the potential negative publicity he might receive if his identity were ever revealed, despite my pledges to conceal it. In another case, a person whom I had previously met, and whose colleagues I knew, agreed to meet with me at his office for a follow-up interview. I arrived a few minutes early, and the receptionist showed me into the boardroom where there was a long wooden boardroom table and windows looking out onto the cityscape. Joining me a few minutes later, he took the seat at the head of the board table. Putting a pad of paper and pen on the table in front of him and leaning onto his elbows resting on the table, he stared at me and said that he did not have as much time as he thought that day, but that if we were going to talk, "today is the day," and there would be no second chances. Hoping to alleviate his concerns, I explained what my research was about, who the research was funded by, and that I was bound by strict university ethics guidelines. Then, without hesitation, he asked, "Why is the EU interested in this? The EU isn't friendly to the US oil and gas industry." He asked why he should talk to me and asserted that it was absolutely no benefit to him to do so. I explained that I was there to better understand the industry by collecting perspectives from people *inside* of it. "What's the end goal?" he asked. I explained that I hoped to publish the findings in a book and in academic articles. Then, he asked, "Are you the sheep or the wolf? I want to know why the sheep in the EU sent you here." Not exactly sure why I or "the EU" would be the "wolf" or the "sheep," I said I was neither and that I just wanted to understand and hear his story and perspective.

After discussing back and forth for about thirty minutes, he agreed to a recorded interview. I gave him the "official" documents, sanctioned by the university ethics board, that I gave everyone who agreed to a recorded anonymous interview, as well as the research consent form. He read over the information and said that I was "showing my hand" by indicating that I was interested in energy ethics, because, he explained, by being interested in ethics, I was suggesting that there was an "ethical dilemma" to be "exposed." I assured him I was not there to preach ethics nor was I there to "expose" him but was genuinely interested in his perspective. He signed the consent form, and agreed to the interview—but then paused and stared up at me sternly from the form he had just signed and said, "Just so you know, I'll do the interview. But, I'm going to treat you like the enemy." I was startled but tried not to let it show. As he pushed through my questions with one- to two-sentence answers and resisted my every effort and prompt to linger, to expand his answers, and lend me his insights, the recorded interview lasted less than twenty minutes.

This might have been my most difficult interview, but his distrust of me and antagonism toward my research was an insightful experience. Although I was genuinely interested in what he thought and not there to assail his ethical sensibilities, issues of energy and hydrocarbons, in particular, are highly divisive, and people inside the industry have come to be suspicious of, and expect criticism from, those outside of it. My goal in writing this book is to give readers an insight into this world while representing what I observed, heard, and experienced in the course of this research in such a way that my interlocutors will see themselves reflected in the pages that follow, even if their analysis and conclusions diverge from my own.

I have organized the chapters that follow in a way that first situates readers within the context in which this ethnographic research takes place. Chapter 1, "The Lone Star State," explores the sociohistorical context that makes Houston, Texas, the location of this project and how this context feeds into the present-day ethical sensibilities of energy financiers located there. At the heart of the American oil industry since its founding, Texas is as rich in oil and gas deposits as it is in present-day discourses, symbols, and imaginaries rooted in its history as an independent republic on the frontier between the US South and the "wild west." These imaginaries are still relevant today, I argue, figuring into the "freedom-loving" capitalist allegories, ambitions, and self-identities of aspiring oil entrepreneurs and financiers alike. Understanding how this history informs future-gazing allegories about Texas's oil and gas industry, as well as present-day notions of risk and responsibility, is crucial for understanding why "fracking" was pioneered in Texas, why Houston is the epicenter for US energy finance, and the ethical sensibilities of the people I came to know.

Chapter 2, "Financing the US Shale Revolution," investigates how the US oil industry has depended on and continues to depend on forms of finance to find and extract hydrocarbons. From loans to investments, the expansion and contraction of the oil industry can be linked to the forms of finance that have fueled it. This was no less true for the most recent expansive phase of the industry, dubbed "the shale revolution," which could not have unfolded without private equity financiers. Seizing on investor fervor to be a part of a new American oil rush, private equity firms offered investors an opportunity to capture part of the wealth that oil "booms" have been known to generate. In doing so, they are part of a long lineage of private investors on which the US oil industry has turned since its founding, who are empowered to define and take risks on our collective behalf in pursuit of profits. I demonstrate how private equity came to be perceived as a "golden ticket" for aspiring oilmen, and suggest that private equity financiers are conduits of responsibility that connect people around the world to oil and gas projects in the United States.

Chapter 3, "Ethical Calculations," examines how oil and gas financiers use constellations of financial metrics and models to construct allegories about future energy projects and companies. While in the early twentieth century there were few methods of predicting how much revenue an oil well could generate, today future-gazing financial metrics that measure financial value and risk over time are the industry norm. I argue that these financial metrics and models play an essential role in the construction of ethical narratives on which energy investments and loans are made. Narrowly defining risk, value, and time, and woven into allegories about the future, they help provide the ethical scaffolding on which moral arguments about oil are crafted. Unpacking these metrics and their meanings is crucial for understanding our present energy worlds and the future energy worlds that are currently being decided on and constructed.

Chapter 4, "Not a Dichotomy: Climate Change and Hydrocarbons," builds on the preceding chapters to explore how my interlocutors' perceptions of time, risk, responsibility, and value become entangled with their views on climate change. My interlocutors have diverse and idiosyncratic perceptions about the risks associated with climate change, the anthropogenic factors that drive it, and what (if anything) should be done to mitigate these risks. This chapter explores how notions of material provisioning and cosmology enter the ethical frameworks of my interlocutors in hydrocarbon finance. If metrics and models are the ethical scaffolding on which allegorical narratives about the near future are crafted, I argue that material provisioning and cosmology are the scaffolding on which allegories of futures beyond the temporal gaze of metrics and models are made.

Chapter 5, "'What the Hell is ESG?' and the Moral Case for Oil," examines the recent emergence of Environmental, Social, and Governance (ESG) frameworks coming to bear on US hydrocarbon financiers. In a few short years ESG frameworks went from being a little-known and little-cared-about acronym in the industry to a central feature of investor presentations, interindustry dialogue, and public-facing corporate strategies. First ignored, then met with skepticism and anxiety, ESG was not only quickly adopted by many hydrocarbon financiers and independent oil and gas firms, but they also integrated it into their forward-gazing narration of the future and their place in the future. Integrated with net discounted cash flow projections, the value of hydrocarbon reserves, barrels of production per day, and EBIDTA, ESG has become another means by which firms can measure their "goodness" and by which they can craft allegorical narratives about themselves for investors and creditors. Lauded for ushering in a new era of corporate climate change responsibility and tolling the death knell for US hydrocarbon financiers, ESG, I argue, has not fundamentally changed the practice of oil and gas finance. By contrast, in this chapter I show that ESG has become yet another tool in the moral "argument for oil."

The book concludes by reflecting on how quickly the prospectus for energy finance and climate change mitigation has changed since the research underpinning this book began and suggests that what the future holds is far from certain. The unprecedented fall in oil prices in April 2020, prompted by the COVID-19 pandemic, caused oil and gas producers to curtail production. Hailed as a "win" for the planet by climate change activists, the short-term fall in greenhouse gas emissions was quickly undone as lockdowns loosened and demand for fossil fuels rose again. Indeed, resurgent global oil and gas prices instigated by Russia's invasion of Ukraine in February 2022 revealed countries around the world to be stubbornly dependent on fossil fuels to meet their energy needs. While soaring oil and gas prices have sparked a cost-of-living crisis and fears of energy shortages in the UK and across Europe, producing oil and gas became wildly profitable again, garnering renewed enthusiasm among investors. These events raise important questions, such as the following: Is a post-fossil fuel world possible? And, if so, will it look much different from the fossil fuel world that preceded it? While the answers to these questions have yet to be revealed, I suggest that real changes are afoot and that we are at a vital juncture with regard to what energy future comes next.

The overarching argument I make is that by understanding how energy financiers ethically and financially value energy, we can understand how people shape flows of capital, and how capital, in turn, shapes the energy worlds we find ourselves in. In this vein, I suggest that the concepts of value, time, risk, and responsibility can tell us something about what people think is important, to whom they feel obligated, where they understand their agency to begin and end, and how the past, present, and future come to bear on their evaluations. I hope this book sheds critical light on the answers to the questions raised above, gives insight into the lives of the people who work at the intersection of the financial and energy sectors, and brings clarity to how different sorts of ethics come to shape our worlds.

1

The Lone Star State

You may all go to Hell, and I will go to Texas.
—Davy Crockett, 1835

John's private office looked like a museum celebrating Texas's settler-frontier history and its oil and gas industry. There were cowhide rugs in the middle of the room and deer heads on the wall. Cabinets along the side of the office were adorned with family photos alongside giant blue, grey, and purple geodes, and on a desk at the far end of the room there were two large computer screens. We were sitting in the middle of John's office at a quad of chairs with a glass-top coffee table in the center. The table doubled as a display case for twenty or so vintage hunting knives. Underneath the table there was a drill head from one of John's previous drilling operations, and there was an antique rifle on the wall on the right. These artifacts bore material witness to not only a long career in the industry but also an attachment to the place where he had made this career. They marked the completion of drilling programs and were representative of John's success in the oil and gas industry. They also drew one closer to Texas's settler-frontier history. I had met John just a couple of days before at the first industry conference on oil and gas finance that I attended, which Tony had told me about when we met at the JW Marriot (see Introduction). I happened to sit beside John at the luncheon keynote. After chatting over lunch, he agreed to meet with me at his office a couple of days later.

John is a rare combination of successful "oil man," investor, and financier. He grew up "in the middle of an oil field out in west Texas," he told me, and started working for his father's engine repair business at the age of twelve. "You didn't need to be very old to drive a truck in those days," and there were a lot of "pumping units" in that "part of the world," he said—by which he meant those bobbing oil jacks that still pepper the west Texas landscape. The mid-twentieth century was a time of unprecedented US oil production, and demand for oil field services such as engine repair was booming. "Internal combustion engine[s]," he said, "usually single cylinder.... They would burn valves up, would start leaking fuel, and wouldn't run properly . . . so we'd go out and change the [engine] heads." Later, he attended the University of Texas, where he earned a master's degree in engineering. Along the way, he worked for almost a dozen oil companies in increasingly senior roles, before becoming a commercial banker, lending money to companies like the ones he had worked for. After a decade in banking, he went back to working for oil and gas companies, before founding (and later selling) his very own successful independent oil and gas business.

For John, the Texas oil and gas industry is the best of American capitalism, with Texas as its center. What makes Texas special, he tells me, is that it "is a pretty damn independent place"—more independent than other parts of the United States. He explained to me,

> Texas, if I'm not mistaken, is the only state that was an independent republic before it was annexed by the United States. The people who came here were looking for opportunity, and they got it. Even when [Texas] went into the United States as a state, there was a very entrepreneurial spirit, because we kept all of our public lands, the state did. Texas did not cede them to the federal government like New Mexico, Oklahoma, Utah, Nevada, all the states, and all the other states before that too. So, there's an entrepreneurial spirit that is in Texas as a whole.

John was not mistaken. When the Republic of Texas—which seceded from Mexico in 1836—joined the United States, the state retained title to its public lands (as I explain below). He continued, "And I think being heavily involved in the oil and gas business just tends to make a person pretty independent. Because, a lot of times you're doing things that other people didn't think you ought to do, or didn't think would work." People like oil magnate Roy Cullen exemplified this Texas "spirit," he said, explaining, "Cullen . . . a lot of what he did was he drilled deeper. So, if he didn't find it when he got to where he thought it was going to be, well then, he would drill deeper, and sure enough a lot of times it was there. Well, I mean, how many people are going to do that?" Occasionally diverting my gaze from John to the artifacts in the room as we spoke,

I began to appreciate the connection between Texas's past and the present manifestations of its oil and gas industry, through the identities of those working in it. While the past is expected to have an impressionable impact on the present—from people to places and industries—there was something about the way that John invoked the past that stuck with me in the weeks and months that followed. Was there something really special about Texas? I wondered. What was the connection between Cullen and the "Texas spirit" that John had described? And, what was the connection between Texas's settler-frontier history and its contemporary oil and gas industry? As my fieldwork unfolded, I kept coming back to these questions as I was reminded time and again of my conversation with John. My interlocutors frequently invoked Texas's independent and frontier past in explaining its present. Representations of cowboys often appeared in the offices I visited and were common sights around Houston; and, many interlocutors invoked the notion of the cowboy in describing the independent oil and gas producers they worked with (as Tony did in the Introduction). Indeed, the more that I looked and listened, the more references to Texas's settler-frontier history I found, and these references were routinely invoked alongside and entangled with notions of the entrepreneur and entrepreneurship.

In this chapter, I explore these representations and the ways in which the past is invoked to ethically orient the present and visions of the future. I begin by briefly unpacking the historical forces that have shaped Texas in order to situate the way interlocutors I came to know draw on the past. I then explore how notions of this past were recrafted to create popular contemporary historical imaginaries and how key figures such as Hugh Roy Cullen provide a temporal-historical bridge that connects Texas's frontier history with its present-day oil industry. If allegories are stories, images, songs, and poems that convey a moral message about people, the "right" ways of living, and the nature of human existence, then historical imaginaries that my interlocutors invoked to explain themselves and the industry and to narrate the future cannot be ignored. Some readers may interpret these historical imaginaries and the allegories woven with them as simply trading in stereotypes. I suggest, however, that there is something much deeper to them that warrants analytical attention. Drawing the past into the present and into the future is a way, I argue, of ethically orienting oneself in relation to well-established norms, which is especially important amid calls for transformation and change. I conclude by reflecting on how the entrepreneur has in many ways supplemented notions of the cowboy as an agent of change and progress, and by suggesting that the notion of "culture" may be analytically applied to ways my interlocutors draw on Texas's history to orient themselves.

An Independent Nation: Cotton, War, and Cattle

I have traveled through many US states. While the national flag is a frequent sight, I can recall few state flags. Yet, in Texas, the state flag is maybe more prominent than the US flag. It adorns many vehicles in the state, and many vehicles are branded "Texas edition" (see figure 1.1). In Houston, major streets are named after people and places associated with its war of independence, such as Lamar Street and San Jacinto Street. Even the city itself is christened with the surname of the Tennessee migrant turned Texas army general who became the republic's first president, Sam Houston (Brands 2005; Campbell 1993). Then, there are the massive murals painted on the sides of hydrocarbon and petrochemical storage tanks just east of the city depicting scenes from the 1835–1836 Texas Revolution (see figure 1.2). Texas, at least in and around where I conducted my fieldwork, is steeped in reminders of its historic past, which John invoked when we met at his office.

Texas was indeed a republic before it entered the United States, and before it was known for producing oil, it was known for its cotton production and, later, its cattle industry. Unlike the states in the Northeast and Southeast, Texas began not as an English or French colony but as a Spanish colony. Following Mexico's secession from Spain, Texas became a northernmost province of Mexico, alongside what are now known as New Mexico, Arizona, and California. Historical accounts that compete with more recent historical analyses narrate Texas's war of independence from Mexico as agitated by a fervor among independent-minded American pioneers seeking to free themselves from Mexican government oppression (Baptist 2014; Burrough et al. 2021). Recent historical analyses have complicated these accounts. Texas's secession from Mexico, they suggest, was not just a product of a fractious Mexican federal government and tensions with its provincial administrations but largely revolved around the issue of slavery. At the time of its war of independence, Texas was wedged between the US South, the state of Mexico, and indigenous peoples on whose land English, French, and Spanish colonies had encroached for three centuries. In the years following Mexico's secession from Spain, the state emancipated slaves within its borders. As historian Edward E. Baptist (2014: 266) notes, however, while "Mexico had made emancipation its national policy . . . Texas was many miles from Mexico City," the nation's legislative capital. In 1835, when Texas settlers entered into an armed conflict with Mexican troops, records indicate that enslaved Africans accounted for 13 percent of Texas's nonindigenous population (Baptist 2014: 266). In the years leading up to the conflict, Stephen Austin, for whom Texas's capital city is now named, was a leading proponent for US settler migration from the southeastern United States to Texas. As Bryan Burrough, Chris Tomlinson, and Jason Stanford (2021) note, Mexican officials hoped that waves of settlers would provide enough population to prevent the nation's Texas settlements from being wiped out by indigenous raids. Accordingly, they made exceptions for slavery in Texas because the only way that Austin could entice US settlers to migrate to Texas was to allow them to bring their slaves and to promise them "virgin cotton land at bargain prices" (Burrough et al. 2021: 19). The context for Texas migration and settlement was rising global cotton prices because Texas had no "heavy"

Figure 1.1: Historical marker on lamppost in downtown Houston (*left*), and "Texas Edition" emblem on vehicle (*right*). Photos by author.

industry at that time, such as iron works. As one interlocutor explained, "There really was no industry in Texas" at that time; there was just "cattle and cotton."

While wholesale cotton prices waxed and waned throughout the 1820s, they began to rise precipitously in the early 1830s, and between 1831 and 1835 the population of Texas doubled as settlers and their slaves streamed into Texas to grow cotton. The vast expansion of cotton production in Texas was premised on the acquisition of new inputs—seed, land, and slaves—which was funded by a wave of new money and credit. New and established banks across the US South issued loans to prospective cotton farmers secured against the financial value of slaves. Bonds, a form of debt-based financial instrument, also facilitated the flow of capital into Texas's cotton boom by allowing investors in the United States and Europe—from New York to Paris—to claim a part of the profits that cotton production generated (Baptist 2014). The Mexican government's enforcement of its emancipation laws in 1835 prompted an armed conflict at the San Antonio military fort called the Alamo, where all but a couple of armed settlers were killed.[1] This is generally understood to have "officially" started Texas's war of independence, although it was preceded by several armed insurrections (Baptist 2014; Burrough et al. 2021; Brands 2005). The difference between this insurrection and previous ones, Baptist (2014) suggests, however, is that it was funded by investors in neighboring US states—principally New Orleans (which was the slave-trading capital of the United States)—who advanced war supplies in exchange for Texas government bonds. In the years immediately following the war and Texas's declaration of independence in 1836, the number of settlers, slaves, and cotton farms in the new republic grew exponentially, facilitated by debt capital (Baptist 2014). A key aspect of Texas's decade as a republic was land reform. To encourage settler migration, its constitution voided land grants by the Mexican government and over ten years issued titles to over 41.5 million acres of land (Baptist 2014; TGLO 2015). For many settlers, including its founders, Texas was indeed an opportunity to escape the debts they had accrued in US states to the east, craft new identities, and seek fortunes.

When it was annexed by the United States in 1845, Texas did indeed (as John said) retain title to all of its public lands, as well as rivers and tidelands, and the mineral rights thereunder (Clark 2016; TGLO

2015). This meant that when oil and gas were discovered on publicly owned land in the 1900s, the state of Texas (and not the federal government) owned these hydrocarbons. Texas retained its lands because the US Congress had declined the republic's treaty for annexation in 1844. Under the treaty, Texas would have ceded 175 million acres of land to the federal government in exchange for the federal government assuming the republic's $10 million of debt, which it had accrued in the process of independence and nation building (Clark 2016; TGLO 2015). Instead, it was annexed under a joint resolution by the US Congress that did not include an exchange of land for debt, although the federal government did assume its debt in the Compromise of 1850 when Texas established its western border (TGLO 2015). Another key implication of its 1845 state constitution is that Texas prohibited the incorporation of state banks and discouraged non-Texas banks from operating in the state, which curtailed industrial development until the early 1900s (Clark 2016).

Figure 1.2: Historical settler-frontier scenes on the large hydrocarbon storage containers just east of downtown Houston. Photos by author.

Cotton was not the only crop that settlers cultivated, however; they also reportedly grew sugar cane, tobacco, and corn alongside raising cattle (Fulgate 1961; Jordon 1969). Cotton cultivation grew steadily well into the 1900s, stimulated by waves of new labor and technological improvements, but global cotton prices slumped (Tomlinson 2014).[2] Cattle ranching also grew throughout the 1800s and into the 1900s. When settlers migrated west to Texas, they also brought with them cattle, Spanish settlers having practiced cattle herding in American colonies since the 1500s and having brought this practice to Texas prior to Anglo-American migration (Brand 1961; Love 1916). Thus, the first "cowboys" were Spanish settlers, Mexicans, and, later, black slaves who raised and managed herds for their owners (Jordon 1969; Massey 2000; Moore 2012).[3] Historian Clara Love (1916) notes that cattle ranching in Texas was largely unprofitable until after the US Civil War (1861–1865), when demand for beef in cities across the United States started to rise. The development of railroads in the latter half of the 1800s gave Texas ranchers greater access to growing urban markets through which they could sell their cattle (Love 1916). As Texas's cattle industry grew with increasing demand for beef, it rivaled and then eclipsed its cotton industry, which suffered from falling prices and the introduction of synthetic fibers in the 1900s (Britton et al. 1976). According to historian Jacqueline Moore (2012: 1), Texas is "the birthplace of the modern cattle industry as well as the birthplace of the [US] cowboy." While cattle ranching spread across the United States in the decades following the US Civil War, she argues that it was Texans who "first adapted Mexican techniques" of cattle handling on horseback (Moore 2012: 1). Migrating north in the post–Civil War period, Moore (2012: 163) says, they brought these techniques, cattle, and "cowboy culture" through to the most northerly central states of Montana and Nebraska.

While Texas would hang on to its cowboy culture, the state would be beset with rapid changes and industrialization following the discovery of oil at Spindletop near Beaumont in 1901. Crude oil that had seeped to the surface had been known by indigenous peoples and early settlers for centuries and had been used for a number of purposes—from sealing boats to topical skin cures. Oil had also been discovered in Texas years earlier in Nacogdoches, Bexar, and Hardin counties (Clark 2016; Stiles et al. 2002; Texas Almanac 2022). It was the Spindletop discovery, however, that would prompt the state's first "oil rush," define its first generation of "oilmen," and be the impetus for a merger of cattle and oil "culture" as the world was on the precipice of an energy transition from coal to oil.

Legends in the Making

In many ways Texas's history distinguishes it from other US states. Its history, moreover, has had a formative impact on the shape and identity of the United States—from the shape of its southerly border and neighboring states to the US cotton and cattle industries and US national identity. While grounded in historical events, contemporary manifestations of these events have in part been crafted. Burrough, Tomlinson, and Stanford (2021) show, for example, that the battle at the Alamo—which marked the beginning of Texas's war of independence—was narrated in the days and decades that followed to serve various purposes. Competing and fictionalized accounts were vital for recruiting volunteers from across the United States to join Texas's revolutionary army, and from the mid-1800s the Alamo was a popular backdrop for US novels. Then, beginning in the 1900s, historical fictional accounts of the battle at the Alamo were crafted for film and television. Walt Disney's 1954 *Davey Crockett* television series and the 1960 MGM film *The Alamo*—directed by and starring John Wayne—were popular contributions to this wave of historical fiction. These fictions overlapped and became entangled with cowboy fictions and tales. According to Moore (2012), between 1865 and 1900, an average of one thousand western dime novels were published per year, and many sold more than half a million copies. Western shows, meanwhile, were a popular form of live entertainment that often portrayed cowboys fighting "Indians." US authors and artists of the late nineteenth century portrayed cowboys as exemplars of American masculinity in a heroic struggle against nature. Between the early 1950s and the early 1960s, US film studios produced over eight hundred western films, many set in Texas, and western television shows accounted for about a quarter of evening programming (Goldberg 2008). While the vast majority of these television and film productions were fictional, they ascribed an "authentic" and "virtuous" character to American settler-frontier life that had been all but lost.

Historical imaginaries associated with cowboys, the frontier, and the American West became entangled with prideful Texas oil narratives following the Second World War. This entanglement was prompted by *Life* and *Fortune* magazines' profiles of H. L. Hunt in April 1948 (Burrough 2009; Life 1948).[4] The discovery of large reservoirs of oil in the eastern part of the state in the 1930s founded several family fortunes, including Hunt's, and supplied the carbonous energy the US military needed during the war (Burrough 2009; Clark 2016; Huber 2013). While there were many "oilmen" in Texas before this time, according to Burrough (2009) there were no popularly known Texas oilmen prior to this 1948 exposé. In the years that followed, "Americans devoured the countless articles and books about 'the big rich,'" a term coined in the *Fortune* article to describe the Texas oil magnates Roy Cullen, H. L. Hunt, Clint Murchison, Sid Richardson, and others (Burrough 2009; Merrill 2012: 201). The 1952 book and subsequent blockbuster movie *Giant* hastened this popular American obsession with historical imaginaries of the American West and its entanglement with twentieth-century oilmen. Filmed in Texas against the backdrop of western motifs, the film celebrated Texas's cattle ranching heritage and charted the rags-to-riches rise of a fictional oil man played by James Dean.

Famous and less-famous oilmen alike helped propel this nostalgia through their appetite for western-themed artworks depicting western cattle, and through the acquisition and establishment of sprawling cattle ranches, which confirmed their status and affirmed this link (Merrill 2012). When oil was discovered in the 1950s beneath their west Texas homesteads, this virtuous connection between cattle and oil was also advanced by ranchers turned accidental oilmen, who retained their cowboy boots, cowboy hats, and rural Texas sensibilities while experiencing a meteoric rags-to-riches rise in wealth (Bainbridge 1961). Merrill (2012) notes that these representations came at an important juncture of American petrocultural history; while the US oil industry experienced a postwar boom in the 1950s, as John worked for his father repairing pumping engines in west Texas, US oil supremacy was already on the decline. By the time it was surpassed by OPEC oil-producing countries in the 1970s, western and cowboy representations took on a new geopolitical significance—signaling a link to a more virtuous way of life that harkened back to the United States' founding settlers. Ronald Reagan harnessed these cowboy motifs in his presidential campaign, as would George H. Bush and George W. Bush[5]—with roots in Midland and Houston, Texas—during their presidencies (Merrill 2012). Since Reagan, and possibly before, adorning cowboy hats has become a presidential tradition (Scudder 2018). It is representative of a connection to US settler-frontier history, regardless of whether US presidents hail from ranching states, and is indicative of Texas's formidable impact in propagating "cowboy culture" in US national identities.

Cowboys and Frontiers

Given this history, there is surprisingly little anthropological engagement with the historical imaginary of the American cowboy, the frontier, and western motifs. What makes the contemporary conceptions of the cowboy a historical *imaginary* is that popular representations of cowboys are rooted in a mixture of historical record and imaginative invention. The idea of the American cowboy is entangled with masculine white representations from the settler-frontier—from the laconic figure of the Marlboro Man to more common representations across Texas and parts of the United States more broadly (Hitchens 2003; Merrill 2012). Cowboy "legends" emanating from Texas often revolve around masculine figures who guard against incursions from East Coast elites and are representative of "the spirit of America"—independent, "brave white men taming the frontier and blazing the path for more timid easterners to follow and settle" (Moore 2012, 2014: 29).

Historically, cowboys were a class of highly skilled labor, hired by ranch owners known as cattlemen (Moore 2012).[6] Between the 1880s and the 1920s, however, they came to be redefined as "manly hero[s], fulfilling America's destiny of taming the continent" (Moore 2012: 13). The recrafting of the cowboy coincided with American anxieties about the disappearance of the "frontier" that had come to be associated with Americans' unique character and strength, as well as nostalgia for an earlier time in the face of rapid industrialization, urban expansion, and European immigration (Baptist 2014; Moore 2012).[7] The articulation of the frontier being entangled with notions of American exceptionalism and strength was advanced by historian Frederick Jackson Turner's celebratory embellishment of US settler-colonialism following 1890, on the precipice of Texas's (and indeed the United States') first oil boom. Turner argued, "The result is that to the frontier the American intellect owes its striking characteristics. That coarseness and strength combined with acuteness and inquisitiveness; that practical, inventive turn of mind, quick to find expedients; that masterful grasp of material things, lacking in the artistic but powerful to effect great ends; that restless, nervous energy; that dominant individualism, working for good and for evil, and withal that buoyancy and exuberance which comes with freedom—these are traits of the frontier." (Turner 1928 [1920]: 37). Turner advanced the argument that it was frontier individualism, to which Texas was central, that promoted democracy in the United States. These sentiments dovetailed with popular representations of cowboys, the frontier, and western "culture" in dime novels and in traveling "western shows" during this time period (Moore 2012: 208). Indeed, Turner's 1893 intervention on the meaning of the frontier and the subsequent volume of essays he published in 1920, *The Frontier in American History*, had a formidable impact on the usage and understandings of the frontier at the same time that notions of the American cowboy were being recrafted.[8] In the wake of Turner's early intervention, the term "frontier" was adopted by hundreds of book titles and came to be associated with the border lands that separated "civilization" from the "wilderness" and "unoccupied territory" (Mood 1945, 1948: 82).

The idea of the frontier, however, has enjoyed a much longer history. Tracing the etymology of "frontier" to the Latin words "*frons*" and later "*fronteria*," Mood (1948) shows that it was first adapted into French before it was taken up in English sometime in the 1600s. Mapping its meanings and applications over the next two centuries, Mood shows that the concept of the frontier was commonly defined as the "bounds or limits" of a country or territory (Mood 1948: 78). It was only in the context of American settler-colonialism following the American Revolution that, Mood (1948) shows, the meaning of the word "frontier" changed from denoting a territorial limit to denoting the edge of an expansive advance.[9] In the decades that followed the American Revolution, US English dictionaries defined "frontier" as not just a limit or boundary but in terms of the "furthest settlement" (Mood 1948: 79). Anthropologist Sonja Dobroski (2022) has shown that US settler heuristics and American identities have developed in relation to notions of frontier, the treatment of Native American peoples, and the capture of their lands.[10] With indigenous territories rebranded as frontier, the protagonists of these imaginaries are Christian European settlers, of which the "cowboy" is a capillary. She suggests that this settler-frontier heuristic has been, and continues to be, central to a wide swath of extractive practices and their moral justifications across the United States.

The notions of the cowboy and the frontier are, thus, integral to one another and tied to the United States' expansive phase of growth in the 1800s, of which Texas was of central importance. In these entangled historical imaginaries, the cowboy is an agent of change situated on the precipice between "civilization" and an unharnessed nature from which he derives strength and demonstrates his independence. Earlier trappers and traders, by contrast, were situated beyond the frontier—crafting lives and livelihoods from the "wilderness" in territories beyond "civilization." Operating in the liminal space between Anglo-American settlements and an unknown nature that offered "gifts of free land" and seemingly endless "opportunity," historical imaginaries of the cowboy continue to excite the imagination of many (Turner 1893: 223, 227; Moore 2012).[11] Cowboy narratives often situate cowboys at the bottom of the socioeconomic strata but endow them with the socially mobile potential of becoming cattlemen, offering not only imaginaries of "adventure" but also hopes of class mobility (Moore 2012).[12] I suggest that for many it serves as a key temporal device by framing "how people contemplate their present conditions and potential futures in terms of the past" (Knight and Stewart 2016: 2). Thus, when my interlocutors invoke the notion of cowboys to describe independent producers searching for oil and gas, as Tony did at the beginning of the Introduction and others do throughout this book, the subterranean strata where hydrocarbons lurk is their frontier and the cowboy is a device by which to historically situate these activities.

My ethnographic encounter with John had a mixture of these frontier and historical markings. The cowskin rugs, the antique hunting knives and rifle, deer heads on the wall, and references to Texas's history as an "independent republic" were not only historical artifacts and registers but a way of anchoring the present in regard to the past. Anthropologist Webb Keane (2015: 27) describes things that come to bear on the "process of making ethical evaluations and decisions" as "ethical affordances."

Adopting the idea of an affordance from psychology, Keane (2016) explains that ethical affordances are not determinate but are available to be drawn on in processes of evaluation—from reflectively evaluating past choices to determining the "right" course of future action and deciphering the behavior of others. Affordances can be objects, as well as experiences, laws, narratives, and habitual practices. The idea of the frontier, I suggest, is one such ethical affordance that interlocutors I came to know drew on to historically orient themselves in relation to the world.

Ethical affordances may also be a way of describing how real and imagined moral exemplars are adopted into people's ethical frameworks—a process by which subjects of moral admiration become objects of ethical reference by which people orient themselves and evaluate the conduct of themselves and others, as well as the broader circumstances in which they are situated. The historical imaginaries of the cowboy and of Texas's early oilmen, I suggest, are examples of exemplars turned affordances for many I came to know. Thus, while John revered the ingenuity and resilience of the oil industry, as a whole, his greatest praise was reserved for independent producers, who perhaps most closely resemble the historical imaginary of the cowboy of the past.

From Cowboys to Oilmen

There is a remarkable amount of overlap between the historical imaginary of the cowboy and that of Texas's early oilmen, in part because some of the earliest oilmen had pre-oil careers in the cattle industry drilling water wells in rural Texas (Clark 2016; Moore 2012). Texas remained a predominantly agricultural state prior to the discovery of oil. The "heavy" industry that did exist consisted of the lumber mills in the eastern part of the state, which produced fortunes for lumber barons John Henry Kirby and Jim West (Burrough 2009). When oil was discovered at Spindletop, few are known to have made and retained the wealth they had hoped for, with the exception of Howard Hughes, who made his fortune by patenting and manufacturing rotary drilling heads, which became the industry standard (Botson 2005). The establishment of dynastic Texas oil fortunes came in the 1930s and 1940s.

Twentieth-century oilman Hugh Roy Cullen not only is a legendary example of the wealth that oil can generate but, importantly, provides a moral and temporal arch connecting Texas's past with the state's present-day oil industry. Born in Texas in 1881, Hugh Cullen was the grandson of Ezekiel Wimberly Cullen, who had immigrated to Texas from Georgia in 1835 and fought in Texas's war of independence (Cullen Foundation 2023). Cullen was raised by his mother in San Antonio—where the Alamo is located—after his father, a cattle buyer, reportedly abandoned the family when Cullen was young (Burrough 2009). Cullen's mother had immigrated to Texas around the time of the US Civil War after Union soldiers (from the US Northeast) burned her family's plantation (Burrough 2009). Cullen left school in the fifth grade and by the age of sixteen found work with a cotton brokerage, where he reportedly negotiated with farmers to buy their cotton crops, traveling from farm to farm on horseback (Burrough 2009; Cullen Foundation 2023). In 1911 Cullen moved to Houston, where he diversified his business from cotton to include real estate investing. According to Burrough (2009), Cullen "accidentally" fell into the oil industry when a real estate developer located in the same office building offered Cullen a job purchasing mineral rights for prospective oil exploration. After drilling three unsuccessful wells and losing $250,000 of investors' money, he marked his first successful "wildcat" prospect in 1920 with a pile of "handpicked cow manure" in the middle of a pasture (Burrough 2009: 19; Cullen Foundation 2023). For many, Roy Cullen is a moral exemplar who is emblematic of a generation of oilmen whose virtues and rags-to-riches stories are both aspirational and characterize the "heart" of the industry.

Continuing our conversation at his office, John explained, "The original Cullen, Hugh Roy, he made a practice of: if you came to him with a prospect, an idea, very often he would give you more money or more interest than you asked for. . . . It got him first look at every deal in town." Beyond Cullen's being a prudent businessman and one of the most successful Texas oilmen, John attributed a "kind of spirit" to him, by which he pointed to a genuine honesty and "goodness" about him. Not only was he more than "fair," John suggested, by sharing the wealth that oil could generate, but he was also willing to give hopeful property owners, lease holders, and prospectors a chance. The gesture of sharing oil wealth and oil luck, John suggested, was demonstrative of Cullen's commitment to contributing to and building a Texan society founded on oil. Other of my interlocutors also invoked Cullen. One of them credited "wildcatters like McCarthy and Hugh Roy Cullen" with bringing "massive amounts of money" to the state and with shaping Texas society as it "exists today," a society built by oil wealth and around "the idea that finding oil is good." Others also pointed to his legacy. "He just gave away enormous amounts of money" even though he could barely read and write, another of my interlocutors claimed, pointing to Cullen's dropping out of school in the fifth grade. He was not suggesting that Cullen's limited ability to read and write was contrary to his generosity but rather pointed to Cullen's limited literacy to emphasize the man's ability to transcend barriers. For many, Cullen and other early oilmen continue to be a "real-life" rags-to-riches moral archetype. No one who invoked Cullen mentioned his political legacy of ultraconservatism or his well-documented racism (Burrough 2009). Instead, he and other early oilmen were invoked as inspirational exemplars.

One interlocutor who was in his early thirties and grew up in Austin, Texas, explained to me, for example, how Roy Cullen, H. L. Hunt, and other early oilmen inspired him to enter the oil industry: "Even as a kid I was drawn to it. You hear about the Hunts, or the Murchisons, or some of these families. It's like, 'Holy crap, you guys did what?' . . . That was part of the appeal. I've wanted to be in the '[oil] well' since elementary school." While giant multinational corporations dominate the US oil and gas industry today, it was independent producers ("wildcatters") who drilled exploratory wells in pursuit of oil—like Cullen—who brought the industry into being and are celebrated as present-day moral exemplars (High 2022).[13] Thus, while most of my interlocutors do not wear cowboy hats, bolo ties, and cowboy boots, figures such as Cullen are a temporal-moral register that orients the ethical sensibilities of many I have come to know. The companies that they built, for many, are testament to their achievement. Quintana Petroleum, founded by Hugh Cullen, and the Hunt Oil Company, founded by H. L. Hunt, still exist today (Cullen Foundation 2023; Hunt Oil Company 2022; Quintana Resources 2023). Other examples include the Gulf Oil Company and the Texas Fuel Company (Texaco), which were established following the 1901 Spindletop discovery just east of Houston (Burrough 2009; Gulf 2022; Texaco 2022). Humble Oil, founded in 1917, by "Houston and Beaumont oilmen" who also began their careers at Spindletop is another example (Burrough 2009: 13). What these companies have in common, besides their Texas roots, is that they were founded by independent oilmen and, for a time, supplied the United States with vast amounts of crude oil (Yergin 2009). Some continue to play a formative role in the world of oil and gas. Others, such as Humble and Texaco, are better known by the names of their amalgamated corporate successors, ExxonMobil and Chevron (Blum 2016; Burrough 2009).

Early Texas oilmen like Cullen were champions of what some called the state's "independence culture" that connected its present with its past. Some described it as encompassing a "distrust of East Coast bankers" and "big" oil companies, as well as an anti–federal government sentiment. One of my interlocutors summarized this sentiment as "we don't like anybody with a lot of power from the East coming down to tell us how to run our business." From Texas's early settlers to twentieth-century oilmen, many invoked the idea of independence as demonstrative of the "culture" that defines the industry, Texas, and Texans.

"An Entrepreneurial Spirit"

For John, this independence was synonymous with what he called the "entrepreneurial spirit," which he credited Texas's earliest settlers for establishing and present-day oilmen for maintaining. Other of my interlocutors made similar conceptual connections. Echoing John, another interlocutor proudly explained to me that being an entrepreneur, being Texan, and the notion of the cowboy were so integrally connected that they were figuratively joined at the molecular level by "DNA": "Texans by nature are just entrepreneurial. . . . We're going to be on our own. It's just an attitude, the way people are here. It's in the DNA to be a cowboy and to go it your own way. . . . It's always going to be that way." In a similar vein, another interlocutor affectionately explained to me that the "culture" within the industry today is reflective of "early-twentieth-century Texas values," which "were pretty libertarian, very pragmatic . . . [and] very entrepreneurial."

Several of my interviewees said that the state and municipalities cultivated and nurtured this independent "culture." Many invoked the absence of personal, corporate, and estate tax collection as examples of how the state of Texas differentiated itself from other states and maintained the libertarian "frontier freedoms" that early state settlers enjoyed—freedoms that many associated with the cultivation of entrepreneurship and innovation, which were allowed to flourish when unencumbered by oppressive tax regimes, they said. One interlocutor explained, for example, "From a regulatory and legal standpoint, we're very, very free-markets oriented and entrepreneurial. We have low taxes, relatively low. No state income taxes. . . . It allows for a lot of innovation." Other interlocutors echoed these sentiments, telling me that Texas has a "friendly tax environment" and that "it's a tax-free zone," which has endowed it with a "friendly economic environment" and a "pragmatic regulatory structure." A managing partner at a private equity firm specializing in oil and gas, whom I call Kyle, explained to me at his office how the state's tax laws dovetailed with its regime of private property and mineral rights to create the right environment for "explorers." He explained, "They have [oil] in Pittsburgh, and they have it in Pennsylvania, and . . . Oklahoma too. But, I think they're different. The rules that we have here in Texas, specifically, I think have encouraged and have helped people who want to be explorers." Here Kyle uses "explorer" in both a specific and a general sense, referring to the exploration for oil and gas specifically and also to the facilitation of more general explorer personality traits, which connect Texas's past and present.

There was also often a temporal-historical dimension to these sentiments that connected the past and present in ways that were stabilizing. This stabilizing temporal dimension was captured by phrases such as "it's always going to be that way" and by references to Texan culture and social "codes" that transverse time. The notion of agential independence cuts across these and other accounts I observed in ways that connected frontier and cowboy narratives with notions of present-day entrepreneurship. When I asked my interlocutors what entrepreneurship was to them, I received various but overlapping answers that intersected with the ethnographic excerpts above. For example, one person replied, "I think that an entrepreneur is different than a small businessman. I think an entrepreneur is someone who can . . . articulate a vision in a way that allows them to attract capital around which they can build an enterprise." Another told me, "Entrepreneurship is creating something. It's creating a business from next to nothing and really going off on your own to build something." Yet another said, "When I say 'entrepreneurial,' it is . . . self-reliance . . . a sense of confidence that they can do it—bootstraps—and they'll do whatever they have to do to make something happen. That goes back to the self-reliance and coming here to create or build, or make something happen." Others echoed these sentiments, replying that what distinguished entrepreneurs was their accumulative capacity to "build" and "create," combined with their ability to be "confident" and "self-reliant" in ways that allowed them to develop a profitable business. The notion of building "something from nothing" not only characterized many of the entrepreneurial notions that my interlocutors described to me but also echoed settler-frontier notions of crafting livelihoods from an underexploited "nature."

Contemporary and popular notions of the entrepreneur can be traced to neoclassical economist Joseph Schumpeter. Prior to Schumpeter, few are known to have distinguished entrepreneurs from "businessmen" and "capitalists" (Taymans 1951). For Schumpeter (2008 [1942]: 131), entrepreneurs are the engine of what he considered to be the "evolutionary process" of capitalism. He argued, "The function of entrepreneurs is to reform or revolutionize the pattern of production by exploiting an invention or, more generally, an untried technological possibility for producing a new commodity or producing an old one in a new way, by opening up a new source or supply of minerals or a new outlet for products, by reorganising an industry and so on" (Schumpeter 2008 [1942]: 132). The "capitalist entrepreneur" is the "mechanism of change," he said, who provides "individual leadership acting by virtue of personal force and personal responsibility for success." In the process, entrepreneurs are at the vanguard of what he famously calls "creative destruction" and are the engine of profits gleaned from "successful innovation" (Schumpeter 2017 [1912]: 72, 2008 [1942]: 81–83, 133).[14] None of my interlocutors mentioned Schumpeter by name but seemingly drew on his ideas of entrepreneurship, and many closely associated entrepreneurs with risk taking, innovation, and value creation.

I suggest that as an agent of change, the entrepreneur—like the cowboy—is a protagonist of tension. Hailed as the harbinger of "progress" and "profit," entrepreneurs instigate change that fits within the historical trajectories of capitalism. The entrepreneur does not, for example, advocate for systemic societal change or a kind of postcapitalist politics. Instead, the entrepreneur allows historical capitalist trajectories with their social stratifications to continue intact, while providing the opportunity for class ascension and wealth accumulation. Like the historical imaginary of the cowboy, the entrepreneur is the individual situated on the precipice of the present and the future, the precondition for a kind of settler-frontier advance that in turn lays the preconditions for future industry and profit creation. If an entrepreneur is, as Schumpeter suggests, responsible for supplying new sources of minerals and providing new ways of producing old commodities, then it is perhaps fitting that the entrepreneur has in many ways merged with, if not supplemented, the historical imaginary of the cowboy for the interlocutors I came to know. What the cowboy and the entrepreneur share is the notion of material provisioning—providing the material means for society to exist. Coinhabiting the world in a material, and indeed moral, tension with society, both protagonist ideal types engender a kind of Ayn Randian libertarianism by challenging and succeeding against external forces that curtail their ambitions—manifest as wilderness in particular, nature in general, or big government. Woven into allegorical narratives about financial and existential risk taking, self-reliance (an individual-oriented responsibility), and progress (a time orientation toward change), they constitute powerful ethical registers by which my interlocutors ethically orient themselves, as well as narrate the present and future.

A Lone Star "Culture"

Many of my interviewees invoked the term "Texas culture" when referring to a variety of contemporary, historical, and historical-imaginative factors that have come to bear on their sensibilities. The concept of culture, as utilized by academics, has been problematized as reinforcing colonial power dynamics, for generalizing entire communities of people, and for ignoring the diversities of life within communities. Anthropologist Canay Özden-Schilling (2021: 8), however, suggests that there is "value in holding on to 'culture'" when we think of it as a toolkit of symbols, stories, rituals, worldviews, and images by which we ethically orient ourselves in navigating the world. This idea of culture can be particularly helpful, she suggests, when we are thinking about expert communities, whose members work with a set of common materials, tools, and problems.

I have suggested that the notion of the frontier, the historical-imaginary of the cowboy, and exemplary twentieth-century oilmen are ethical affordances in the cultural toolkits of the interlocutors I came to know. These affordances are tied to Texas's long settler-colonial history and the state's history of commodity production that began with cotton. The cowboy, I have also suggested, remains an important historical imaginary that, over the decades, has become entangled with contemporary notions of the entrepreneur. This entanglement is perhaps not unique to Texas, as similar iterations are likely to be found across the central and southwestern United States. It is, however, relevant within the community of interlocutors on which this book centers, and it is linked to notions of agential action, an "American way of life," and specifically a Texas way of life. Drawing on these notions, some of my interlocutors told me that the shale revolution, which I discuss in chapter 2, could have started in Oklahoma or Louisiana, but it did not. The reason it started in Texas, they said, is that Texas had the "right" culture; and, just as "cowboy culture" and cattle farming had spread from Texas to states across the United States, so too would a new way of extracting oil and gas—"fracking"—and a land grab on which this new form of resource extraction depended. I agree with Özden-Schilling (2021) that there is value in holding onto the concept of culture when it is analytically applied to expert communities in specific contexts.

While my interlocutors may share financial knowledges, modes of expertise, and tools of analysis with financiers in New York, Chicago, London, Paris, and Tokyo, evidence presented from ethnographies conducted within these financial communities does not indicate that industry professionals in these places invoked similar cowboy notions so readily, if at all. Indeed, if finance is "borderless" because of global flows of capital and because of shared knowledges, expertise, and tools among those who direct this capital, it is perhaps these regional cultures—manifest in regional historical imaginaries and ideal types that ethically orient people and their allegories—that differentiate how capital is deployed and to what end. This historical regional context is vital for understanding the sensibilities of the financiers, as well as the engineers and technicians they funded, because shared historical imaginaries are vital to the allegories interlocutors tell about themselves, the industry, and hydrocarbon finance. As a result, I suggest, these allegories can tell us something important about an ethical orientation that my interlocutors share in common and what might analytically be described as culture. In the next chapter, I build on these themes in discussing an oil rush that came to define the early 2000s and changed the world in profound ways.

2

Financing the US Shale Revolution

Rich people make their money in the private markets while poor people try to make it in the public markets.
—Houston private equity financier, Twitter, 2020

I was excited to meet up with Arthur again. We had met for lunch at a Tex-Mex restaurant a few months earlier and he agreed to meet me at his office, located southwest of Houston's downtown core. It was a cool and misty day in January 2019, and when I arrived at the eleventh-floor suite, Arthur was meeting two men in the boardroom adjacent to his office's lobby. I chatted with the receptionist for a moment and then took a seat. The wall separating the lobby from the boardroom was clear glass, and I could see that the two men he was meeting with were wearing suits, while Arthur was wearing a collared white shirt with a fleece vest and slacks. Sitting across from one another, they looked engaged in their conversation and occasionally looked down at some documents. The two men looked as though they were presenting something. I wondered if they worked for one of Arthur's portfolio companies or if they were pitching a business plan in hopes that Arthur's firm would invest. A few minutes later, the men got up, rolled up what appeared to be some large maps, shook hands with Arthur, and emerged through the boardroom door before exiting the office through the lobby where I was seated. Arthur emerged a few seconds later. With a grin, he extended his arm to shake my hand and invited me in. We sat at the boardroom table where he and the two men had just met. Arthur said I should sit facing the window so I could enjoy the view of the mist-swept cityscape while we talked. There was a large black-and-white map of the United States on the table between us, just off to the left. Tiny squares on the map divided the United States into a massive grid, and thousands of tiny blue, green, and brown dots were speckled across it—clustering around Texas, the Northeast, and up through the Midwest. The colors, he explained, denoted the quality of oil deposits, from high to low. Pointing to the map as we talked, he explained that his firm "only goes for high-quality" deposits. Arthur is not an "oil man," though; he is a managing partner at a Houston-based private equity firm specializing in oil exploration and production. Private equity firms provide a way for institutional investors, such as pension funds, and wealthy clients to invest in companies that are not traded on stock exchanges (Souleles 2019), and firms like Arthur's specialize in creating, buying, selling, and trading private companies.

We began by chatting about his early career and how he became a private equity financier. He grew up in Austin, he said, and earned a degree at the University of Texas, where he interned with Enron. When he graduated, he was hired by the Houston office of a major US investment bank on a "two-year analyst program,"[1] which laid the foundation for the rest of his career.

> My partners that I have today, I was working with them right out of undergrad at Bull Capital . . . doing energy investment banking in the early 2000s. . . . I loved the financial modeling. I used to joke that I was a coder, a computer coder, but my language was Excel. . . . I loved putting together, or working on, deals that you would see in the *Wall Street Journal*. I loved the exposure that I had at that age of twenty-two, twenty-three, twenty-four . . . flying around on the private jet with CEOs and CFOs on the road show to talk about whatever was the latest deal that they did, or whatever capital markets deal they wanted. They were trying to sell some equity or some debt. . . . At the time, we were definitely number one in energy for Wall Street. . . . It was great exposure to the energy business, and to the financial world.

This was the training for his career as a private equity financier, he told me. When he left investment banking, he worked for a couple of private equity firms and oil and gas firms, before he and his current partners raised their first "fund." He explained, "A lot of our investors are college endowments, pension funds, foundations, and insurance companies. We started that first fund in 2014 and we finished [fundraising] in 2016. We invested all that capital, committed all those funds to various portfolio investments, and then we started raising a second fund at the end of

2017. We finished that [fundraising] about a year ago . . . and so we're investing out of that fund right now." "Funds" are the vital pool of capital on which the private equity business turns. Private equity firms raise "funds" from investors, then invest this money. Since the early 2000s, private equity firms specializing in US onshore oil exploration and production, like Arthur's, have been vital to an expansive phase of growth in the onshore US oil and gas industry, dubbed "the shale revolution." By channeling billions of dollars into unconventional exploration and production companies, Arthur and his peers turned a sunset industry in the United States, with most of its onshore oil resources extracted at the turn of the millennium, into an expanding sector in the midst of a technological renaissance. In the process, they profoundly changed the energy landscape of the United States, and indeed the globe, by unlocking previously unthinkable quantities of oil and gas (Haines 2013a; McLean 2018; USEIA 2016, 2018, 2021b, 2021c, 2024).

Arthur has crafted a career, indeed an identity, as an oil and gas private equity financier. Being a managing partner at the firm makes him "feel very entrepreneurial," he tells me; but, he explained, "It took me a while to kind of discover that in myself because it wasn't modeled at home." While he was born in Texas, his parents are from New England and do not have the same Texas sensibilities, he suggested. They wanted "company jobs," he said—but not Arthur. He is not a pension taker, like his parents; he is a pension maker and, for him, what makes being a private equity financier entrepreneurial is that it puts him in a position of control. He explained, "To me, entrepreneurship just means that you are in control of your own destiny. . . . I mean, there are always things that are outside of your control. . . . But to me, it just means you are applying what you have learned throughout your life throughout your career to go and address some need. And in doing so, you are . . . in control of your own destiny . . . and trying to make the most of this opportunity that you see." He told me that he "loves" Houston, small to medium-sized oil and gas companies, and hydrocarbon private equity finance because they are full of "entrepreneurs" and "the entrepreneurial spirit." He likes being the bridge between "noble" organizations and oilmen who have "seen an opportunity . . . but they just need the money to be able to do it." He sees it as his responsibility to make this connection and seize this potentiality. It puts him in a position where he can make the "golden ticket" dreams of aspiring oilmen come true (or not) while shaping society in profound ways—from morally provisioning hydrocarbons to generating the wealth that institutions need (High 2022: 740). In many ways Arthur echoes the cowboy sentiments explored in chapter 1 and the entanglement of these sentiments with notions of value creation, entrepreneurship, and risk taking—in a way that bridges high finance and the contemporary US oil industry.

In this chapter, I explore the world of US hydrocarbon finance and argue that without private equity firms like Arthur's, the shale revolution could not have unfolded as it did. While other types of financiers also played a role in channeling capital into exploration and production companies, such as commercial lenders, it was private equity financiers who gave the shale revolution its financial momentum. Seizing on investor fervor to be a part of a new American oil rush, private equity firms offered investors an opportunity to capture part of the wealth that oil "booms" have been known to generate. In doing so, they are part of a long lineage of private investors on which the US oil industry has turned since its founding, who are empowered to define and take risks on our collective behalf in pursuit of profits. I begin by explaining why investor capital has been and continues to be the "oxygen" on which small to medium-size exploration and production companies thrive. I then show how private equity came to be a vital conduit connecting institutional investors and E&P firms at a time when domestic energy security concerns were rising and investor returns were low in the wake of two successive financial crises. In the process, I demonstrate how private equity came to be perceived as a "golden ticket" for aspiring oilmen, premised on a model of what one of my interlocutors called "venture capital real estate." I conclude by returning to Arthur. I suggest that as agents who direct private capital flows, private equity financiers are conduits of responsibility that connect people around the world to oil and gas projects in the United States.

The "Oxygen" of the Industry

Finding and producing oil, and more recently gas, is expensive. Exploration and production require a lot of specialized equipment and highly skilled labor, and prior to more sophisticated geological survey methods, my interlocutors told me, it was standard to drill nine "dry" holes for every one well that produced oil. As one industry veteran exclaimed, "The oil and gas business is always out of money.... It just inhales capital" (Clark 2016: i). Other industry experts, meanwhile, have remarked that investment capital is the "oxygen" on which the US oil and gas industry depends (McLean 2018: 28). In the industry's earliest days, the cost of drilling wells was measured in the tens of thousands of dollars (Burrough 2009; Clark 2016). These were conventional wells, however, composed of oil and gas that had migrated from source rock into pools trapped beneath impermeable geological strata (Everett et al. 2012). Conventional wells involve drilling down vertically and puncturing the impermeable layer to access the reservoir; subterranean pressure would then push this oil to the surface.[2] Unconventional wells are more expensive to drill and complete because they are longer and require more inputs. They require drilling down to the source rock where the majority of hydrocarbons remain trapped, then drilling horizontally, and releasing the trapped oil and gas by injecting a mixture of fluid and proppants (such as sand).[3] A veteran reservoir engineer explained to me that unconventional wells can cost up to $30 million each. Other interlocutors confirmed this figure. "Good" drillers, however, can produce unconventional wells for about $10 million depending on input costs, which can fluctuate in price.

The oil industry, in the United States and abroad, is well known for its "major" integrated oil companies—such as Shell, BP, ExxonMobil, and Chevron. The United States is also home to several independent oil companies.[4] These major and independent oil companies often have large budgets for exploration and production, but they are vastly outnumbered by small to medium-sized exploration and production companies that do not have large capital expenditure budgets and are constantly in search of capital. Between the 1940s and the 1980s, for example, there were reportedly one thousand small to medium-sized independent exploration and production companies for every major oil company operating in the United States. In 2015, it was estimated that about seven thousand independent E&P companies were operating in the United States in comparison with only a dozen majors (Clark 2016: 5).

The challenge for these small to medium-sized oil companies has been and continues to be that commercial lenders rarely, if ever, provide all of the capital they require. In the first part of the twentieth century, a limited number of bankers were willing to risk losing depositors' life savings on loans secured by prospective oil reserves as "collateral that could neither be measured nor seen" (Clark 2016: 43).[5] Greater technological sophistication in estimating potential oil reserves expanded commercial reserve-based lending to independent oil producers beginning in the 1950s, but lending practices rarely provide all the capital E&P companies require (Clark 2016). Commercial banks can provide companies with reserve-based loans if they can prove they have reserves that can be leveraged.[6] The goal of exploration and production companies is to find oil and gas; this makes reserve-based loans difficult because the oil and gas, in many cases, has yet to be found and proven. Reserve-based loans, moreover, are risky for lenders because underground reserves are just *estimates* and the projected "value" of these reserves changes with fluctuations in oil and gas prices (which I explore in chapter 3). There is no guarantee that companies will *profitably* produce these reserves, many told me, because costs can rise and companies can be mismanaged. Many small to medium-sized E&P companies have been, and continue to be, reliant on private investors to fund operations—a gap that private equity firms bridge by connecting investors with companies.

The first oil-and-gas-specific PE firms in the United States were established in the late 1980s in Texas.[7] Houston-based EnCap and Dallas-headquartered Natural Gas Partners were the pioneers of this genre of PE in the United States. Established by experienced commercial oil and gas bankers, these firms were founded, one interviewee joked, by a "bunch of unemployed bankers" who turned oil and gas PE into something that "you can make a lot of money" doing. At first, they acted as private lenders and consultants, my interlocutors explained, but by the mid-1990s they had crafted a model to buy direct equity ownership in small to medium-sized private companies. The strategy behind this model was to grow the asset "value" of these companies, then sell these assets (and the companies that owned them) to larger companies, such as integrated majors or large independent producers. These larger companies would then further exploit these assets. My interlocutors referred to this process of developing assets and companies to be sold to larger companies as the "food chain" (see Wood 2016). For private equity firms, selling to larger companies was their "exit strategy," whereby the transaction allowed them to recover the capital they had invested, plus a profit. They could then return capital to their investors and claim their performance fee.

The relationship between private investors and private equity firms is a partnership.[8] The private equity firm is known as the "general partner" (GP) and is responsible for making all decisions related to fund management, investing, and generating profits. Often, the managing partners at the private equity firm, like Arthur, invest some of their own money into each of the funds that they raise. Their investors are the "limited partners" (LPs). In exchange for maximizing the returns for LPs, the private equity firm earns a management fee and a performance fee. Funds can range in size from several million to several billion dollars. Management fees range from 2 percent to 3 percent of the total fund size, while performance fees (known as "carried interest") can range from 5 percent to 20 percent of the return (profit) generated from the fund's investments (Souleles 2019: 7; Kati 2022).[9]

The preference of oil and gas private equity firms to invest in small to medium-sized E&P companies is part of what distinguishes this subsector from the broader US private equity sector described by anthropologists Karen Ho (2009) and Daniel Souleles (2019). The origins of private equity finance can be traced to the middle of the twentieth century, to early venture capitalist firms (Wilson 1985). In the 1980s, private equity became closely associated with "corporate raiders," "hostile takeovers," and "leveraged buyouts" (Burrough and Helyar 2008 [1989]; Ho 2009: 139; Souleles 2019: 64).[10] Using a leveraged buyout strategy, private equity firms would raise debt capital by selling high-yield ("junk") bonds and combine this with a small portion of private equity capital to purchase a firm. They would then use the purchased company's cash flow to pay down the bond debt, increasing their equity stake as the debt decreased. They could then sell the company, as a whole or in pieces,[11] for many times the amount they paid for it.[12] As a result, Souleles (2019) notes, "generalist" PE firms have tended to prefer large and mature corporations as their target of acquisition. Houston-based private equity firms specializing in US oil and gas are different from these older generalist firms. They are more akin to venture capitalists because they prefer smaller, younger companies and endeavor to grow the asset "value" of these companies. Relatedly, they also do not utilize leveraged buyouts, because large, publicly traded companies are not their target of acquisition.

The advantage of private companies is that they do not have to regularly publish financial details or comply with regulations stipulated by regulatory bodies such as the US Security and Exchange Commission.[13] This not only makes what these companies do and how much they profit more secretive, but it also means they can take greater financial risks than the regulators and shareholders of public companies might allow. As multinational management and consultant firm Ernst & Young (2018: 5) notes, "Not all businesses are suited for life in the public eye." Oil and gas private equity depends on utilizing asymmetrical information about investment opportunities, gathering information from people with "deep" local knowledge that is not publicly known, and confidentiality (High 2022). A managing partner at one firm told me that his firm depends on "boots on the ground," which, he explained, meant that they employ informants in key locations who source and collate information for his firm. Collating information from various sources, they can identify emerging investment opportunities and better evaluate "pitches" from entrepreneurs and aspiring oilmen seeking private investment.

Private equity is, thus, different from other forms of finance, such as commercial lending, in several ways. Private equity has a higher risk of financial loss but also aims to generate higher returns for investors. Equity means ownership, whereas forms of lending mean debt, which comes with different sets of legal relationships. The loan agreement binding lenders and borrowers has "covenants" that spell out the terms and conditions of the debt arrangement.[14] While lenders may monitor a firm's health, they do not typically take an active role in managing companies. Loan agreements aim to reduce future uncertainty for the lender by specifying courses of action associated with potential future events, such as payment default. Private equity firms, in contrast to commercial lenders, tend to take a direct role in managing firms in their investment portfolios—from selecting senior managers to working closely with management teams to ensure firms meet their goals. They exercise more control.

Commercial lenders tend to target "proven" operations in the oil and gas industry by focusing on established businesses with producing, rather than potential, hydrocarbon reserves. Commercial lenders, a managing partner at a PE firm explained, have been and continue to be unwilling to lend capital for "exploration plays" not only because if exploration fails their loans default but also because they have no financial incentive to do so. If an oil and gas prospect turns out to be hugely profitable, lenders will only get their contractual principal and interest. Moreover, one former oil and gas commercial lender explained that "the margins in the banking business are so small, that if you ever make a bad loan, you might as well quit. You won't live long enough to make the money back." Private equity general and limited partners, meanwhile, stand to benefit from the entirety of the profit-making potential of prospective hydrocarbon reserves. On the vanguard, PE firms and their portfolio companies specialize in proving the "potentiality" of reserves and their future profitability, where profitability is "less a concrete number" and more of a geofinancial probability imbued with capitalist hopes and dreams (Miyazaki 2013; Weszkalnys 2015: 617; Wood 2016: 45). Arthur explained that, as with other private equity firms, he expects that some of his portfolio companies will lose money but hopes that others will cover these losses and exceed expectations. He said,

> There's real risk involved in this business . . . the risk of just losing almost everything on an investment. That's why when you're doing private equity investing, you've got a portfolio of companies, maybe six to ten companies in any one fund. Maybe one is going to be a loser. But, hopefully, you've got a real winner in there and you make three times your money on it. Then the others are all just like, "You did pretty well," "You didn't do great, but you didn't lose your shirt on it." Hopefully, it all averages out so that you made one and a half to two times your money.

Figure 2.1 situates private equity on the spectrum of oil and gas finance. This figure is a reproduction of similar diagrams I collected during fieldwork and is demonstrative of the type of visual representations used by interlocutors I know when they are speaking with prospective investors.

A "Golden Ticket"?

As anthropologist Mette High (2022) shows, independent oilmen and oil entrepreneurs have, over the last two and a half decades, been

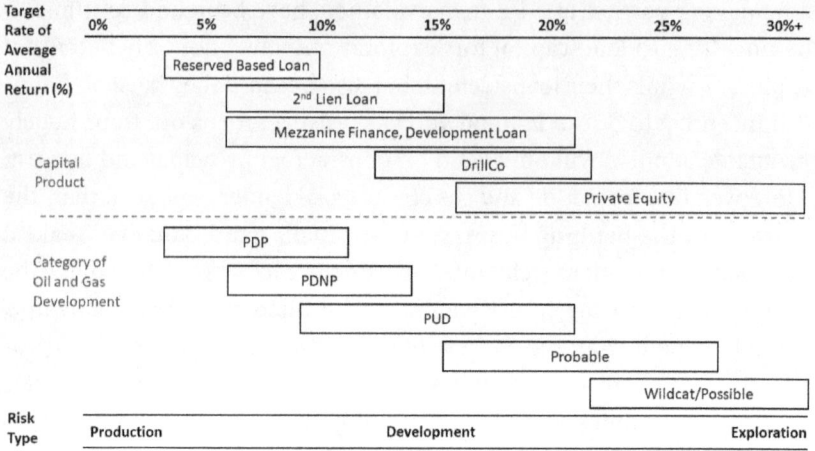

Figure 2.1: Risk-return matrix example. A reproduction by the author of similar visual diagrams collected during fieldwork. The acronyms represent stages of oil and gas E&P: PDP is "proven developed producing," PDNP is "proven developed not producing," and PUD is "proven but undeveloped."

dependent on private equity financiers to breathe life into their dreams of founding their own companies. It is not only potential investors who are captivated by the potential returns that private equity finance can provide; oil and gas entrepreneurs have tirelessly competed to secure private equity investors since the shale revolution began. Documenting the impact of private equity finance on Colorado's oil and gas sector, High (2022) observes, "It was approached as a golden ticket that could turn any dream, any wild idea, into reality. It was seen as an invitation to do something different and to try to capitalize on what had not yet been explored. So much money, just sitting there and waiting for an entrepreneur to put it to work" (High 2022: 740). Many I came to know have shared and continue to share this euphoria, although they are aware that it often comes with pressures. John provides a demonstrative account of the tensions that independent oilmen can experience when working with private equity investors.

He and his partner had invested thousands of hours evaluating and bidding on prospective reserves. They invested time in understanding the particular geology of each prospect, they meticulously calculated how much oil and gas was estimated to be underground, and they prayed their calculations were correct. Then, John and his partner "won" a bid and found a private equity investor to finance the acquisition. "A company called Capital X was the equity partner that put up the private equity money that let us do it. . . . We did equity with two or three different tranches. Then we did a senior loan facility, and a subordinated loan facility with Bank Y." Without private equity investors, John did not have enough capital to purchase the oil and gas reserves that he and his partner wanted to drill. Without the reserves, he did not have the collateral assets to secure the first and secondary loans that he needed to cover some of the operational costs of getting started. Private equity was the vital oxygen that allowed John to start his independent oil and gas company.

Within a few years of founding his firm, his company was producing over sixty-five million btus of gas per year,[15] plus oil, with many more wells to be drilled and potentially "fracked." He explained to me with great excitement, "We got to do everything. We had pipelines and compressors, we had gas processing, you know we had drilling, we had recompletions . . . It was just great." As an experienced financier, John knew his company was not a "forever" project, or a company he was building to pass down to his children. It was the mid-2000s, the shale revolution was just beginning, and big oil and gas companies increasingly wanted to buy reservoir "inventory," of the sort that John's company owned. This worked well for John's private equity partners, who wanted to sell the firm and its assets within three to five years—the "exit strategy." John wanted to "hang on" for longer, five to seven years maybe, but he ultimately knew it was a terminal endeavor. Recalling this ongoing tension, John said, "They kept saying . . . we need to be out of this . . . in three to five years. And, I said: maybe five to seven. They said: three to five. Five to seven. And we kept bouncing back and forth, and finally I said: look, I don't know how long it's going to take us." John lauded private equity financiers as being "as smart as hell," but most of them did not understand the complexities of exploration and production, he told me. Elaborating on this tension, John explained, "Private equity guys are not operators. They're not geologists. They're . . . financial investors. . . . They need the guys who *know* how to do it and *can* do it." With pressure from his private equity investors and oil and gas prices rising— which increased the value of the firm's reservoir assets—he explained that they "began showing the company for sale, much sooner than I had ever anticipated."

The timing, as I explain below, was opportune because to John's surprise, big independent oil and gas companies "needed stuff to drill," he said. "I'm not really sure what did it," he told me, because "when we bought the field," big oil companies only wanted reservoirs that were 75 to 80 percent developed and producing (PDPs), with the remaining 20 to 25 percent proven but yet to be developed (PUDs). This was a problem for John and his investors at first, because, he explained, "Well hell, every time we drilled a well, we thought we had three more to drill." But then, in early 2004 he said companies developed an "appetite" for PUDs. Big independent oil and gas companies, he explained, "needed to be able to go out and say [to their shareholders], 'This is what we're going to [drill] over the next three or four years and here's where it is. What we have to do is: drill this well, this well, this well, this well . . . and we've got tons of them.' So, they didn't want PDPs anymore, they wanted more drilling." John was overwhelmed by the sudden interest from big oil companies in his very productive but largely undeveloped oil and gas field. He joked, "We were practically like the Baskin-Robbins ice cream store and had everybody take a number." Some of his colleagues were confused by his willingness to meet the time demands of his private equity partners to "exit" earlier than he anticipated. Recalling a particular encounter, he explained,

> And when we sold that company, one of the guys that was helping us with financing said, "John, I cannot believe you're selling that drilling company. I mean, business is the best it's ever been. Prices are better than they have ever been. You're going to make money hand over fist." I looked at him and I said, "Well, let me tell you something, if you've got some son of a bitch dumb enough to buy this company for more money than what I'm going to sell it for tomorrow morning, then, you get him over here. But otherwise, at ten o'clock tomorrow morning, it's going."

John's account is illustrative of the temporal shift that happened at the beginning of the shale revolution, when "undeveloped" hydrocarbons locked underground became more sought after by large independent oil companies than those currently being extracted. Prompted by the advent of modern "fracking," this shift may be interpreted as a stretching of these companies' view toward "value creation" as they accumulated reservoir "inventories" to be drilled. It is also illustrative of the relationship between "oilmen" and private equity financiers, in particular the tensions between them that turn on competing time horizons on the terminal life cycle of private equity–owned firms. As a driving force of the shale revolution, private equity finance has, in part, guarded against the construction of dynastic oil and gas companies, and, for a time, incubated a feedstock of small to medium-sized firms to be consumed by larger ones. In the process, this form of finance has, at the same time, fueled the hopes of aspiring oilmen who dream of carving out an existence, a reputation, a fortune, via small, privately owned oil companies in an industry dominated by oil majors. To understand why oil and gas private equity financiers like Arthur came to shape the US oil and gas industry, however, it is vital to understand the "perfect storm" of circumstances that converged in the early 2000s, around the time John sold his company.

"There's No Going Back"

After Mitchell Energy and Development Corporation's petroleum engineer, Nick Steinsberger, "cracked the code" of "fracking" in 1997, it took several months to confirm that his "slick-water frack" method could profitably produce natural gas from shale rock (Zuckerman 2014: 110). It took another three years to convince others in the industry that Mitchell's fracking method was "real"; "people didn't believe what we were saying," George Mitchell is reported to have said (Zuckerman 2014: 109). One of my interlocutors explained, "George is famous for having put his company up for sale in '99 and 2000 and getting no offers. None. Zero." After selling a Houston real estate development, the Woodlands, to Exxon "because he needed cash to keep his company going," this person explained, Mitchell Energy was able to "prove that fracking could work. . . . That's when he was able to sell [the company] to Devon for a couple of billion dollars." While many in the industry remained skeptical of Mitchell's fracking method, Devon Energy acquired Mitchell Energy and Development Corporation for $3.1 billion in 2001 after several months of collaboration between their exploration and production teams.

According to Gregory Zuckerman (2014: 109), who chronicles the acquisition, George Mitchell is reported to have said, "We convinced Devon. . . . They got it." Over the next couple of years independent oil and gas companies became increasingly convinced of the productive merits of "fracking" as Devon's success producing gas using this new method became known (McLean 2018). Independents Chesapeake, EOG (a spinoff of Enron), and Continental also began experimenting with and refining Mitchell Energy's fracking technique. By concentrating where the fracturing occurred and "fracking" wells in stages, called "multistage fracking," EOG not only showed that the method could be improved but also discovered how to extract oil from source rock—making unconventional extraction much more lucrative (McLean 2018; Zuckerman 2014).

These early adopters began competing to purchase more and more prospective acreage and developed what John described as the sudden "appetite" for proven but undeveloped hydrocarbon reserves. One of the most aggressive land purchasers was the independent Chesapeake, which was led by a charismatic entrepreneur, Aubrey McClendon (McLean 2018; Zuckerman 2014). "He was charismatic, tall, good looking, well-spoken, [and] came from a good family," one of my interlocutors explained. Another oil entrepreneur turned oil and gas financier said, "There are certain people that are the true entrepreneurs at the forefront. There's no doubt that George Mitchell is the Father of the Barnett Shale. But, it was Aubrey McClendon that everybody wanted to be." By aggressively purchasing prospective unconventional reserves, this interlocutor explained that he "changed the map" of the United States and convinced other large independent producers to also be "aggressive" in purchasing land because he was buying it all up. This was around the time when John started the process of selling his company at the behest of his private equity partners.

Rick, an executive with a major oil market intelligence firm, explained to me how the shale revolution unfolded in "phases." Rick's firm collects and analyzes vast amounts of data, then interprets this data for what he calls "our financial clients . . . pension funds, hedge funds, investment banks, private equity guys . . . [and] E&P companies." Previously, Rick led the strategic planning unit of a big independent US oil and gas firm for several years in the early 2000s and was an active participant in the shale revolution. Sitting across from me in a small conference room, gyrating with almost unbridled excitement as he explained how the shale revolution unfolded, he said, "In essence, all we did was put together two technologies that we already had: horizontal drilling and multistage fracking. And, bam! We access this enormous resource. . . . There's no going back." He continued,

> Shale plays, shale areas, pass through certain phases that are more or less identifiable life stages. The first stage is what we call "prove it." This is the stage where people are going to drill wells, maybe verticals, maybe horizontals, they don't care because they're not trying to make money. All they're trying to do is show that a reservoir is going to cough up some oil or gas in sufficient quantities. . . . The next stage is what we call the "optimization stage." Now, the cat's out of the bag, and you and everybody runs around, and it explodes. Now, people are trying wells over here, and wells over there, and twenty miles away, and two hundred miles away. . . . discovering where it's good, where it's bad, and what's the best way to drill and complete these wells. . . . We have now reached a phase where pretty much every major play has a third stage, called "standardization." There is very little risk left. We basically know how to drill and complete these things . . . I just got a whole lot of wells to drill. Ten thousand, twenty [thousand], fifty thousand, one hundred thousand of these wells yet to be invested in. This phase is mostly about trying to get your cost down. It's cookie cutter. . . . It's very different from the "cowboy" [optimization] phase . . . where I take a chance to buy some acreage over here for 750 dollars [per acre] and hope it turns into 20,000 dollars an acre. Now everybody knows that over there actually it didn't work and it's still 500 an acre. This over here has been dynamite; it's 40,000 dollars an acre!

It was in the early phase of this land-buying frenzy when established private equity firms capitalized on the sudden appetite of large independents for proven but undeveloped unconventional reserves.

A managing and founding partner at one of these first and very successful oil and gas private equity firms, Myles, explained, "In our early days we did very, very little drilling." Instead, they focused on "acquiring producing properties on behalf" of their institutional investors. He explained, "Then, all of a sudden, [there was] horizontal drilling and unconventional reservoirs. The challenge was not necessarily finding or determining the existence of hydrocarbons in a reservoir.... We knew the hydrocarbons were there to some extent. The question is, Can we develop an economic equation with the right cost structure recoveries? ... And, we made an awful lot of money at it." The private equity "model" that they developed and specialized in, Myles explained, involved "identifying high-quality management teams, agreeing on a strategy, agreeing on the capitalization appropriate for that strategy, controlling the board, [investing] the capital, and building those companies ... and ultimately either selling them to the larger independents and majors or occasionally taking those companies public.... That has been our basic model."

Low interest rates in the years following the dot.com bubble,[16] which undermined the value of debt-based financial investments and rising oil and natural gas prices (see figure 2.2), cultivated excitement for US oil and gas private equity among some institutional investors. At the same time, there was growing anxiety within US policy circles about rising hydrocarbon prices and the need to increase domestic oil and gas production following a spike in natural gas prices in December 2000 and January 2001 (Morse and Jaffe 2001; NEPDG 2001). These anxieties were exacerbated by fears that global oil supplies were running out and that the world was heading toward a supply-induced energy transition. It was also exacerbated by the September 11, 2001, US terrorist attack and the associated buildup to the invasion of Iraq in March 2003. During this time, political turmoil in other oil-producing states threatened to disrupt world supplies while US and global oil demand continued to rise and domestic renewable energy production capacity remained underdeveloped (CNNMoney 2001; Sosa and Desnyder 2003; Yergin 2009).

Additionally, the collapse of Enron in December 2001 and the merger of a couple of large independent oil and gas companies in the years that followed created a surplus of unemployed but highly skilled financiers, geologists, engineers, and technicians. "When Conoco Phillips bought Burlington, I think we got two [exploration and production] teams out of there," Myles said. "Normally" these skilled workers would look for work with another established oil and gas company, he explained, but then they started to get hired by private equity firms and some, with an "entrepreneurial bent," started their own drilling and PE companies.

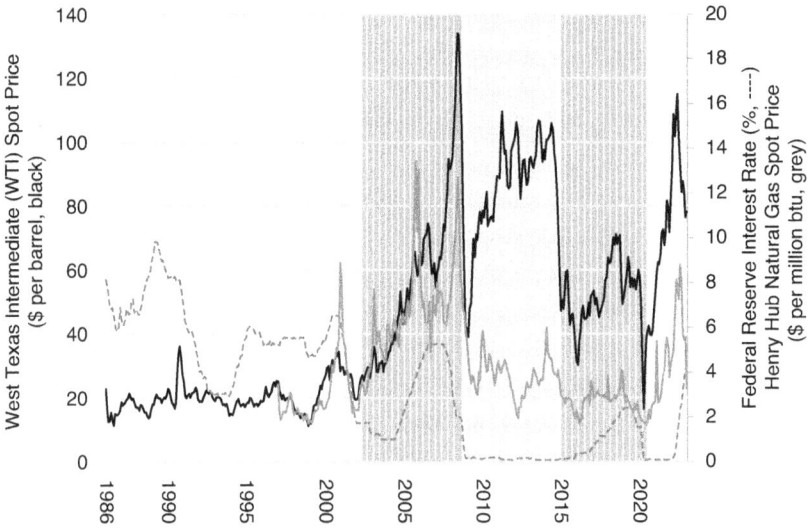

Figure 2.2: Graph of US crude oil and natural gas average spot prices with Federal Reserve interest rate. Data sources: USEIA (2023a, 2023b), St. Louis Federal Reserve (2023).

For institutional investors looking to invest in US unconventional extraction, private equity firms specializing in exploration and production had the capacity to absorb a lot of capital because, as Rick explained, "It's so capital intensive it's amazing." Moreover, because of the "food chain," private equity investors did not have to wait to produce oil and gas to earn a return on their investment. They could sell the prospect to a large independent company to produce the oil and gas, but claim a large share of the future expected "value." "Seventy percent of the value" of oil and gas is in "the upstream," Rick said. As I looked at him curiously, Rick explained what he meant:

> If you take a prospect, or a patch of land that you're going to try to [drill], it will literally be five hundred dollars an acre. And that value won't change. But if you discover [oil and gas] there, all of a sudden it will go to fifteen, twenty, thirty . . . let's say to twenty thousand dollars someday. It's in the Eagleford. I spent maybe I don't know fifty million dollars to drill seven or eight wells on this patch of land, and I estimate that this patch of land can take, or will take, seventy-five wells to develop. I've spent about 10–11 percent of the capital that needs to be spent there. But

if you sell it, I'm going to get probably 70 percent of the NPV [net present value] because I've derisked it. Everybody can see there is no risk to other capital because you took the risk. You could have drilled there and wasted your thirty to forty million dollars on the way to finding out that it was not good.

In this quotation, Rick captures the oil and gas private equity model and the "cowboy phase" that dominated the US oil and gas industry for over a decade and a half, starting in the early 2000s.

Echoing Rick, a director at a transnational investment bank, Vincent, described this model of private equity to me over breakfast as "venture capital real estate." Large independent oil companies "had an obsession" with growing their inventory of unconventional reserves that were proven but undeveloped (PUDs) and their shareholders, he explained, rewarded these companies with higher share prices. "Whoever grew more, whoever showed more inventory, more production, the investors rewarded with higher valuations. In seeing that, a lot of private equity firms said, 'Well, these guys are obsessed with inventory. I'm going to feed them inventory.'" He continued,

The private equity community was like, "Well, let's go and lease-up a bunch of land," which they did, "and then, let's go and let's drill two wells here, two wells here, two wells here, and two wells here. Since we've now surrounded our acreage position, let's go sell all this land to Concho, Diamondback, Anadarko, and Newfield, Encana, you name it . . . sell them the hope and dream of, 'Look, I drilled these wells and they're all excellent wells. You're going to be able to, when you come here, to drill thousands of these wells with the exact same results across this full position . . .'" That initiated [the shale] boom. That's what these private equity firms did for ten years, just this. The [E&P] teams that [private equity] would back were typically groups of three to five guys led by a land guy.

From the early 2000s until 2008, a few oil-and-gas-specific PE firms that were in the "right basins" at the "right time," like Myles's, dominated this subsector of finance. This was the first financial phase of the shale revolution.

When the 2008–2009 global financial crisis (GFC) happened, oil and gas PE ascended in popularity among institutional investors because interest-bearing investments and other investment vehicles were performing poorly in the wake of the GFC (McLean 2018; St Louis Federal Reserve 2023). While the typical time horizon for PE investments ranges from three to seven years, this horizon shifted to three to five years during this phase because demand for these "derisked" prospects meant proven prospects could easily and quickly be sold. Jacob, a managing director of oil and gas lending for a large multinational corporation that works with PE firms, explained, "You had a declining interest rate environment. You had these big pension funds out there looking for ways to hit their actuarial return targets. . . . It's a recipe for private equity to just be a huge force in terms of an asset class, and the window was wide open in the E&P space, given what was going on with shale."

It was a perfect storm—the technology was established, the private equity model was proven, and macroeconomic conditions were right. With few investment vehicles with which to make their target returns, investors channeled billions of dollars into PE firms, hoping to capitalize on what many "prayed" would be the next meteoric rise in oil prices (Haines 2013a, 2013b). As the *Oil and Gas Investor* magazine's 2013 special issue on PE, subtitled "money well spent," exclaimed, "The institutional investor crowd love energy and the kinds of returns it can deliver" (2013a: 4). By contrast with just a few PE firms specializing in E&P prior to 2008, like Myles's, there were 379 PE firms funding approximately three hundred E&P companies in the United States by 2013 (Haines 2013a: 4).[17] Newly established PE firms amassed hundreds of millions of dollars of institutional investments, while well-established PE firms continued to raise multibillion-dollar E&P funds.

This was the second financial phase of the shale revolution, characterized by relatively high crude oil prices, very low interest rates, and explosive growth in the number of US oil and gas private equity firms. This phase ended in late 2014 when global oil prices collapsed following the announcement by OPEC that its member states would not cut crude oil production (BBC 2014; Clark 2016; Kottasova 2014). Although the price of oil fell precipitously, oil and gas PE firms continued to fund raise, money continued to pour in from institutional investors, and PE managers forged ahead with derisking. Blackstone, for example, raised a $4.5 billion energy fund in February 2015, only three years after raising a fund of $2.4 billion (Kumar 2015); and EnCap raised its twentieth fund (Capital Fund XI) worth $7 billion in 2017 (EnCap 2023).[18] Between 2015 and 2019, US PE firms spent $64 billion, of which $44 billion was spent on unconventional E&P in the United States (Flowers 2019; Kumar 2015). In the process, small to medium-sized oil and gas companies and their private equity investors fundamentally transformed the US energy landscape in previously unthinkable ways. Conventional US oil production peaked in 1970 (USEIA 2024; Zukerman 2014). As a consequence of unconventional extraction, however, the United States became the globe's largest producer of natural gas in 2011 and the globe's largest producer of crude oil in 2013 (USEIA 2016). In 2020, the United States became a total petroleum net exporter (where "petroleum" includes natural gas, crude oil, and refined petrochemicals; USEIA 2022a).

The problem for this burgeoning number of private equity firms was that the forty to fifty-five dollars per barrel of oil price range, which persisted between 2014 and 2019, made it difficult for PE firms and their portfolio companies to meet their profitability targets. With so many PE firms competing to prove the potential economic value of unconventional reserves, there were fewer and fewer resources to be derisked. The flurry of PE-fueled E&P activity had derisked the most lucrative acreage, my interlocutors told me, exposing where unconventional extraction was profitable and where it was not. By 2019, the big oil companies at the top of "the food chain" that PE firms depended on to "exit" their investments stopped buying their "derisked" unconventional reserves because, as one person explained, the big companies "got full up on acreage." The combination of oil and gas private equity finance and unconventional extraction was transformational. "The risk profile of the industry truly did change from a subsurface standpoint," Myles said. "But," he continued, "When you look across the industry, it totally destroyed a ton of capital because [the industry] spent so much money on acreage and drilling. Did they transform the supply equation of the world? Yes. Our industry did it, but at what cost? We spent so much money doing it that there were no returns available to the investor or lender." Since mid-2019, some of my interlocutors have commented, money invested in oil and gas private equity was perhaps not "money well spent" after all. While the United States produced more oil and gas than it had for over half a century and some people made billions, many investors and companies lost money as the most recent stage of the shale revolution came to a close in 2020. Some small to medium-sized private equity firms have since dissolved while some large firms have begun consolidating and reorganizing their portfolio companies hoping to survive the downturn. The surge of investor capital into financially high-risk, high-reward oil and gas PE created "overdrilling," people now told me. This activity helped depress US crude oil and gas prices, scuttling investor profits. By aggressively derisking unconventional hydrocarbon E&P, PE financiers exhausted the profits that could be earned from these activities. One message that can be gleaned from this is that in the process of fulfilling their fiduciary responsibilities, PE financiers collectively contributed to a classic crisis in overproduction—one that stretched the United States' land-locked oil infrastructure to its limits (Harvey 2006 [1982]; High and Field 2020; Labban 2008). Some non-PE interlocutors I know, in part, blamed private equity financiers for ushering in the "bust" in the US oil and gas sector—even though, for over a decade, these financiers were the risk-taking stars of the industry that helped revitalize US onshore production to the applause of investors.

"Derisking" the Potentiality of Oil

The conceptual pairing of financial risks in pursuit of financial rewards has been around in various forms for a long time. Economist Frederick Hawley (1893) conceptualized risk taking as a factor of capitalist production alongside the classical economic factors of land, labor, and capital. He argued that what distinguishes profitable enterprises from nonprofitable ones are individuals' entrepreneurial appetites for risk taking. Economist Frank Knight (1964 [1921]) advanced this risk theory of profit by arguing that it is entrepreneurs' ability to take financial risks on uncertain futures that is the source of capitalist profits. For Knight (1964 [1921]), risk can be expressed in terms of odds or probabilities on which imagined futures will or will not materialize, whereas uncertainty describes the unknowable. Anthropologist Arjun Appadurai (2011, 2016: 30) has taken up Knight's conceptualization of risk and uncertainty in his analysis of the "spirit" and mechanics of short-selling derivatives. For Appadurai, it is financial speculators' capacity to take speculative financial risks on exploiting uncertain futures that allows them to earn profits where others will not. According to Knight's (1964 [1921]) and Appadurai's (2011, 2016) definitions, Mitchell Energy and Development Corporation engaged in this kind of uncertainty by taking financial risks on an unknowable future when it was trialing modern fracking—few could imagine it working, and even fewer could probabilistically calculate its success. The distinction between uncertainty and risk, which pivots on what is probable and what is imaginable, is perhaps less distinct than some might suggest. What is probable for some might be unimaginable for others, as was the case during the time when George Mitchell was trying to sell Mitchell Energy but could not convince industry rivals that unconventional extraction worked.

This narrow focus on the financial risks and rewards of exploiting uncertain futures rarely enters the anthropological literature on energy, and fossil fuels in particular, most likely because of the various and complex ways that risk can be conceived. Some of the closest scholarly work in this vein is Gisa Weszkalnys's (2015) exploration of "first oil" in São Tomé and Príncipe. With the blessing of state actors and the help of technical experts whose job it is to estimate the uncertainties of hydrocarbon production, Weszkalnys (2015: 625) shows that profit-seeking "risk-taking entrepreneurs" play a central role in E&P activities in the country. Caura Wood's (2016, 2019) ethnography is particularly insightful. She shows that hydrocarbon E&P entails grappling with multiple externalized and internalized risks—ranging from market price volatility to competing corporate practices of evaluating the financial worth of hydrocarbons deep underground (explored in chapter 3). These financial risks not only threaten investors' capital but are entangled with the moral obligation of managers to return capital to shareholders in ways that challenge their durational ethics of responsibility and commitment (Wood 2016).

The concept of "derisking," meanwhile, encapsulates the idea of making the potentiality of hydrocarbon reserves known, then "redomaining" these largely untapped reserves as financial objects with future economic "value" that can be sold (High 2019: 32; Shever 2012: 78). It implies exposing investors to the uncertainties of exploration and production and can be located in the time between when prospective mineral-acreage rights are purchased (or leased) and when profitable extraction and production can be proven. In this time, "a heterogeneous set of practices" ranging from seismic mapping to drilling test wells to estimating and valuing the size of hydrocarbon reserves are deployed to prove the existence of geological matter that can be profitably exploited for the purpose of capitalism (Weszkalnys 2015: 617). This process of actively taking financial risks in E&P is broader in definition than the risks associated with buying and selling derivatives contracts or financial arbitrage, because E&P involves a whole set of activities associated with redomaining (or recommodifying) the biophysical world (Weszkalnys 2015). The financial risks are multiple—the risk of finding the "right" mix of hydrocarbons and applying the "right" drilling and completion techniques to profitably extract them; the commodity-price risk of oil and gas prices falling and eroding the financial worth of reserves; and the market risk associated with being unable to sell the oil, gas, and assets because there are no buyers.[19] Combining technical expertise with financial expertise to turn unseen hydrocarbon containing rock into future expected profits is the creative "alchemy" in oil and gas finance (Zaloom 2004: 365).

Derisking, then, turns on a dichotomy of what is known and unknown, and in particular evidencing what is considered to have "value." For interlocutors I came to know, derisking is not applying a new technology to inaccessible hydrocarbon reserves, as in the case of Mitchell Energy. Instead, it is about applying a proven technology to known hydrocarbon reserves from which extraction was previously unthinkable but became possible. This is different from other definitions of derisking. The process of derisking in banking, for example, is a retractive rather than an expansive activity that involves closing or restricting the accounts of people and institutions, such as remittance companies, that do not generate enough profit and are considered a risk for money laundering, which banks could be fined for (World Bank 2016). Derisking in the pharmaceutical industry, as business scholars Donald Drakeman and Nektarios Oraiopoulos (2020: 44) show, turns on medical breakthroughs where the "estimates of potential success" are unreliable. Viagra was considered a low-priority drug for Pfizer until it was shown to be effective for treating a different condition than it was originally developed for. Once it had been proven—becoming a multibillion-dollar "first-in-class drug"—similar drugs were quickly developed because uncertainty about its effectiveness had dissipated and the financial risk associated with its development removed (Drakeman and Oraiopoulos 2020). While overlapping with notions of derisking raised by my interlocutors, derisking in the oil and gas industry is somewhat distinct from similar notions in other industries and centers on the process of subterranean exploration.

The Responsibility to Take Risk

Arthur, with whom I began this chapter, explained that derisking was about demonstrating "the likelihood of being able to make money drilling a well." Derisking for Arthur and his contemporaries is about proving the profit-making potential of future oil and gas extraction. While he could not control oil and gas price volatility, what he and others could do was show that profitable oil and gas extraction was possible. Indeed, he explained that, as a private equity financier, it was his responsibility to take risks where other financiers would not: "That's our job, is to say, 'Hey, this is a risky asset. This is a risky area, a risky proposition.' We're going to take on that risk. We're going to go spend money to derisk it so that somebody else can come along and say, 'I see what you did here. I can see that these wells do work in this either new area or an extension of an existing area. Now that you've spent money to derisk it, I can value it more.'"

In a way that echoes Frederick Hawley and Rick above, he explains that risk taking is the crucible of financial value creation. In this regard, he and his contemporaries, he suggested, are at the vanguard of capitalism. Anthropologists of finance have explored similar entanglements of financial risk taking, value creation, and feelings of responsibility. Hirokazu Miyazaki (2007, 2013), for example, has documented how Japanese traders enthusiastically engage with the financial risks of arbitrage not only to generate profit but also because these traders believe in the "power of money" to positively make the Japanese economy more "efficient" (Miyazaki 2013: 15, 51–52). According to Miyazaki (2013: 92–93), arbitrageurs internalize their role as the "strong individuals" who are "willing to take on risks and responsibility" to seize economic opportunities, provision their own well-being, and usher in free-market reforms for the perceived benefit of the Japanese economy.

In yet another dimension of responsibility, Arthur told me that he took seriously his responsibility to take calculated financial risks with his limited partners' capital. He said, "I feel an enormous sense of responsibility. . . . Our investors are primarily college endowments or pension funds. That's not something you take lightly. I genuinely think about the fact that we're taking this money from such-and-such university. They're believing in us. They're investing with us in our projects. If I lose their money, it's very bad for the university, very bad for scholarship programs and infrastructure on campus. If I can grow this money, there's a lot of good that can be done with this. Same for pension funds. These are peoples' retirements." "I really do think about that," he told me, "just the responsibility that comes with that," by which he meant managing financial futures on which people's livelihoods depended. Being a private equity financier, thus, is not *just* about maximizing investor capital or fulfilling his own capitalist goals, although these are important to him. There is a dimension of responsibility that is connected to but goes beyond his fiduciary responsibility to include material and moral provisioning of energy. He sees it as his responsibility to contribute to a greater national and global good. He is motivated to do "impactful things . . . I like to help people," he says, and he feels that being a private equity financier allows him to do that. "We are producing hydrocarbons that are able to be used here in America," and fossil fuel production, he told me, reduces "poverty across the world" by creating wealth and by making energy more inexpensive. Overall, "I think that what we are doing is good." At the intersection of the oil and gas industry and the financial sector, Arthur is able to claim the moral position of materially provisioning the energy people demand, maintaining an American way of life, and underwriting the financial well-being of students and retirees through institutional investors. He helps provide, he tells me, the "comforts of life that Americans and the British and the Canadians . . . have enjoyed." Other private equity interlocutors echoed these sentiments associated with contributing to a "greater good." Myles explained to me, for example, "I've got some God-given abilities that I think I have a responsibility to try to utilize in a productive way, that maybe contribute something positive. That's my very basic fundamental responsibility."

The way that Arthur and Myles describe their personal sense of responsibility to take financial risks on the uncertainties of oil and gas exploration and production is reflective of a kind of ethics. It resembles the notion of using their agency as financial experts to act "on behalf of another" to yield envisioned future outcomes (Laidlaw 2014: 188; see also Raffoul 2018). This conception of agential responsibility is not limited to the causal efficacy of people to be held responsible or liable for adverse or unforeseen outcomes—Arthur's sense of responsibility does not gaze into the past, nor is his agential sense of responsibility rendered through his opposition to "systems of value and power" (Laidlaw 2014: 182). Nor is it limited to his fiduciary duty as one of the general partners in a contractual private equity relationship. Instead, his sense of ethical responsibility to take financial risks is forward looking and gazes toward materializing envisioned outcomes that are rooted in the (re)production of the fossil fuel economy and financial modes of capitalism. It is suggestive of what Laidlaw (2014: 181) calls the "complex processes of the attribution of responsibility" that expose the connected and ethical dimensions of human actions.

These feelings of responsibility are never more tested than in the face of loss and failure. Talking with me in mid-2020 after the downturn and historic plummet in the price of US crude oil, Kyle—a contemporary of Arthur's at a competing private equity firm—told me, "It's not an easy situation. . . . All of our companies are underwater," by which he meant that the financial value of his companies and investors' capital in them had all been wiped out. Now, Kyle was trying to balance his multiple responsibilities—to his employees, to his investors, and to his own capitalist project. He explained,

> If we make them money, then we get money. That's not going to happen on any of our companies today based on where they are at, and what's happened in the industry. It would be very easy, or tempting I should say, . . . economically rational . . . for my partner and I to say, "Listen, we're not going to make money. We're out." That's not what we're doing. That's not what we've done. We feel an obligation to our investors to do the best that we can to generate the best returns as we possibly can. That's what we've been focused on and that's what we're continuing to do for our investors.

Speaking with me around the same time, Arthur told me that his firm had managed to weather the crisis that had swept across the industry.

A handful of committed investors and some price hedging had given Arthur's firm an edge over some of their competitors. It had not been easy, however; during a meeting with some of his institutional investors to review their fund performance, he told me he nervously watched on his phone as the price of oil plummeted, eroding the asset valuations his team was in the midst of presenting.

Anthropologist Caura Wood (2019: 83) observes that "oil at . . . the end of profit" involves a slightly different set of moral responsibilities than it does at the beginning of an oil boom. Instead of moral horizons full of promise and the potentiality of profit, oil at the end of profit tests individuals' sense of responsibility to persevere in the face of dismal financial outcomes, failed promises, and future uncertainty. Kyle is an example of this; once ignited by a sense of responsibility to use his financial expertise to generate "value" by engaging with financial risk, in 2020 he saw it as his responsibility, indeed his moral "obligation," to minimize losses for his limited partners. It has been "very painful," he said, with strain in his voice, followed by a long sigh. Arthur, Kyle, and others I know take solace in contributing to a new phase of American petrocapitalism, in which the United States is again a major producer, and indeed exporter, of global hydrocarbons. They could not have done this, however, without the financial backing of institutional investors and wealthy clients. Private equity financiers, as such, may be understood not only as a conduit for capital but also as a social conduit of responsibility—a way for investors to harness the financial benefits of hydrocarbon exploration and production and engage with the excitement of finding oil, while outsourcing the blame for any potential losses and adverse social and environmental outcomes. As Souleles (2019: 187–88) contends, PE financiers form a powerful yet underresearched "interstitial" conduit for money within a larger financial system that we are all connected to.

Financial Cowboys

Private equity financiers are not like commercial and investment bankers, although this is how many of them started their careers. As I have documented in this chapter, the first Texas-based hydrocarbon private equity firms emerged in the late 1980s from the ashes of the oil price crash that decade, founded by suddenly unemployed commercial hydrocarbon lenders. From these early beginnings, they crafted a model that was, and continues to be, distinct from other forms of private equity and more akin to venture capital. They operate on the spectrum of finance where things are probable and possible, but not certain. Even the idea of "exploration," by contrast with production, encapsulates a kind of frontierism that is situated in the liminal space between what is known and what is unknown, between what is possible and what is. Here there is a conceptual connection between the idea of derisking subterranean strata and the frontier separating the wilderness from territory that has been settled. It is perhaps the most lucrative form of finance in the US oil and gas sector because exploration deals in the commodification of "new" resources that are yet to be captured, a kind of "primitive accumulation" on a subterranean frontier (Marx 1990 [1867]). By "capturing" them and demonstrating the future "value" of these resources in terms of envisioned profitability, private equity financiers (and their portfolio companies) help turn these earthly materials into assets that enter the economy as commodities to be exploited, bought, and sold. This is a realm where few people, companies, and financiers have historically operated.

This form of private equity finance could have been started in another oil-producing state, such as Colorado or Louisiana, but it was not. As with the advent of contemporary multistage fracking, my interlocutors suggested to me, there was a reason this form of finance was founded in Texas, and centered on Houston in particular. There was what economic geographers call an agglomeration of firms, labor, and resources clustered around Houston that provided the necessary preconditions for this form of private equity finance, but there was also something more. Indeed, many of my interlocutors could have forged careers in real estate or worked for a large investment bank or hydrocarbon firm. Many, like Arthur and Kyle, left jobs at large investment banks to start their own private equity firms because they wanted to be more "entrepreneurial" and because they wanted to work with "cowboy" oil entrepreneurs needing $50–500 million to find and produce oil. Connecting "resource making" with "high finance," they not only work with self-described cowboy oilmen but embrace identities as entrepreneurs working on a frontier of sorts—first, by financially provisioning the returns needed by institutional investors who depend on them to meet their actuarial targets, and second, by easing national anxieties about dwindling hydrocarbon resources at a time of eroding US global hegemony and geopolitical tensions that threaten to disrupt the hydrocarbon "lifeblood" on which the United States turns. Hydrocarbon private equity provided interlocutors such as Arthur and Kyle the means by which to exercise their entrepreneurial spirit while working in the finance sector, where few entrepreneurial opportunities exist. They are the cowboys of hydrocarbon finance. The metaphor that the investment capital they provide is the oxygen on which the US oil and gas industry turns dovetails with Matthew Huber's (2013) lifeblood metaphor. If oil is the lifeblood of the United States, investment capital is the oxygen on which oil production depends.

For the allegories that private equity financiers craft about themselves and the allegories that they craft for their investors, these considerations are important. By participating in US hydrocarbon private equity, these financiers and their limited partners are engaging in a kind of nation-building exercise—this form of finance not only produces profit (at least some of the time) but also perpetuates, and indeed advances, a petroleum-based American society. Moreover, I have shown in this chapter that hydrocarbon private equity acted as a catalyst for change by providing capital for exploration and production activities that oil majors were uninterested in and that other financiers would not provide capital for because it was considered too risky. If the historical imaginary of the cowboy is an agent of change, who engages with risk and is in control of his own destiny, this is perhaps why it is invoked in conjunction with exploration and production activities and is entangled with the often-invoked ideal type and self-description of the oil entrepreneur.

In the next chapter, I explore the financial models and metrics that those in the industry use to stabilize these imagined future "values" on which the industry, the "food chain," and the private equity model turn. More than just a vocabulary on which hydrocarbon narratives are woven, I argue, these models and metrics form a lexicon that is an integral part of the ethical scaffolding on which allegories about oil and gas are made.

3

Ethical Calculations

There can't be reserves unless there is economics.
—Alex, 2019

Alex trained as a reservoir engineer and worked for several well-known oil and gas companies with exploration and production activities in the United States and around the world. Now, he is the vice president of a medium-sized oil and gas E&P firm, and his role straddles the divide between financial expert and in-house reservoir engineer. There is a large poster with interlocking squares and rectangles superimposed on a map of the Gulf of Mexico on the wall in Alex's office showing how the area is divided up for oil and gas production leases. On the white board beside me there is a hand-drawn picture of an oil well with numbers scribbled beside it in dry erase marker, and there is a letter-sized piece of paper with a colorful seismic graph plotting the geological layers of a drilling prospect taped to the wall. These artifacts reveal the engineering side of his work—estimating the location, size, and quality of hydrocarbon reserves.

Alex tells me that he does "the economics" for his firm. I ask, "When you say you're doing 'economics' . . . what do you mean specifically?" "It's the reason I'm here," he says. "I do the economics for the exploration, and I also do the economics for the acquisition." Whether a company is looking to drill a new well or buy a new land prospect, the most important thing he has learned, he tells me, "is really people want to make sure they're going to get their money back, and if you can't show them . . . you're not going to get anybody to do anything." He learned how to do "economic analysis" when he worked at AnaOil.[1] He explains, "What I learned with them is that the economics are everything. You got to have reserves to boot the economics, and that's what guys like me do. We do the reserves, too, but then we usually run the economics. . . . It's critical. We got investors coming in to look at these blocks [of land to drill]. They want to see how much money they can make." By "economics" he means financial metrics and models that anticipate—that "see"—the future and inform decisions about which hydrocarbon projects should be materialized based on what is profitable. Investors are not interested in the material aspects of extraction; that is Alex's job. Instead, they want to know what it financially means for them. If a company cannot make "a 20 percent rate of return" for its investors, he says, "you don't do it. . . . That way, you cull a bunch of stuff . . . separate all the junk off." He shows me how he puts all the information about various oil and gas wells into a program on his computer and runs a probabilistic distribution on the development of each. "I run all the probabilities, all the outcomes . . . all the way through to your dollars-per-share impact" for investors, he says. The data he includes in his calculations are price decks, expected oil well decline rates, and discount rates. Discounted cash flow analysis and metrics like IRR and PV10 (which I explain below) are key to Alex's analysis. "We're big into discounted cash flow. We'll look at what [investors] are going to get back in time, at a discounted rate. . . . We do a full suite of the economics. . . . They're very rigorous. . . . Nothing gets done without the numbers."

    Figuring out the value of an oil well or oil company is "the biggest part of an acquisition," he says, "because unless you can figure out a value on it, it's worthless." He tells me, "There can't be reserves unless there is economics. . . . You have to show that it has value. That it has more cash flowing than it costs, or you can't call it reserves." His observation that hydrocarbon reserves exist, insofar as they can be imagined as having future financial value, reveals insight into the power of metrics and models in shaping allegories about what energy futures should be materialized, or even imagined. Hydrocarbons locked underground cannot be classified as energy reserves if they do not have financial value. Using economic models and financial metrics, he separates which imagined futures have value and which futures are "worthless." The allegories he weaves are not inconsequential—they are the basis for whether wells are drilled, hydrocarbons are extracted, and companies and acreage are bought and sold. Alex's job is to "make sense" of oil and gas futures, as he puts it. In the world of energy, the metrics and models he uses are more consequential than the Black and Scholes formula, which is hailed as one of the most important concepts in contemporary financial theory (MacKenzie 2001; Maurer 2002).[2]

Alex is not unique in this regard. As he said, this sort of economic-financial analysis is "what all these big companies do." My other interlocutors also perform similar economic analyses—weaving stories of future value with economic concepts and financial metrics. Alex frames what "makes sense," imagines the future, and crafts allegories about energy in the financial lexicon of the industry. By contrast with the Texas-oriented cowboy narratives, this lexicon of metrics and models is not drawn from a unique Texas brand of oil capitalism. With a few exceptions, these models and metrics are imported from the broader US finance sector, which is indicative of hydrocarbon finance being situated within US and international financial markets. Modularly applied to companies and assets, they synthesize the diverse and heterogeneous world of hydrocarbons into a homogeneous set of indicators that can be compared and woven into allegories about the futures and the right course of action for capital providers. Alex, like Arthur in the chapter before, crafts part of his identity around being able to manipulate these metrics and models to fit a complex world and show what has "value" and what does not. They work as the interface that ties the financial world to the US hydrocarbon industry.

In this chapter, I examine how financial metrics and economic models are used to craft allegorical narratives about hydrocarbon futures. These metrics and models provide the economic and financial scaffolding on which moral arguments about the "rightness" or "wrongness" of particular energy futures rest. While my interlocutors may use different techniques for defining "value," as I will show, what these metrics and models share is an ethical orientation that places investors and lenders at the center of their calculus. Forming a lexicon that defines notions of value and the time frames worth considering, these models and metrics orient my interlocutors toward common ways of envisioning the future and toward materializing these visions. In an era defined by growing public concern about anthropogenic climate change and calls for the decarbonization of capital (Langley et al. 2021), future energy projects are pitched, mineral rights are transacted, wells are drilled, pipelines are built, infrastructure is constructed, and money is invested and loaned on the basis of the allegorical imaginaries woven with this lexicon.

This chapter also further unpacks the story of the shale revolution explored in the previous chapter. In chapter 2, I showed how the shale revolution unfolded with the help of private equity financiers whose goal was to "prove" prospective hydrocarbon reserves and sell these reserves to larger oil and gas companies. Here I show how the future value of hydrocarbon reserves is estimated and situate these financial practices within the history of practices within the US hydrocarbon industry. Formatively shaping how and when my interlocutors see "value," I suggest, these financial practices dovetail with the historical imaginary of the cowboy turned oil entrepreneur, which I discussed in chapter 1, as a key ethical register by which the interlocutors I came to know navigate the world. Indeed, the metrics and models explored in this chapter are vital tools in the toolkits of both oil and gas financiers and exploration and production companies.

I begin by examining the entanglement of hydrocarbon expertise, financial metrics, and economic models, as well as the importance of framing expert narratives as allegorical. I then unpack the mainstay metrics highlighted in my opening vignette, before turning to an ethnographic encounter at an early morning breakfast meeting. I conclude the chapter by reflecting on how these metrics, models, and allegories are coming to bear on new forms of energy extraction.

Financial Imaginaries and Energy Allegories

Caura Wood (2016) shows that shareholder value is not just produced through a company's *current* E&P activities. Instead, the financial value of hydrocarbon companies is based on the estimated value they will produce in the *future* in the form of oil and gas reserves to be extracted. Financial calculations and economic models that are entangled with the geological estimates of a company's reserves are essential to the apprehension of "hydrocarbon potentiality" and "future cash potential" (Wood 2016: 44, 46). Geological estimates combined with forward-looking productivity-decline curves, and the financial metrics of net present value (NPV) and discounted cash flow (DCF), collectively "liquidate the future" into the present by framing future hydrocarbon extraction into "a temporal rate of return" (Wood 2016: 45, 51). For Wood (2019), economic models and financial formulae take on another temporally entangled dimension. They foster a shared imagination of future "value creation" and, echoing Fabian Muniesa (2017), offer a "shared moral horizon" among investors, lenders, and entrepreneurs (Wood 2019: 68). Metrics orient financial counterparties and collaborators toward common profit-seeking goals and prompt them to collectively imagine the materialization of anticipated outcomes. This is important for attracting and retaining investors and lenders because hydrocarbon finance fundamentally turns on performances of credit. Derived from the Latin word "*credere*," meaning "to trust or to believe," a defining feature of credit is its function in linking the past, present, and future (Graeber 2012; Hart 2001; Maurer 2010: 146). Investors and lenders are exchanging money in anticipation that they will get their money back plus a profit at a future date. As one of my interlocutors explained to me, "The investor has to believe in what he's investing in" because investors, as well as lenders, must anticipate that they will recoup their capital. Financial metrics and economic models lend a sense of imaginary assuredness, "thickening" expectations into anticipation (Bryant and Knight 2019: 22). Charts, tables, and illustrations, Stefan Leins (2018: 12) shows, "stabilize" these financial imaginaries and make them more creditable. Financiers play a critical role in crafting "imaginaries" of the future using metrics and models, Leins (2018: 12) argues, leading to the subsequent allocation of investment capital in pursuit of these imaginaries. Doug Holmes (2014) makes a similar point; central banks, he argues, recruit their respective publics to collaborate on the monetary goals of price and currency stability. To do this, bankers compose economic narratives with supporting data and charts to project what will happen in the future and propose interventions to materialize imagined outcomes. From *Stories of Capitalism* to *Banking on Words* to *Economy of Words*, it has been shown that economic models and financial metrics play a central role in the construction of narratives about the future (Appadurai 2016; Holmes 2014; Leins 2018).

As with my opening vignette and in line with these works, I suggest that narratives built on models and metrics are the impetus for flows of capital in the US hydrocarbon industry. It is not possible to bring investors and lenders down the well hole to show them how much oil and gas there is, nor is it possible to transport them into the future to show them what oil prices will be and how much money is to be made. It is possible to imagine this, however. Financial metrics and economic models provide ways of imagining how much oil and gas is underground and how much it is all worth through virtual "as-ifs" woven around tables of numbers and graphs. In this regard, they constitute what David Sneath, Martin Holbraad, and Morten A. Pedersen (2009: 11) describe as technologies of the imagination, "concrete processes by which imaginative effects are engendered" by producing imagined hydrocarbon futures and the place of lenders and investors in these futures. Commonly used in the way described in the vignette, they are in line with what Laura Bear (2015: 408, 410) describes as "styles of imagination associated with capitalist practice" that are "wielded by exemplary figures . . . who work with the performative power of words" to "invoke an invisible realm" in order to explain the future (also see Zaloom 2003 and Ortiz 2014).

Metrics and models are more than just the building blocks of narratives, however—they double as moral calculative devices about the "right" energy futures. They project a speculative ethics (Bear 2020). In his analysis of the Black and Scholes (B&S) formula as a model for estimating options prices, Bill Maurer (2002) makes a similar suggestion. The B&S formula is a "moral argument," he argues; it "is a deontology of the way things 'ought' to be," and the metrics it produces for options prices are a moral appraisal about the value of things (Maurer 2002: 29). To take this argument one step further, the persuasive power of these models and metrics is not measured by the numbers they produce but by how they are woven into allegorical narratives. In this vein, Deirdre McCloskey and colleagues have drawn attention to how economic narratives are allegorical, with economic concepts and calculus lending the rhetorical authority of being "right" (Klamer and McCloskey 1992; Donald McCloskey 1995; Deirdre McCloskey 1998). Even general terms like "economic" and "uneconomic" not only communicate profitability, or a lack thereof, but also communicate a "rightness" and "wrongness" about particular presents and futures. Holmes (2014: 95) argues that central banks regularly deploy econometric allegories to instill public confidence in banks' projections and render the economy "susceptible to policy interventions." For him, allegories are notable for "the persuasive labour these narratives are called upon to perform" to render support for monetary policies (Holmes 2014: 11). In the hydrocarbon industry, the concept of allegory draws attention, first, to the ethical frameworks that models and metrics furnish economic narratives. Secondly, it draws attention to the fact that they are also moral arguments about what are the "right" courses of action and the "right" futures to strive for. In this regard, models, metrics, and the allegories constructed with them are endowed with a sort of energy ethics (High and Smith 2019; Smith and High 2017). Common arguments (supported by metrics) among my interlocuters—such as "the economics of the project," "it has to work out on an economic basis," "the economics are challenged," "none of that drilling is economic," "are these resource plays truly economic?" and "the economics suck"—are not just hollow rhetoric but ways of conceptualizing what is right and wrong, and advocating for certain energy and hydrocarbon futures. Financial metrics and economic models are the scaffolding upon which allegories about which energy presents and futures are good and valuable are built.

Metrics and Models: NPV, IRR, EBITDA, and FCF

Donald MacKenzie's (2001: 118) now-classic examination of the Black-Scholes-Merton options pricing theory (B&S) is an excellent and instructive example of opening the "black box" of financial formulas. He shows how the application of Brownian assumptions from physics to finance are flawed but have, nonetheless, had wide-ranging effects on the performance of finance, envisioning of the future, and the materialization of economies. While not nearly as sophisticated as the B&S formula, the financial metrics of EBITDA, FCF, PV10, IRR, and NPV are mainstays in the US hydrocarbon finance community and no less important. It is common to hear my interlocutors describe companies and oil and gas assets in the lexicon of these metrics. In casual conversation they say things such as "target returns of 20 percent IRR or 2x ROI," "median EBITDA was 1.7 billion," "you could probably get double-digit IRR out of a deal," and "generate free cash flow." They are central to the everyday discourse of oil and gas financiers and the practice of economic evaluation, and they help determine what energy futures are materialized. While my interlocutors may be guided by coexisting idiosyncratic regimes of ethical registers—their faith in God and variants of Texan and nationalistic pride, for example—when they talk about, conceptualize, and evaluate hydrocarbons, they often do so in the constellation of financial-economic value articulated by this lexicon.

This has not always been the case, however. The integration of metrics and models into US hydrocarbon finance has evolved over the last ninety years. In the early part of the twentieth century, few US oil companies were able to secure commercial loans because banks were "unable to predict future production rates and prices" that would allow them to figure out if they were likely to be paid back (Clark 2016: 65). According to Bernard Clark (2016), the few short-term loans that were made considered the net worth of the borrower and were secured against real estate and the value of oil in-transit (also see Wilson 1966 [1962]). Historical bank documents show that DCF methods were not yet applied in the US oil and gas industry in the 1930s. Correspondence between the vice president of First National Bank in Dallas and the vice president of First National Bank in Houston, dated August 14, 1934, indicate that the "most important feature [of an 'oil loan'] to consider is the matter of title"—referring to the land to be collateralized with little consideration for the value of future oil production.[3]

Modern DCF methods can be traced back at least to the 1930s, although the principles of DCF can be traced back much further (Parker 1968). Irving Fisher (1930), notably, applied the concept of discounting to the theory of interest rates. He argues, "The basic problem of time valuation which Nature sets us is always that of translating the future into the present, that is, the problem of ascertaining the capital value of future income" (Fisher 1930: 14). By the early 1950s, US hydrocarbon finance had changed. More reliable reservoir engineering, economic price forecasting, and the integration of DCF made calculating future profitability possible (Clark 2016; Wilson 1966 [1962]). Reserve-based lending and other financing schemes flourished alongside these calculative techniques (Clark 2016). A paper presented by two vice presidents of Chase National Bank of New York on February 17, 1953, for example, mentions the incorporation of DCF in assessing the worthiness of hydrocarbon commercial loans: "The method of valuation generally used by the institution with which the authors are associated is the estimation of the present worth of future profits at that discount rate which it is believed will result in the fair market value" (Terry and Hill 1953: 1). Since the 1950s, NPV and DCF analyses have been at the core of US hydrocarbon finance, in lockstep with their adoption across the US finance sector (Biondi 2006; Svetlova 2012). NPV expresses the current value of future expected cash flow, less expenses, and is the end result of DCF analysis; it allows investors and lenders to imagine the future, evaluate its financial value, and decide what projects should be materialized. It is central to the superficially benign but critically important political vernaculars of financial valuation (Muniesa 2017; Ortiz 2021b). For hydrocarbon companies, DCF and NPV are crucial analytical lynchpins linking anticipated future income and profits to present-day financial values—financializing the value of material geological reserve estimates into imagined temporal rates of return (Wood 2016). Not only do they inform investing and lending decisions, but they also prompt assets and companies to be bought and sold today for a portion of the value they are anticipated to produce in the future (Field 2022a). The equation for calculating NPV is as follows:

$$NPV = \sum_{t=0}^{T} (R_t/(1+i)^t) \quad (1)$$

R_t stands for anticipated net revenue for one time (t) period in the future; i represents the discount rate (the rate by which the value of future money is eroded),[4] t represents specific time periods (ex. year 1, year 2, etc.), and T refers to the total number of time periods under consideration.

The internal rate of return (IRR) metric is an adaptation of NPV. It presents future economic value as a rate of return, in the present, that is readily comparable across a diverse range of investments. The higher the IRR metric, the more profitable an investment is expected to be. The IRR can be reiteratively calculated using this formula (Ahmed and Meehan 2012 [2004]; Wright and Gallun 2008):

$$IRR: 0 = NPV = \sum_{t=1}^{T} [C_t/(1+IRR)^t] - C_o \quad (2)[5]$$

C_t stands for net cash inflow during time period t; C_o stands for total initial investment costs; t represents specific time periods; and T refers to the total number of time periods. These metrics are among the most common techniques of calculating the "time value of money" (Wright and Gallun 2008: 61, 361; Souleles 2019), a way of imagining the future expected profitability in the present.[6]

My interlocutors also often refer to EBITDA and free cash flow (FCF). An industry veteran explained to me that when he first started as a financial analyst in the 1970s, he used to look at companies' FCF and DCF. Then, he explained, "somehow, EBITDA came into the mainstream, and then that became the nomenclature of purpose." "EBITDA" stands for earnings before interest, taxes, depreciation, and amortization; it was popularized by US billionaire and media CEO John Malone in the mid-1970s (Forbes 2003; Petacoff 2016). FCF was popularized by Michael Jensen (1986). My interlocutors tell me it was used well before Jensen, but became a common metric used by analysts and investors after it was popularized. There is no unitary definition of "FCF," but it is typically defined as cash available to company managers after capital expenditures (Bhandari and Adams 2017). EBITDA and FCF provide a financial snapshot in time. They allow people to imagine how much money is flowing through companies, how much debt companies can service, and how quickly this debt can be paid down, adding to the equity value of shareholders (Souleles 2019). As current measures of profitability and financial health, they help investors and lenders imagine the likelihood of near-future profits—whether companies will be profitable tomorrow, next week, next month, or next quarter (Ahmed and Meehan 2012 [2004]; Wright and Gallun 2008).

What EBITDA and FCF share in common with DCF, NPV, and IRR is that they are imported from economics and finance into the hydrocarbon industry. They are economic-finance metrics invented for investors, lenders, and analysts to modularly apply across assets and companies. They were brought to bear on the US hydrocarbon industry, alongside their broad-scale adoption in the US lending and investing communities (Biondi 2006). My interlocutors, combine these metrics with other terms in the lexicon such as "return on investment" (ROI),[7] "rate of return" (ROR),[8] and "total enterprise value" (TEV) to weave allegorical narratives of imagined futures.[9] The use of these metrics to imagine, value, and decide on future hydrocarbon projects and companies forms part of the changing financialization and economization of US oil and gas (Çalişkan and Callon 2009; Hann and Kalb 2020)—"changing" because the US oil and gas industry has been increasingly financialized and economized since its founding. As I have shown above, an evolving assembly of qualification and analytical practices has rendered hydrocarbons the subject of economic logic, transformed underground deposits into assets to be exploited, and determined whether they are extracted on the basis of allegorical financial narratives. These allegories, in turn, have been pitched to increasingly wide swaths of investors, as discussed in chapter 2. Reflecting on this trend toward economization-financialization, an industry veteran lamented to me that she longed for the days when the industry was driven by charismatic oilmen with "two-day shadows [beards] and cowboy vests." Now, she said, everything is more driven by financiers.

PV10 and Price Decks

Adapted from the more general NPV, the most important financial metric in the oil and gas industry is present value 10 (PV10). It incorporates the material specifics of estimated hydrocarbon reserves underground with the expectation that the financial value of these reserves will be eroded by interest and inflation at a rate of 10 percent per year (i.e., the "10" in "PV10") and, thus, is a key metric in the "assetization" of hydrocarbons (Birch 2017: 468; Ouma 2020: 70). In 1982, the US Security and Exchange Commission (SEC) standardized it as the reporting measure for proven oil and gas reserves for publicly traded companies—solidifying it as an industry benchmark ever since.[10] Reservoir engineers make PV10 calculations on the basis of reserve estimates of how much oil and gas is underground, expected production costs, expenses, production decline over time,[11] and projected energy prices (called "price decks").[12] Determining how much recoverable oil and gas there is and valuing it have been described by those at the center of hydrocarbon finance as the "single most important determinant of how much money a producer can get" from capital providers (Shearer 2000: 7; also see Boone 1980; Sherrod 1968). It is the fulcrum where the qualitative composition of hydrocarbons, the number of units, and the cost of extracting them are synthesized into monetary values to be realized over time and given a present-day dollar value. As one of my interlocutors explained, PV10 allows people to imagine "the actualization of the future cash flows" and is the basis for all other metrics. Table 3.1 shows a simplified PV10 calculation for a hypothetical unconventional set of hydrocarbon wells.[13]

TABLE 3.1: Simple Hypothetical DCF and PV10 Calculation.

Year	Expected Oil Production Volume (Barrels)	Decline Rate Year-to-Year (%)	Average Expected Price per Barrel ($US)	Simple Gross Cash Flow ($)	Lease Operating Expenses, Other Expenses, and Taxes ($)	Simple Net Cash Flow ($)	Discounted Cash Flow (PV10, $)
Initial Investment				−12,000,000			−12,000,000
1	300,000		55	16,500,000	2,000,000	14,500,000	13,181,818
2	105,000	65	60	6,300,000	2,039,669	4,260,331	3,520,934
3	73,500	30	58	4,263,000	2,072,531	2,190,469	1,645,732
4	58,800	20	58	3,410,400	2,108,264	1,302,136	889,376
5	49,980	15	57	2,848,860	2,143,987	704,873	437,671
6	44,982	10	56	2,518,992	2,180,941	338,051	190,821
7	42,733	5	55	2,350,310	2,219,191	131,119	67,285
8	42,306	1	55	2,326,806	2,259,539	67,267	31,381
	717,300		57	40,518,368	17,024,122	23,494,246	7,965,018
						PV10	7,965,018
						IRR	56%

Note: Table 3.1 is an analysis of a hypothetical unconventional oil well. Source: Author.

An interlocutor named Peter explained that when he started in the industry in 1982, PV10 was a standard metric for evaluating drilling projects. He started as a reservoir engineer but later moved into hydrocarbon finance, holding senior roles as a private equity financier, endowment investor, and director. He explained, "NPV10 was a standard metric," although, he added, "We also used other NPV hurdles (twelve, fifteen, twenty, etc.), IRR, ROI, [and] pay out times to evaluate projects." Used in combination with other metrics such as IRR, Peter said, "PV10 . . . is a consistent, standard metric for comparative purposes." Like numbers and metrics for Zaloom's (2004) traders, for Peter, PV10 and IRR convey objective information distilled from heterogeneous materialities and are critical for comparative informational transparency.

Integrating future price forecasts into the metrics of the industry has been standard practice since the 1950s. Formalized into "price decks," these forecasts integrate current and historical data into probabilistic

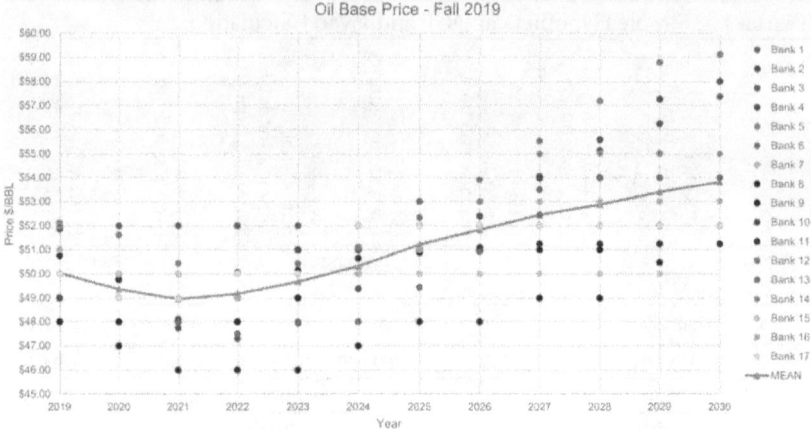

Figure 3.1: Energy bank price deck survey. Source: Haynes & Boone LLP (2019: 3). Reproduced with permission.

models that predict future hydrocarbon prices (Duff & Phelps 2017). Figure 3.1 is a graph of the oil price decks of several banks, published in the fall of 2019.[14]

These price decks are integrated into metrics and are used by lenders and investors to imagine, value, and decide on hydrocarbon loans and investments (Haynes & Boone 2019). Price decks are important, one person explained, because, "If you have a price deck that is flat, instead of a price deck going up every year, it is a completely different PV10. For the same property, you could have a one hundred million [dollar investment] going down to twenty-five [million]. All because of the flat nature of the price deck." As central factors in calculating NPV, DCF, IRR, and PV10 metrics (through their R_T and C_T variables), price decks are powerful economic forecasting models for imagining, valuing, and deciding on energy futures in monetary terms. In this way, price decks are not entirely dissimilar to central banks' GDP growth projections or US Treasury yield curves, in that they represent expectations of economic futures that incorporate uncertainty about what lies ahead (Holmes 2014; Zaloom 2009). They offer financiers' collective assessment of future hydrocarbon prices and illuminate economic allegories about what energy futures should or should not be materialized on the basis of how much economic value they are calculated to have.

Time Horizons

PV10, NPV, and IRR cast future profitability in terms of the present through the variables that segment time into units and the total time horizon under consideration.[15] These metrics encourage users and audiences to imagine time as simultaneously linear and circular (see figure 3.2)—linear, because they have starting and ending points that coincide with loan and investment time horizons; circular, because their purpose is to represent the future in present monetary terms. While the time horizons of major oil companies range up to twenty-five years, time lines are much tighter for nonmajors and their financiers. The time horizon for oil and gas investments typically ranges from three to five years, many told me, while the time horizons for loans typically span from three to eight years. The far distant future for both investors and lenders lurks at around ten years; by that time, many told me, so many things could change that the reliability of financial metrics and models fades into the fog of the future. Metrics and modeling are tailored around these times. The choice of metrics to use has a lot to do with whether oil prices are rising and falling, instigating a "boom" or "bust," and associated growth or discipline allegories. In a boom, financiers may focus more heavily on EBITDA than FCF because EBITDA conceals from investors changes in asset values and how much a company is spending on equipment and land.

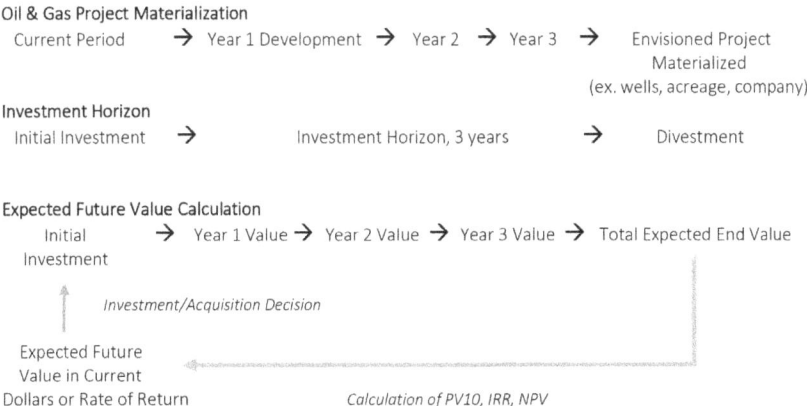

Figure 3.2: Example of the linear and circular temporality of investment. Source: Author.

If the future looks optimistic, financiers and their clients may accept EBITDA and are "happy . . . talking about things like net asset value" several years in the future, one of my interviewees explained. In a bust phase, however, financiers and their clients want to see more immediate signs of profitability. As prices stagnate or fall, as they did in the latter half of 2019, the sentiment and the lexicon shift to emphasize positive FCF, as well as near-term NPVs and IRRs. The shift between "growth" and "discipline" narratives and the metrics of choice, thus, reflect lenders' and investors' anticipations about when they will be paid back.[16] There are some disagreements about which metrics best reflect financial value and when, but there has been no critical upheaval in terms of how value is measured and imagined in the future over the last forty or so years. How these metrics and models define time, and how time is woven into allegorical narratives, is a formative part of the ethics they advance and the moral conclusions they precipitate—excluding the distant past and non-near future. Framing the near future in terms of its present financial value, these metrics and models remind me of Richard Irvine's (2019: 79) discussion of presentism: "What is striking . . . is that the closely drawn time horizons of economic activity in the present lack sufficient depth to understand the very environment upon which that economic activity depends."

Distilled Life

As moral calculative devices that illuminate allegories about hydrocarbons, these metrics distill all factors associated with making oil and gas finance decisions (including people, places, the environment, etc.) into unitary measures of current and future anticipated financial values. They distill information about hydrocarbon assets and companies into net cash inflow, net revenue, initial investment, and the discount rate. In doing so, they exclude a wide range of qualitative information about people, places, and things outside of their modular calculus. Synthesizing the materiality of hydrocarbons, companies, and assets into financial metrics allows a wide range of objects inside and outside the industry to be readily compared and evaluated on the basis of their future anticipated profitability. The narrow objective focus of these devices lends a sense of transparency and authority to their resulting figures and to the allegories they support. They cut out all the messiness of hydrocarbons—the places of extraction, the people it affects (for better or worse), and the outcomes of refining and consumption—and construct rational and numerically "clean" imaginaries of value creation from the perspective of investors and lenders. In doing so, they make a double move: distilling the calculative variables under consideration, while at the same time presenting totalizing imaginaries of assets and companies. As technologies of the imagination, they provide calculative reasons as to why oil and gas investments, loans, and projects should or should not happen, and illuminate the moral process of assetization. I demonstrate this in the following vignette drawn from an ethnographic encounter in late 2019.

The Breakfast Meeting

It is 7:30 in the morning and the dining room is packed. "Capital discipline has been demanded," the speaker says, looking out into the crowd of faces staring back at him. He continues:

> The Fidelitys of the world introduced this concept called capital discipline.[17] The general definition is grow within cash flow, pay dividends . . . 4 percent dividend yield . . . 4 percent production growth within EBITDA. . . . The definition of an E&P company is the antithesis of capital discipline. . . . We now have valuations at twenty-year troughs, whether you look at TEV, EBITDA . . . TEV to PV10. . . . Investors are rightfully skeptical. . . . Are companies just borrowing time? Can they really achieve this?

We are at a monthly breakfast meeting of the Houston Oil Finance Association in late 2019,[18] a monthly ritual in the Houston hydrocarbon finance community. The speaker is a managing director at a well-known private investment firm founded by two prominent US arbitrageurs. He has done the math, he says, and the prognosis for US hydrocarbon exploration and production companies is bleak. Companies that have led a renaissance in the US hydrocarbon industry with the advent of unconventional extraction have been financially "imprudent," he says, and many will not be able to make the transition from "growth" to "discipline" in the months ahead. He explains, "Eighty to 85 percent of the companies cannot achieve capital discipline. Something between 15 and 20 percent can. We were being very generous in our math when we got to this. There's another way of running this math that says no one can. It's somewhere between zero and 15 percent that can achieve capital discipline."

The story he is weaving is an allegorical narrative of a US industry in transition following a fifteen-year "boom" associated with the shale revolution. For over a decade, investors and lenders poured capital into US onshore unconventional hydrocarbon extraction during a growth phase in the US oil and gas industry not seen since the early 1980s. This created a flurry of E&P activity predicated on "proving" the future profitability of prospective hydrocarbon reserves that could be sold for a portion of their expected net present value, as I discuss in chapter 2. Investor fervor for US unconventional E&P was hastened by the early success of private equity financiers specializing in E&P in the mid-2000s and by the global financial crisis that challenged institutional investors to meet their actuarial targets. By late 2019, however, the industry entered a "bust" cycle with stagnating and, later, falling oil prices, challenging E&P companies to make profits. This is what he refers to when he talks about the shift from "growth" to "discipline." The "right . . . strategy going forward" for investors, the managing director argues, is "to buy PDP for cheap and . . . make all kinds of money." The "right" strategy for lenders is "PDP-covered loans" that are "priced up relative to [the] history" of the borrower.

While this language may have little meaning for people outside of oil and gas finance, for people in this community it constitutes prescriptions about the appropriate way capital should exploit US onshore hydrocarbon resources. Investors and lenders *should* focus on extracting profit from "proven developed producing" (PDP) US hydrocarbon assets, and the companies that own them, by imposing cost-minimizing strategies—discipline. Investors and lenders, by contrast, *should avoid* "proven undeveloped" (PUD) hydrocarbon assets and the companies that want to drill these prospects with the hope of making a profit from future expected extraction—growth—at least for now.

He is weaving this allegory with the lexicon of hydrocarbon finance. The sea of blue and grey suits crested with peaks of white, grey, and salt-and-pepper hair is watching and listening intently; they know, or seem to know, what he is talking about because they too speak the language. They are private equity partners, investment bankers, commercial lenders, asset managers, insurance brokers, financial consultants, and lawyers all specializing in oil and gas finance. They connect investment and loan capital from all over the world with small to medium-sized E&P companies operating in the "lower 48" states of the continental United States. Their clients are some of the largest institutional investors in the world, and they are the people who financially fueled the US shale revolution. The meeting and the presentation reminded me of Arthur Mason's (2007, 2012, 2019) work on economic experts in the US hydrocarbon industry. Using neoclassical economics, he shows that experts have been architects of future energy imaginaries for decades, building "consensus around imagined futures" (Mason 2012: 89). For Mason (2019: 128, 137), the concepts and language of economics allow experts to "speak in the name of the market" and appear to "transcend proprietary attachments" because of economics' near universal currency in industry circles. The imaginaries these economic experts craft achieve an "egalitarian" quality in their calculation by displacing the "idiosyncrasies of judgment" with "depersonalized, highly quantitative approach[es]" to energy markets (Mason 2019: 126, 128). In this regard, they are a modular-like counterpart of hydrocarbon's material infrastructures highlighted by Hannah Appel (2012a) in her exploration of offshore oil platforms. They have a universal-like quality that can evacuate the specificity of particular companies and assets, making them comparable across times and places.

(Hydro)carbon Capital

The metrics and models highlighted in this vignette and in the opening vignette are the ethical scaffolding on which allegorical narratives are crafted. Allegories are important for highlighting the moral messages embedded in the hydrocarbon narratives of financial experts, whose job it is to weave imaginaries of the future and how the future should be acted upon by capital providers—lenders and investors. The concept of allegories highlights that financial narratives are not just descriptive but also prescriptive evaluations about which energy futures have value and which should be materialized. Unpacking these metrics, where they came from, how they are used, and their components helps us better understand how they define time and value, as well as the allegories that are constructed with them. The temporal horizons defined in these metrics, I have shown, are not one hundred years, or fifty years or even twenty-five years. The futures they imagine and the decisions they inform about energy projects are much shorter than that. Moreover, what constitutes value becomes starkly clear. From the diverse and heterogeneous universe of things that might be considered values—or, crudely, what we consider to be important (see Introduction)—value is very narrowly defined in terms of profitability (Graeber 2012). While these are not new revelations, unpacking these metrics clearly renders how energy financiers conceptualize value and time and make energy decisions on our collective behalf from the opaque fog that shrouds the American hydrocarbon industry from those outside it. The significance of the prevailing economistic value concepts explored here is not how they are measured in dollars but instead how they index people toward shared capitalistic orientations of what has worth and how that worth should be measured.

Beyond understanding how these metrics, models, and allegories have come to shape the present energy landscape in the United States, they have broader implications. As the US energy industry pivots toward a mixture of renewable and hydrocarbon energy, these and similar metrics, models, and allegories are coming to bear on new forms of energy extraction and potential futures—helping people imagine, evaluate, and advocate what should and should not be materialized. Paul Langley et al. (2021) have noted that private capital is being championed as central to climate-change mitigation. This has made the decarbonization of capital and divestment from high-carbon assets "contingent, contested and compromised" (Langley et al. 2021: 511). While the shift to "low-carbon" investments is real, investors' need to meet their actuarial targets remains the same. The decarbonization of capital, many tell me, has more to do with dismal investment returns in oil and gas between 2015 and 2020 than with a "green" shift in investor sentiments (which I explore further in chapter 5).

Understanding how this lexicon makes sense of the world, the imaginaries it creates, and the realities it materializes opens opportunities to better shape (or oppose) the larger energy worlds we find ourselves in. Moreover, it provides an occasion to reflect on whether the ethical frameworks embedded in this lexicon and the moral conclusions of its allegories coincide with our own ethical frameworks and moral ambitions for the future we want to create. This is particularly important in the face of climate change, which I explore in the next chapter.

4

Not a Dichotomy

Climate Change and Hydrocarbons

We better hope it's man-made, because if it's not we're in trouble.
—Lindsay Graham, quoting Mitt Romney, 2019

Arthur called to tell me that he would be a bit late. It was a warm, sunny day in late September and I had invited Arthur over for dinner. He and Katie, his girlfriend, arrived at our modest apartment a half hour later. I saw Arthur's white SUV pull into the driveway of the apartment complex and went out to greet them in the sun-baked parking lot. I led them up the outdoor stairway, down the terraced corridor, and into our air-conditioned flat. They brought a bottle of wine and a chocolate meringue pie that they had picked up the day before from a small German-style bakery halfway between Houston and San Antonio. We chatted over some appetizers out on the large square ottoman. As we chatted, Arthur occasionally checked his phone before excusing himself for a few minutes to take a phone call; he said that he was working on a deal and needed to confirm a few details with the counterparty. When dinner was ready, the four of us sat down at the small, round dining table. As we took our places, Arthur excitedly showed me a picture that an employee had sent him from one of his portfolio firms that was operating somewhere in the southwestern United States. The picture was of a drilling platform with a torch-like natural gas flare atop a boom set against a rural scenic orange sunset—visual evidence of his firm's oil exploration and production activities.

As we dug into our homemade curry, Katie asked me what I thought about climate change and calls to stop oil and gas extraction. Climate change was something that Arthur and I had talked about, and I knew that he and Katie had talked about it as well. Almost everyone I had come to know had told me that climate change and the anthropogenic impact of hydrocarbons were topics of conversation at home. Often it was the source of tension and intergenerational conflict—some said that their children and their children's friends "hated" the oil and gas industry (Field 2023). For many, this disapproval was cause for introspection and an ethical appraisal of their work, the industry, and their place in the world (as with Tony in the Introduction). Katie seemed to be both genuinely curious about what I thought as well as slightly provocative, asking me to step into what I understood was an ongoing conversation between her and Arthur. With a moment of pause, I said that I believed in climate change and that oil and gas was contributing to it, but that the focus of my research was understanding how people within the industry *themselves* ethically navigate the world, including how they approached climate change. Arthur then chipped in. He said that the infrastructure and technology was just not in place for an energy transition. He believed in climate change and said that "I really hope we invent completely renewable energy," but until then he was going to produce oil and gas. Hydrocarbons are an essential resource that "saves lives, makes wealth, and makes jobs," he said. Weighing the conversation, Katie seemingly agreed with Arthur and nodded her head. It is hard, she said, for her to counter the predominant narrative she hears, that the production of oil and gas is "causing climate change and is destroying the world." Then, enthusiastically, Arthur retrieved his phone and showed me a graph of falling carbon dioxide in the United States. In the moment, I couldn't tell if the graph was describing emissions, atmospheric concentrations, or something else; nor could I inspect the figure more carefully. There were more figures, he said—swiping to the right, and showing me figure after figure. What was I looking at? I wondered. "It's an app," he said enthusiastically, called "Inconvenient Facts," and it had all sorts of data that he could draw on when talking about climate change. I should download it, he said, to which I wholeheartedly agreed—I had not come across it before.

Dinner went on and the homemade curry seemed to be a hit. Arthur had two extra helpings. We chatted and ate, and by around 9:30 p.m. Arthur and Katie prepared to depart so that we could "put the kiddies to bed," he said. Before they left, I asked Arthur if he had ever read *The Moral Case for Fossil Fuels* by Alex Epstein. I asked because the arguments that Arthur had made about the benefits of the oil and gas industry in the face of climate change sounded strikingly familiar, not only because I had heard others recite similar claims but also because they echoed the arguments made by Epstein. Arthur said that he knew of the book, which had obtained near-gospel status within the industry,[1] but he had not yet read it. Like others in the industry and like the self-described moral philosopher of oil and gas Epstein, Arthur did not see a dichotomy between believing in anthropogenic climate change and perpetuating hydrocarbon exploration and production. His approach to climate change drew on his economic evaluations of the US hydrocarbon industry's contribution to economic growth and value creation, his self-described libertarian ethos, and his cosmological sense that what he was doing in the world was "good." In many ways, the manner in which Arthur ethically navigated climate change and calls to curb oil and gas production was indicative of how many of my interlocutors navigated these issues.

In this chapter, I explore my interlocutors' idiosyncratic perceptions of climate change, the anthropogenic factors that drive it, and what (if anything) they think should be done about it. The challenge, I suggest, is that while the effects of climate change are observable, it is a complicated phenomenon in which contemporary considerations are future oriented. As such, it challenges people to consider what they value (monetarily and more broadly), why, how, and when, while also considering a quandary of risks and uncertainties, and who is responsible (individually or collectively) to act on these considerations. Climate change is, thus, fundamentally an ethical problem that requires attention to cross-cutting notions of time, risk, value, and responsibility. To explore my interlocutors' perceptions of climate change, I first return to Arthur before engaging with the work of Alex Epstein, illustrating how he is invoked, and how his arguments are mobilized by my interlocutors. I then return to Arthur and my ethnographic encounters with other interlocutors to show how these provisioning arguments are set alongside and, indeed, entangled with their Judeo-Christian cosmologies. I conclude the chapter by suggesting that the climate crisis is not a crisis of emissions or particular forms of energy per se but a crisis of the future and how people see themselves in these futures.

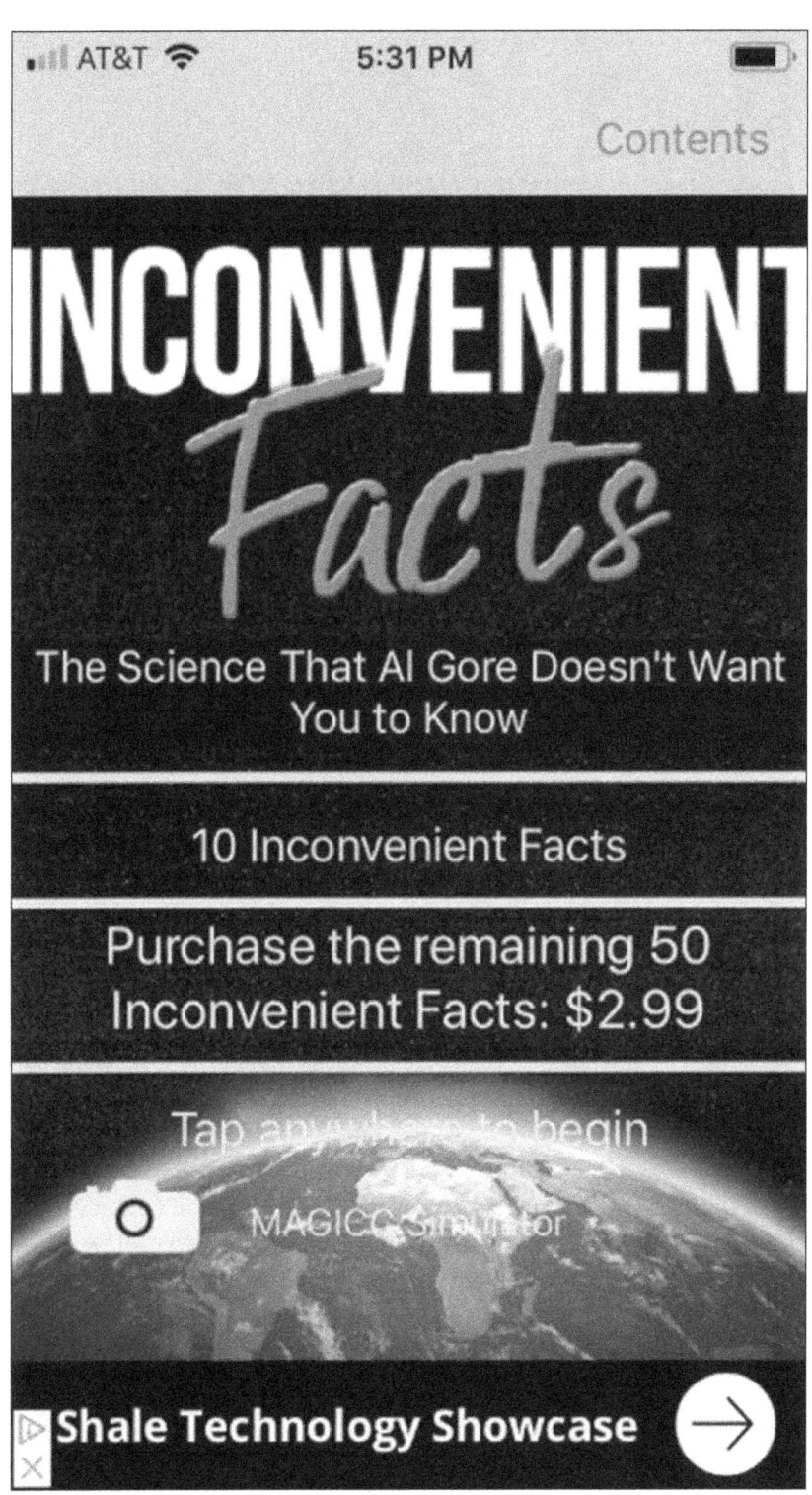

Figure 4.1: Screen shot of Inconvenient Facts App. Source: Author.

The Moral Case

Arthur and I first talked about climate change when we met at his private equity firm's office in early 2019. When we talked then, he said that he was open to a future energy transition but was skeptical of its near-term likelihood. He said that "maybe" oil demand will peak at "some point, and as a human and resident of the world . . . it would be amazing if we could all drive solar cars and live off of wind energy, but the reality is that we're not there yet." For him, a so-called clean, renewable energy future was a pipe dream. Joking, he said that "there's a great song" by "Merle Haggard, a famous country singer . . . I think it's called 'Rainbow Stew.'" He continued, "The lyrics are, 'When they find out how to burn water and the gasoline car is gone. When an airplane flies without any fuel and the satellite heats our home. But one of these days when the air clears up and the sun comes shining through, we'll all be drinking that free bubble love and eating that rainbow stew.'" For Arthur, the song was a powerful—albeit funny—allegory that epitomized calls to move away from fossil fuels and toward a renewable energy transition as far-fetched, verging on ludicrous. "It's just funny to me," he said, "because . . . people have been talking about this for forty years and during that time the demand for hydrocarbons has more than doubled." By "this" he referred to a transition away from hydrocarbons. His skepticism was not rooted in a fundamental disbelief in climate change or how human activity was expediting its effects. Rather, his skepticism was rooted in his understanding of the limits of nonhydrocarbon energy technologies and how a rapid energy transition would undermine an "American way of life" (Huber 2013). "Power is life, life as we know it," he said, and there are "real physical limitations to what clean energy can provide, at least based on currently available technology." Realistically, he told me, "you're going to need oil and gas for a long time to come still," and calls "to shut down fracking" and to "criminally prosecute oil and gas company executives" are "general hypocrisy." People had better be ready for higher "prices at the pump," and anti–fossil fuel campaigners had better be prepared to give up flying and combustion-engine vehicles, he said. For him, a transition away from fossil fuels seemed to be more of an existential threat than climate change—both more immediate and more of a threat to what he understood to be a good and right way of life, both professionally and personally. "I'm not . . . a climate denier," he told me, continuing, "I'm not denying that the climate changes over time. What I'm wondering is if we can have a more balanced discussion about what is the impact of all this. What are the trade-offs of trying to address it?" In many ways his arguments echoed not only what others told me but also the arguments advanced by Epstein.

Later in 2019, Arthur would reference Epstein to me over lunch. In this time, I had subsequently discovered a remarkable overlap in the evidence cited by Epstein and by the Inconvenient Facts app. The figures featured in Inconvenient Fact #7 in Epstein's book are identical, for example; both show a man standing beside a series of larger and larger pine trees holding signs indicating higher and higher concentrations of carbon dioxide, suggesting that higher levels of carbon dioxide are good for plants and, by extension, good for planetary vegetation.[2] While there are similar books, including Gregory Wrightstone's (2017) app turned book *Inconvenient Facts*, few purported public intellectuals have become as popular within the US hydrocarbon industry as Epstein. The reason why Epstein's arguments have resonated with so many of my interlocutors and have become so morally expedient—beyond the observation that his worldview coincides with their own and that he provides moral cover for hydrocarbon exploration and production—is that he taps into deeper ethical registers. Thus, his arguments warrant critical attention.

I first became aware of Epstein in early 2018. He famously debated environmental activist Bill McKibben at Duke University in late 2012 and, as I later came to understand, was adopted by many in the US oil industry as its moral philosopher and champion. I first encountered Epstein's book when I visited Tony at his office. *The Moral Case for Fossil Fuels* was sitting on the shelf in Tony's office, and he recommended that I read it because, he said, Epstein explained what the oil industry has done for society. Others also recommended Epstein's book to me. One person recommended it because, he said, "it is a good read," and another, James, who founded an influential oil and gas private equity firm, similarly said, "Have you read any of Alex Epstein's [books]? His *Moral Case* . . . is pretty good . . . I think for a guy knowing nothing about oil and gas, he's a very smart guy. I was just mad because he wrote it, and I didn't think of it!"

Epstein (2012: 13) posits that his book is about "morality, about right and wrong," and explains that he takes a capitalistic anthropocentric perspective in his assessment of fossil fuels. He asks, "What will promote human life? What will promote human *flourishing*—realizing the full potential of life?" (Epstein 2012: 13). From this position he argues that there has been a fundamental failure by environmental experts to adequately predict anthropogenic climate change and to fully consider the benefits and risks of fossil fuels. Moreover, experts are ill equipped to assess whether hydrocarbon usage is "good or bad" in the context of climate change because this is a "complex interdisciplinary question" about which everyone is on equal footing, he says (Epstein 2012: 27).

Taking a libertarian approach to economic growth and a cosmopolitan approach to climate change, Epstein flips prevailing notions of climate responsibilities. The fossil fuel industry, he argues, is responsible not just for heralding the present energetic era but for underwriting all of the benefits, technologies, and advances that define contemporary civilization. Climate scientists and environmentalists, he argues, are responsible for undermining this by overemphasizing the risks associated with climate change and, thus, threatening the life and happiness of people the world over. Vacating the legitimacy of climate scientists' expertise, he compels and gives moral license to my contacts within hydrocarbon industries to shape the future using the tools and technologies of the industry for the sake of humanity. Advancing his material-provisioning argument further, he argues that fossil fuels have been and continue to be morally justified because the "cheap" and "reliable energy" provided by hydrocarbons has "enabled billions of people to live longer and more fulfilling lives" (Epstein 2012: 30).[3] "Ultimately, the moral case for fossil fuels is not about fossil fuels; it's the moral case for using cheap, plentiful, reliable energy to amplify our abilities to make the world a better place—a better place *for human beings*" (Epstein 2012: 34). In this vein, my interlocutors within the industry reminded me of the material importance of hydrocarbons and pointed to many of the mundane and everyday products that are derived from fossil fuels on which lives and livelihoods depend—from textiles to pharmaceuticals (see High 2019 for a similar account).

Matthew Huber (2013) shows that material-provisioning arguments have circulated since the mid-twentieth century and in many cases were propagated by oil majors. Among the many mid-twentieth-century examples that Huber highlights, two are Esso's advertising tagline "Petroleum helps to build a better life" and Shell's "From A to Z—An alphabet of good things about petroleum," which celebrate durable fabrics, stain-resistant paints, heavy machinery, and modern medicines as products of the oil industry (Huber 2013: 76). What is newer about the material provisioning arguments advanced by Epstein, and recited by others, is that his argument is not just about an "American way of life" but also about a broader call to level up the world's poor (Huber 2013: xiii). While ignoring deep global inequalities along the cleavages of region, race, gender, and class, his moral-provisioning argument draws on the material abundances of the United States' twentieth-century past and its present in order to illustrate a vision of an abundant American and global future that is dependent on hydrocarbons. As Huber (2013: 169) observes, "Countless petroleum products . . . make up so much of American life" that a shift away from fossil fuels will entail a social and political transformation, not just a technological revolution. This does not precipitate a predetermined hydrocarbon future, however; instead, he suggests, fossil fuels are a material condition of a potential "emancipatory future" that does not involve continued extraction and production (Huber 2013: 169).

The material-provisioning arguments advanced by Epstein and circulating within the industry subscribe to what Jane Guyer (2007: 410) has described as a "combination of fantasy futurism and enforced presentism"—in this instance, imagined capitalistic-techno-utopias grounded in the hydrocarbon technologies of the present. Situated in the language of techno-realism about available energy sources, demands, and technologies, these envisioned futures turn on maintaining a "kind of 'freedom'" that has been engendered by over a half a century of US hydrocarbon infrastructural development—from automobiles to electricity generated from hydrocarbons—and its political economy. These material-provisioning arguments make a double temporal move: first, they project present modes of value production into not just the near but also the distant future as the only viable future worth imagining while excluding other emancipatory possibilities; and second, they cast present and near-future material needs as taking precedence over the potential impact that fulfilling these needs will have on future generations (which I return to below).

Beyond these moral material-provisioning arguments, Epstein's argument becomes more existential and strikes a biblical Judeo-Christian tone. Fossil fuels, he argues, are essential to human existence because "Mother Nature" is "hostile" (Epstein 2012: 86). Elaborating on this point, he says, "There is no climate that man is ideally adapted to, in the sense that it will guarantee him a decent quality of life. Nature does not want us to have a life expectancy of seventy-five or an infant mortality rate below 1 percent. Nature, the sum of all things on Earth, doesn't care about human beings one way or another and attacks us" (Epstein 2012: 128). The more fossil fuels people use, the "safer" people are "from climate-related dangers," he posits (Epstein 2012: 124). Indeed, the more fossil fuel energy people have access to, the more people can "master" the climate: "It's actually hard to imagine a dilemma that might justify restricting fossil fuels, for our potential climate mastery is so great" (Epstein 2012: 132, 134, 138).[4]

The framing of nature as a primordial and an autonomous force has been shown to stem from Enlightenment ontologies that frame it as external to and separate from people (Goldman and Schurman 2000). The root of this ontological orientation, however, can be traced even further back to the Judeo-Christian cosmology in the Book of Genesis:[5] "And God said, Let us make man in our image, after our likeness: and let them have dominion over the fish of the sea, and over the fowl of the air, and over the cattle, and over all the earth, and over every creeping thing that creepeth upon the earth" (Genesis 1:26, King James Version). The enduring idea emerging from this cosmological root is that people have not only the right but the responsibility to "master" nature, and its manifestation as climate change, for anthropocentric purposes.

Mike Hulme (2009: 348) locates the mastery-of-nature narrative in the biblical myth of Babel, wherein "a confident and independent humanity, repopulated after the traumas of the Flood," builds a tower that rises above the flood plain and into the heavens as a testament to humans' mastery over nature. Such narratives are not novel. Historically, these narratives have dovetailed with the political-economic projects of Victorian imperialism, wherein tropical places were framed as dangerous and in need of "conquering," and of American capitalism, wherein the burning of large tracts of the landscape to induce precipitation was trialed across the United States, including in Texas (Hulme

2009). Since then, the notion of "climate control" has manifested across scales—from ambient air control systems within buildings and vehicles to geo-engineered weather patterns induced by the seeding of clouds with silver iodide (Hulme 2009). It has also taken other forms, such as genetically modified and edited food varieties that are resistant to pests and drought, and pharmaceuticals and treatments that have facilitated "the medical mastery over nature," where nature manifests as infectious parasites, bacteria, and fungi (Yearly 2006: 13).

By invoking and anthropomorphizing nature as a "hostile" external force that "doesn't care about human beings" and "attacks us," Epstein draws on this history in order to situate hydrocarbons as the vital ingredient needed for nature's "mastery" (Epstein 2012: 86, 128, 138). Many of these hostile nature–related arguments are cited and echoed by my interlocutors with specific reference to modern medicine, agricultural technology, heating and air conditioning, and construction materials needed for human survival. Thus, what makes Epstein such a powerful moral touchstone is that he invokes enduring ideas and posits that without fossil fuels, an American way of life, and indeed society, would collapse. He provides a powerful allegory by combining well-trodden material provisioning arguments that are ensnared with a particular era in the capitalist political economy of the United States with Judeo-Christian fables. Not all of my interlocutors invoked Epstein, nor did they equally invoke the arguments that he advanced, which also circulate within the industry independent of him. What is vitally important about these arguments, however, is that they tune in to something fundamental about how my interlocutors ethically orient themselves in the world in ways that intersect with historical imaginaries and financial calculus.

Arthur's call for assessing the "trade-offs" of curbing hydrocarbon exploration and production in the face of climate change is one such intersection. This call took a contemporary-leaning tendency, whereby a near future when hydrocarbons were curbed by climate change policies put "lives," "wealth," and "jobs" at risk. This cost-benefit framing was echoed by others such as Tony (as well as Epstein). Like Arthur, Tony argued that we need to "add up the positives and negatives" of fossil fuels in the context of anthropogenic climate change, and that this cost-benefit analysis was an "important basic framework" for deciding what is "good" for society. In the face of calls to phase out hydrocarbons, Tony asked me, "When society understands the choice they're making, will they push back?" There is "a huge correlation" between "energy and the eradication of poverty," he told me. Set alongside conversations about the financial metrics by which the industry is financially judged and the economic value of companies and assets is determined (see chapter 3), these future-gazing cost-benefit analyses incorporated an implicit social discount calculation. Akin to the notion of net present value calculations (NPV), social discount calculations place an economic set of values on future things—jobs, production, the environment, climate change costs—and then express these future values in present economic terms by eroding these valuations according to a future social discount rate. Incorporated into a cost-benefit analysis, social discount calculations allow people to consider, for example, whether the benefits of reducing the greenhouse gas emissions of hydrocarbons (now and in the near future) outweigh the costs—now, in the near future, and in the distant future. Economists Nicholas Stern (2007) and William Nordhaus (2007) have popularized formal social discount calculations regarding curbing greenhouse gas emissions in the face of climate change within scholarly and policy circles. As evidenced by testimonies of Arthur and others, such calculations do not have to be formalized, however, but can instead take the form of implicit time-preference judgments weighted toward the present that are situated within the calculative rhetoric of economic value. As John Broome (1992, 2008) has shown with regard to the social discount rate, and as I demonstrate in chapter 3 with regard to net present value, the higher the discount rate is assumed to be (explicitly or implicitly), the more the present outweighs the future (also see Gardiner 2004). For Arthur, Tony, and others with whom I spoke, these implicit presentist-leaning calculations conceptually and empirically dovetail with their explicit presentist-leaning financial calculations, explored in chapter 3. Even if they agreed that the economic cost of mitigating and adapting to climate change increases several-fold in the coming decades, conceptually discounting these economic costs significantly reduces their present value toward zero.

There are, moreover, temporal considerations of risk and uncertainty. Weighed against concerns that the anthropogenic effects of hydrocarbons jeopardize the lives, wealth, and jobs of more distant future generations, Arthur explained, "What I don't know is, what are the chances that there will be some incredible breakthrough that happens that we can't even see? In the year 2000, could anybody have foreseen the iPhone?" Here, Arthur juxtaposes near-present material and economic risks with the uncertainties of distant futures. As discussed in chapters 1 and 3, the notion of risk has long been conceptualized and, indeed, operationalized in terms of knowable probabilities on which imagined futures will or will not materialize. Uncertainty, by contrast, describes unknowable futures. In the calculus of finance, the unknowable lurks beyond eight to ten years. This foggy unknown invites, as Arthur does here, possibilities for technological market-led innovations. This is akin to what Stephen Gardiner (2011) calls the mitigation of "the invisible hand," whereby market forces will reveal unknown solutions as well as future prosperity. Entangled with uncertainty, the invisible-hand argument not only leaves open the possibility of yet-to-be discovered technological fixes to anthropogenic climate change and its causes but also posits that future generations will be harmed by restricting economic growth in the present and near terms.

The moral impetus of present and near-term material-provisioning arguments are cross-cut with attributions of responsibility and notions of justice. As I discussed in chapter 3, financiers like Arthur assume a forward-gazing sense of responsibility to take financial risks in oil and gas exploration and production to yield envisioned financial outcomes, fulfilling their fiduciary duties and (re)producing a mode of political economy they see as "right" and "good." Calls to curb hydrocarbon exploration and production in order to combat climate change not only challenge their ability to fulfill these sets of responsibilities but add another layer of responsibility in the form of liability. As Tim Hayward (2012: 1) observes, public and scholarly debates on the ethics of addressing climate change revolve around who has the responsibility of shouldering the "costs and burdens" of addressing it and its effects. In this vein, debates gravitate toward notions of causal responsibility ("polluter" pays), beneficiary responsibility (beneficiaries pay), and economic responsibility (ability to pay). My perception is that attributions of causal responsibility are what incited Arthur to invoke the claim that environmentalists were "hypocrites" because, as he explained, everyone benefited from the work of the oil and gas industry—although unequally. Transposed onto prescriptions for the future and the role of people in shaping these futures, notions of responsibility merge with notions of justice and agential capacity—that is, what is "right" and the ability to make right. At the intersection of responsibility, justice, and agency come further considerations about the necessity to act individually, collectively, or somewhere in between in manifesting future prescriptions. This is why I suggest that allegories about climate change tune into something fundamental about how interlocutors ethically orient themselves in the world—because they tap into fundamental existential questions about the present and future, what constitutes risk, who has responsibility to whom and what, and what they value and why. In this way, climate change calls on my interlocutors to use the tools at their disposal to navigate the world—such as the normative tools and lenses of economics and finance—but evades the ability of these tools and lenses, as well as the agential capacities of individuals, to adequately address it. As I show in the next section, for some interlocutors this evasion manifests as a loss of control in a world in which they are socially and economically empowered. For others, as I show in the section that follows, it is cause to put their faith in higher powers.

"It's Not about the Climate"

It was late October, and I was sitting at "Tom's table." Tom is an engineer turned financier and is a senior contemporary of Arthur's. He has worked for some of the biggest oil and gas companies in the world, is a prominent member of Houston's hydrocarbon finance community, and has profoundly shaped US oil and gas finance over the last few decades. Sometimes I would see him at closed-door industry events, but when we met one on one, he liked to meet for lunch at his favorite downtown luxury steak and seafood restaurant. I had already been seated when he called to say that he was on his way and would arrive shortly.

Tom arrived a few minutes later, sporting a blue-collared shirt and suit jacket with his usual air of confidence. The server promptly came over to take our order, seemingly conscious that most business-attired patrons at this bustling lunch hour likely had to get back to the office or had an afternoon meeting to attend. We chatted about Brexit and the Houston Astros game, before I asked him about how the industry had changed and how calls to address climate change affected him and others in hydrocarbon finance. "Boy, that can be a whole new study," he said with a mixture of excitement and irritation. Rhetorically taking a step back and preparing to deliver his thoughts, he said, "Let me frame the answer," before continuing: "The progressives, the Left, whatever you want to call them, liberals, began twenty years ago in the schools in America trying to instill bias in our children that the government's good, and capitalism is bad, and this is an existential threat. None of that is based on fact." By contrast, he explained, "The facts are clouds attribute for 97 percent and 98 percent of the global warming effect on the planet. That has been a historically accepted fact forever. You never hear about that. All you hear about is the 2 or 3 percent of gases, mostly of CO_2, that impact global warming. Why is that? Well, because politicians can't legislate clouds, but they can [legislate] CO_2 emissions."

Tom understood climate change as an impetus to reorganize the political economy of the United States to be more centralized and government controlled, centered on what he called "political elites." "The conclusion of the matter is it's not about the climate," he said; it is about "manufactur[ing] a catastrophe" in order to take "control of the economies and all the little people out there." He elaborated, "I draw the analogy: if you've watched the *Hunger Games* movies, where the people live in the Crystal City, then all the rest of the folks are toiling to make their lives wonderful. That is the visual of the liberal Left. The elites and the educated—the chosen—must control the masses for the benefit of the elite. That's what that's all about." "It's all about control," he said.

The specific challenge for Tom and others in the industry is that concern about climate change "had now infiltrated into the investment community, starting at universities, pensions, and endowments." As a result, it was challenging their ability to persuade investors and to raise oil and gas private equity funds. Tom expressed deep frustration at the "insanity" of investors not supporting the material necessity of hydrocarbon exploration and production while potentially earning sizable profits. Turning his perplexity to the temporal tensions between nearer-term profits and material needs, and longer-term climate change predictions, he exclaimed that even if one believed in climate change, "You're talking about something decades in the future." He asked me, "Are you really willing to change your entire life, and your economy, and impoverish the planet over a concern that's generated from a computer model that says temperatures, fifty years from now, are going to be two degrees different?"

For Tom, climate change, which he understood as linked to naturally occurring slow-moving changes to the earth's environment, manifests in the present as a guise for adverse political economic change. Continuing, he said, "If you haven't read *The Moral Case for Fossil Fuels*, you should. He's coming to town next Wednesday to speak. He's got a lunch sponsored by CIBC. You send me a reminder and I'll see if I can get you in the lunch, or at least . . . see if you can spend some time with Alex." Excited by the possibility of an ethnographic engagement like this and the chance to possibly engage with Epstein, I enthusiastically agreed to send Tom a reminder that afternoon.

We spent the rest of lunch talking about "investment-grade" exploration and production companies couched in the language of financial metrics and the changing "cost of capital." It was clear to me that he ethically assessed much of the world through the tools that afforded him a financial-economic analytical lens. It was also clear to me that, by contrast with the threat posed by climate change, he perceived the possibility of an energy transition as an existential threat to what he understood as *his* way of life. Financial experts like Tom funnel capital, steer managerial decisions, craft financial imaginaries of the future, and decide on what kinds of hydrocarbon energy projects are materialized. Well-compensated and in positions of decision-making authority, he and his peers are empowered to execute elite agential action, by defining what has "value" and the time horizons worth considering (see chapter 3). They can exert control on the world around them through the purchase and ownership of assets, companies, and labor, and they can exert control within their personal worlds by using their wealth for philanthropic activities and to make consumer choices beyond the reaches of the poor and middle classes. They have what Dominic Boyer (2014: 322) describes as "energopower"—a means by which to use their expertise and authority to intervene on issues of energy and the Anthropocene, which emerges as the ability to control and influence the conduct of others within the shifting hierarchical social structures, institutions, and norms of the United States (Field 2021b; Foucault 1994). This is why Tom was incensed by the loss of "control" that an energy transition would, according to him, entail. It seemingly breached the Gramscian bargain between politicians and hydrocarbon capitalists that facilitated his place in the upper-class social hierarchies of the United States.

The first time Tom and I met in June, for example, he told me that the climate has been changing for millennia, and he assured me that humans are excellent at adapting. When we met for lunch that day at his favorite restaurant, he apologized for being late. He had been managing "a bit of an emergency," he said. Before I could ask if everything was alright, he told me that he had been driving his "high-end" sports car into work early the previous morning. A tropical storm had flooded low-lying areas, and he drove through what *seemed* to be a shallow pool of water. These "high-end [sports cars] intake air into the engine from the bottom of the car," he said, and when he drove through the pool of water it sucked water into the engine. His emergency was that he was on the phone with the mechanic, who was looking into it. The car might be a "write-off," he said, but luckily insurance would probably cover it.

I had also been driving through the storm and flooding that disabled Tom's car the day before to take our minivan in to get the air conditioning repaired because the heat and the humidity of the burgeoning Houston summer were making it impossible to not sweat through my clothes on the way to meet my interlocutors.[6] As I drove southwest from our Braeswood neighborhood, the city changed from mixed residential to industrial to residential again. It also changed from racially diverse to predominantly African American, testament to the city's historical and deep social-spatial segregation. In this part of the city, the boulevard separating the east and west traffic was adorned with large piles of moldy-looking furniture, mattresses, and garbage bags. There were also rotten-looking furniture and garbage piled in front of some of the houses. None of these piles looked new, and I remembered reading stories in the *Houston Chronicle* about how segments of the city had not yet been repaired or cleaned up after Hurricane Harvey in 2017, twenty-two months earlier.[7] While most Houston-area residents were affected by the storm, the severity of the damage experienced and the capacity of households to recover have divided the city along the intersections of race and class (Smiley et al. 2022).[8] Low-income households in Houston were more likely to be located in flood-prone areas, and poor and non-white residents were less likely to receive financial recovery assistance than their higher-income white counterparts (Boyer and Vardy 2022;

Blackburn and Bedient 2018; Capps 2018; Lin 2018).[9] Many of the homes that were condemned or remained damaged were owned or rented by people who could not afford flood insurance (Foxall and Schuetz 2022; Watkins 2022). While Houston is well known for tropical storms and regional flooding, the severity of both have increased in recent decades, culminating in what Dominic Boyer and Mark Vardy (2022) describe as a "slow catastrophe." There has been almost one recorded flooding event for every year of Houston's 184-year history,[10] but in the span of twenty-four months between 2015 and 2017, Houston experienced three five-hundred-year flooding events. Moreover, so-called unnamed tropical storms more frequently cause catastrophic flooding in the city (Boyer and Vardy 2022).[11]

There was a sense among most of my interviewees that flooding had gotten more frequent and severe in recent years. The wife of one of my interlocutors told me, as we surveyed the backyard garden at their home, that the weather had really changed since they had moved to Houston decades earlier. Assessing her stunted tomato and pepper plants with me, she said that her garden no longer grew as well. Another person, meanwhile, told me that while flooding had always happened, it now seemed to happen all the time. They did not share the same view of climate change as Tom, nor did they evaluate calls to curb hydrocarbons with the same apocalyptic visions of the future. What they *did* share in common with Tom, besides working at the intersection of the financial and hydrocarbon industries, was a sense of control over their lives and their futures afforded by their socioeconomic status, which allowed them to live at higher elevations and to financially insulate themselves from the effects of climate-related catastrophes. From climate-controlled vehicles to flood-resistant homes, and from flood insurance to accumulated savings that could be drawn on in times of need, my interlocutors enjoyed more control over their lives and their futures, and they experienced climate-related events differently than others in the city. These seemingly ordinary luxuries, which were out of reach for the city's poorest and most flood prone, were not just a product of the wealth that the finance and hydrocarbon industries are known to generate but also provided a sense of anticipatory planning against the risks and uncertainties of the future. They individualized responsibility for climate adaptation in terms of insurance premiums and deductibles, afforded a sense of mastery over the city's heat and tropical deluges, and reinforced the "rightness" of normative structures of capital accumulation. It made sense to me, then, why calls to curb hydrocarbons incensed Tom and invoked dystopian visions of the future—because they undermined his control over *his* future. While others shared his sense of indignation, they took solace in Christian cosmology in managing the vicissitudes of the climate and the industry.

"You Need to Put Your Faith in God"

Like many of my interlocutors, Arthur's Christian cosmology is another ethical register by which he orients himself in the world. "I am a believer," he told me when we first met at his office in early 2019, and "I do attend church." It was a bright, warm Sunday morning when my family and I attended church with him several months later. We arrived early and found seats near the center of the main space where a stage was set up in the middle, and where the service would start a few minutes later. Arthur spotted us in the crowd and excitedly came over to sit with us. Sporting a travel mug of coffee, black golf shirt, jeans, and running shoes, he seemed at ease, and the occasion felt like a community barbecue. "This is probably different than what you are used to," Arthur said to me. It was. Located in a refurbished factory complex, it was very different from the Methodist church we had attended several times with another of my interlocutors and the Roman Catholic churches I had attended growing up. It was furnished with new, hip-looking partition walls that divided up the expansive open space inside the reclaimed factory, there were children running around playing, and most people were dressed in weekend casual wear, such as jeans and hoodies. There was a long lineup of people, young and old, wearing baseball hats, piercings, tattoos, and flannel, waiting to buy coffee and baked goods at the café in one corner of the complex. It felt like a "hip" community center. Arthur told me that he came to join this church after he attended a number of other denominations around town. What he liked about this church, by contrast with others, was that it was "stripped down" and focused on what he understood to be core Christian values. By contrast with another church that he considered joining that built an expensive athletic facility for its parishioners, which he described as hypocritical, he said that "through my church, we do a lot of homeless outreach," which he was involved in. "I like being able to go to the store and buy . . . four hundred dollars of food that we're going to feed the homeless. I like that. it's fulfilling to me that everything that I've done in my career has got me to this point, where I can do that. It's just something that makes me feel good. It is a motivation."

There was a striking comparison in the way he invoked the notion of hypocrisy both regarding hydrocarbons and climate change and regarding homelessness and Christian cosmology. My sense was that this comparison was borne out in the way he felt he needed to act in the material present in ways that were congruent with his own Christian cosmology. He could not solve homelessness in the city, but he could partially alleviate the immediate hunger of the unhoused using his wealth. Similarly, he could not solve climate change, but he could work to supply the hydrocarbon energy people needed in the present with his financial expertise. The charismatic and self-described "holistic missional" ethos of Arthur's church provided him positive affirmation of his place and agency in the world. Arthur could tether himself to the moral mast of the church while weathering the storm of growing calls about curbing fossil fuels and while living by his own libertarian Christian ethical sensibilities. The prosperity of being an oil and gas private equity financier facilitated his faith-filled sense of agency—his material contributions to the church's outreach program justified and lent moral credence to his work. It brought him emotional and spiritual "fulfillment" and a sense of moral justification that his work at the intersections of the finance and oil and gas industries was, in the deepest sense, "good" amid calls that the industry was "evil," "bad," or otherwise "destructive."

This juxtaposition at the intersection of "good" and "bad" is where his claim of hypocrisy was located. Even in the face of climate change, how could financing oil and gas be bad if it provided people with material energy that they needed in the present? And, how could it be bad if it allowed him to use his wealth to help the poor? If others made their wealth in non–fossil fuel industries but used this wealth in ways that did not subscribe to what he understood as "authentic" Christian values, was this more or less good? These were some of the questions Arthur appeared to be grappling with when we talked about his faith alongside concerns about climate change.

Examining the role of agency in his study of Methodists and Adventists, Hirokazu Miyazaki (2000) argues that what makes religious rituals and practices consequential for practitioners is not *necessarily* rendering the intentions of nonhuman spiritual entities accessible, but the interplay of agential action. He observes, "Religious practitioners may even explicitly reject an anthropomorphic rendering of nonhuman entities to insist that what is at issue is not so much the agency of these entities as the limits of human agency—their own or others'. In other words, what makes religious rituals consequential is not the intentions of experientially inaccessible entities from religious practitioners' viewpoint but the limits placed, at least temporarily, on their own capacity to make sense of events or even their capacity to act" (Miyazaki 2000: 32). This observation provides an insightful analytical premise for understanding Arthur's faith and broader ethical orientation in navigating the world. He did not anthropomorphize God or nature in any of our conversations, unlike others whom I discuss below. Rather, he approached Christianity and climate change as a set of limits in which his agency could be activated or vacated. Within this cosmology, his own socially situated agential power found abeyance at the limits of spiritual and earthly processes beyond his control. Describing his life as a kind of path set within a broader landscape ordained by God, he explained to me, "I am still on my spiritual journey." Others expressed similar agential sentiments with regard to the future in both a personal and a worldly sense. A petroleum engineer turned senior banker at a major US oil and gas industry lender told me at his office, for example, "I came to know the Lord . . . [and] I just put more of my faith in Him to take care of us." He continued, "I felt like God was guiding my life and that I didn't need to control everything. If you work hard and are ethical, just let Him be in charge of where your life goes." For this interlocutor, as well as Arthur, there was a productive tension between their agency and the agency of a grander spiritual Christian entity that guided not only *their* path but the collective path of the world more broadly in ways that included climate change. This tension allowed them to exercise their libertarian political economic sensibilities and entrepreneurial spirits in ways that echoed a Protestant kind of ethic in the present with regard to things that they perceived to be within their agential capacity, while letting go of phenomena they understood to be beyond and outside of their agency and the agency of humans, such as climate change.

Others expressed similar but distinct Christian cosmologies. James, the founder of the influential oil and gas private equity firm whom I introduced earlier and who had asked me if I had read Epstein's book, explained to me, for example, "I do believe in God. I'm a Christian, and so I do believe that there is an afterlife. I do believe that, and I have believed it for a long time, that we need to have God and have Jesus be part of our lives. And, that we need to give ourselves, our companies, everything that's valuable to us, to God." James, like Arthur, saw his Christian cosmology as congruent with his work at the intersection of the finance and oil and gas industries. James, in fact, saw his work in oil and gas private equity as even *more* strongly entwined with the work of God. He understood his life, his work, and the process of capitalist value creation as all tied to his faith and spiritual service in ways that extended beyond Christian notions of charity and material contributions to society at large. For James, his work and his faith were inseparable. Thus, while he admitted that the industry might be "very unpopular," he insisted that his work could not be "bad" not only because it yielded material benefits but also because it was in service of God.

Another corporate veteran, whom I met at one of the monthly hydrocarbon finance meetings, explained to me that Christian cosmology was not only "fundamental" to the lives of those who worked in the "oil field" but was also the cosmological ethos that ran through the industry—from the well heads to the corporate suites. Christian cosmology, he told me, "is core to the fabric of business leadership" in the industry. Evidencing what he meant, he explained, "There's some Christian business lunches that occur in town that are very prominent, very well attended. One is downtown at the top of the Shell building. . . . Another one is at the Houston Country Club." Echoing this sentiment, the CEO of a start-up hydrocarbon private equity firm explained to me at his office that "I came to faith because of the [oil and gas] community." He came from a secular scholarly family, he said, where faith was not a central part of his life growing up. When I asked him why he gravitated toward Christianity, he suggested that it was not only because others in the industry attended church but also because it was a kind of cosmological way of dealing with risk and uncertainty. He explained, "Oil prices go up, and oil prices go down. What do you do? You pray. A lot of prayers have been answered. You need to put your faith in God." This sentiment extended not only to the boom-and-bust cycles of the industry but to factors beyond his control like climate change. The "common lay person," he said, "cr[ies] foul that we're destroying the environment and changing the climate," and "we do account for a lot of the carbon emissions, greenhouse gases," he admitted, but he was not worried. At ease and with what appeared to be a sense of self-assuredness as he leaned back into his chair, he explained, "I'm a firm believer that the goal of any business is to create shareholder value. That's number one. I don't care if anybody says any differently, but that's why companies were created, to create shareholder value." Merging his capitalist sensibilities with his Christian cosmology, when it came to climate change and the vicissitudes of the boom-and-bust cycles of the oil industry, he relinquished his agency and put his faith in God.[12]

In another instance, Sam cited divine intervention after oil prices collapsed in 2014. Sam worked as a commercial lender to oil and gas companies, an investment banker with Enron, an executive of a medium-sized independent exploration and production company, and an industry consultant. We first met in the elevator of the Total building on our way to a monthly luncheon at the ornate Houston Petroleum Club (Field 2021b). When we met a few weeks later over lunch at a pub on the west side of Houston, he said to me, "I don't know if you're a Christian man, but I honestly believe that the good Lord stuck his hand into it . . . Hurricane Harvey." Clarifying what he meant, he said,

> At the end of '14, '15 when prices tanked . . . there were tens of thousands of apartments that were coming to fruition, being built and finished just at that time . . . and everybody was going, "My gosh, all these apartments are about to be completed, and these prices are tanking, and people are being laid off right and left. There's going to be the biggest problem there's ever been in this city." . . . Just at that time, Hurricane Harvey comes in, wipes out all of these houses, wipes out apartment complexes and stuff, and guess what? For two years, all those people have to live somewhere. Guess where they all have to go? Brand new apartments. It was uncanny. . . . I'd say the man upstairs had a lot to do with it. I really believe that. How else could it happen? We would have had . . . probably forty to

fifty thousand units on the market that would have been empty. In our church, I bet we had thirty families that were affected. . . . having to move out of their homes or apartments, because they were under water.

Invoking divine intervention in a way that invites comparison to elements of the biblical story of the flood, Sam understood God to be intervening to "save" the city's economy—through its real estate and construction sectors—at a time when the oil and gas industry was experiencing a negative price shock and facing an uncertain future. While this is an idiosyncratic view, what it shares in common with the Christian cosmologies of other of my interlocutors is a sense that God is watching over those within the industry and working through them. Thus, beyond the gaze of economic models and financial metrics that illuminate imaginaries of the future, and outside of the moral material-provisioning arguments that activated my interlocutors' sense of agential authority in the present, Christian cosmology provided a means by which many of them ethically oriented themselves in the face of the uncertainty of climate change.

A Crisis of the Future

Climate change is an environmental phenomenon that calls into question people's relationship with the earth, each other, and nonhuman entities. It is a physical phenomenon involving the earth's processes, but unlike the wind, the rain, and the sun, climate change cannot be directly experienced through our senses. It is an idea that people use to describe changes in complex earthly processes, culminating from a multitude of observations in specific places and times over the last half-century. The leading authority on climate change, the Intergovernmental Panel on Climate Change (IPCC), was established in 1988 to provide governments with state-of-the-art assessments on exactly how the earth is changing and why. The six assessment reports it has released since have evidenced with increasing scientific confidence that humans are changing the rhythm of the earth's systems and affecting its nonhuman species in profound and irreversible ways (see for example IPCC 2022). The problem is that although there is an ever-growing consensus among policy makers, scholars, and publics about the necessity of curbing anthropogenic climate change and adapting to its effects, how this should happen, by what means, at what cost, and for whose benefit are at the heart of the biggest existential challenge facing the planet. Anthropogenic climate change is not simply a scientific problem to be solved with technological innovation but a deeply human problem imbued with historical patterns of inequality, diverse needs and desires, an array of cosmological orientations, unequal access to resources, and asymmetrical power dynamics.

What I have highlighted in this chapter is how notions of material provisioning and cosmology enter the ethical frameworks, and indeed the allegories, of my interlocutors in hydrocarbon finance. If metrics and models are the ethical scaffolding on which allegories about energy and the *near futures* are crafted, material provisioning and cosmology are the scaffolding on which allegories about *uncertain distant futures* are crafted, including my interlocutors' place in these futures.

This is why I suggest that climate change arguments are unlikely to be "won" on the basis of scientific evidence. While people may disagree about the "facts" and how these facts should be interpreted—as I have shown above—disagreements about climate change are much more deeply rooted. They are rooted in people's cosmological worlds, how they envision the non-near future, and their place in these futures. From invoking dystopian visions of the *Hunger Games* to suggesting that a rapid energy transition would spark a new American "civil war," most of my interlocutors understood hydrocarbons to be the lifeblood of a Judeo-Christian American way of life that they were fighting to preserve. Timothy Mitchell (2009; 2011), Ewan Gibbs (2021), and Daniel Knight (2017) have argued that the way we produce, move, and use hydrocarbons is connected to meanings of modernity and belonging to particular energetic eras. I agree, and I suggest that the climate crisis is not a crisis of emissions or particular forms of energy per se but a crisis of the future and how people see themselves in these futures.

Without addressing the specific tools with which people evaluate the value of worldly things (chapter 3), the way people draw on the ethical registers of the past to situate themselves in the present (chapter 1), or the way material and cosmological registers come to bear on the ways in which people evaluate the uncertainties of the future (this chapter), it is difficult to appreciate how people in hydrocarbon finance ethically navigate their worlds. In the next chapter, I explore how my interlocutors in the industry are addressing climate change concerns from within the investment and finance communities, which are collated under the banner of Environmental, Social, and Governance standards (ESG).

5

"What the Hell Is ESG?" and the Moral Case for Oil

The new buzzword in business in 2019 was Environmental Social Governance (ESG), and the term is on track to become mainstream in 2020.
—Tyne Thygesen, 2019

Charlie asked me if I "remember[ed] when Martin presented in January to our Houston Oil Finance Association."[1] "No, I wasn't there," I replied. "Well, he was talking about ESG," Charlie continued, before pausing for a moment, looking somewhat exasperated, and throwing his hands up into the air. "Like, what the hell is ESG?" he asked, signaling that it was a little-known and little-cared-about acronym in the industry at the time. It was early November and Charlie and I were meeting for lunch near his office downtown. He is one of the association's founding members and has been at the center of the US hydrocarbon finance sector for decades—his family is steeped in the industry's corporate echelons. I had joined the association in mid-2019 after Charlie had invited me to attend a few meetings. "I know now," he said, reflecting on how quickly the language of ESG had percolated through the sector over just eleven months.

Its percolation was rapid but not complete. In late 2019, a few of my interlocutors still asked me, "What is ESG?" when I raised the topic with them. Charlie agreed with how quickly talk of ESG had washed across the Houston hydrocarbon sector, but he said that he had not seen any "practical application" yet. There was a lot of "lip service," but few had implemented meaningful changes, he asserted. Moreover, he was skeptical of how ESG standards were to be *assessed*. He explained, "Fitch, the rating agency, is going to have some sort of scale for whether or not companies are self-reporting and asserting that they're complying with ESG. . . . They're not going to independently verify it. They're just going to keep track of whether companies say it, or they're paying attention to

[ESG] ... in their SEC disclosures." ESG was not new, but it was new to the US hydrocarbon industry.

Since late 2018, Environmental, Social, and Governance (ESG) frameworks went from being a largely unknown acronym in the US hydrocarbon industry to being a central feature of investor presentations, interindustry dialogue, and public-facing corporate strategies. In recent years, ESG has usurped CSR, and its close investment-oriented cousin, socially responsible investing (SRI), as the commonly accepted framework for ethical corporate behavior. Emerging in the context of sustainable or ethical investing, rather than in response to anticorporate activist critiques, ESG has come to replace other corporate ethical registers and has become the go-to acronym for socially responsible business practices. As exclaimed by *Forbes*, "The new buzzword in business in 2019 was Environmental Social Governance (ESG), and the term is on track to become mainstream in 2020. It refers to a company's commitment to do more than make a profit, such as actively strive to contribute positively to the environment or social causes and to conduct themselves responsibly" (Thygesen 2019). By 2020, *Forbes* triumphantly declared that ESG had become "mainstream ... driven by united demand from employees, investors and customers" to force companies to take action on climate change and social injustice (McClimon 2020). Proponents of ESG claim that it tackles one of the largest shortfalls of CSR and SRI by being measured, quantifiable, and criteria led, allowing organizations to be held quantitatively accountable and comparable within and across industries (McClimon 2020). Critics, however, have suggested that ESG does not meet these claims (Fancy 2021; Richie 2022).

In the sections that follow, I document how and why ESG has been adopted by oil and gas financiers. I show that demands by institutional investors have been central to the adoption of ESG within the industry and that *when*, *why*, and *how* it was adopted must be understood within the broader trends of US corporate finance. Framed in the terminology of "risk," increasingly represented on "scorecards," and integrated into narratives crafted by financiers and pitched to investors, ESG has become a new tool in the ethical scaffolding of the allegories of my interlocutors. I show that ESG has, over the last several years, transitioned from a tool used against the hydrocarbon industry to a tool used in the argument for oil. Drawing on themes and concepts explored in the preceding chapters, I argue that when situated in the long history of corporate moral codes, ESG may be best understood as integral to the financialization of the corporate gift.

New Corporate Ethical Registers: ESG

The well-known predecessors to ESG are CSR and SRI. CSR arose from NGO and activist campaigns against corporate malfeasance and the expansion of global corporate capitalism in the 1990s, calling for corporations to clean up their acts. As Dinah Rajak (2011) notes, however, once companies took up the CSR banner beginning in the early 2000s, they became the purveyors of best practice and ethical standard bearers—usurping the moral high ground of NGOs that had helped usher in the era of CSR. Since then, scholars have shown that CSR programs have allowed corporations to pursue capitalist political-economic objectives while diffusing responsibility for poor business practices and reinforcing unequal gift relations in the communities where they operate (Gardner et al. 2012; Cross 2014; Rajak 2011; Rogers 2015b). In the global hydrocarbon industry, Douglas Rogers's (2015a) examination of Lukoil in Russia's Perm Region shows, for example, that company-sponsored cultural festivals and community projects are a way of distracting attention away from the economic inequalities that exist between oil workers and people in surrounding communities, and the toxic impact of extraction on the region. In its various manifestations, CSR appears as a collaborative venture among diverse interests and values, under the guise that corporations are assuming responsibility for the social and economic well-being of the communities where they operate, endowing corporate citizens with a public-facing morality and the authority to shape social orders while pursuing corporate interests (Rajak 2011).

Building on a longstanding history of faith-based organizations' avoidance of "sin stocks," SRI emerged alongside CSR in the 1960s as a framework for restricting particular types of investments (Eccles et al. 2020: 591). According to Robert Eccles and colleagues, SRI gained momentum in the context of the Vietnam War, the US civil rights movement, and environmental concerns among politically active investors. By contrast with strictly financially driven investment concerns, SRI demanded the integration and consideration of "nonfinancial information" so that churches, charities, and NGOs could make better, more socially informed investment decisions (Eccles et al. 2020). One purported problem of SRI (as with CSR), however, was that the way it should be defined—let alone measured—was heterogeneous (Sandberg et al. 2009). There was no single definition and, therefore, no single way of measuring it. Thus, while it provided a means by which to incorporate broader moral concerns into the world of investing, it was subject to criticism for being too ambiguous. ESG emerged to fill these gaps.

While claiming a similar ethical ethos as SRI and CSR, ESG has captured the interest of investors and corporate leaders by moving away from the wedding of social "values" with financial analysis and toward a closer integration of social *values* with economic *value* (Eccles et al. 2020). It first appeared in the United Nations 2004 report *Who Cares Wins: Connecting Financial Markets to a Changing World*, its introduction accompanied by an invitation to asset managers, brokers, and analysts from UN's secretary general to "better integrate environmental, social and corporate governance issues" into their financial assessments (Eccles et al. 2020; UN 2004). This invitation was endorsed by nearly two dozen financial institutions, including HSBC, Morgan Stanley, and BNP Paribus (UN 2004). Just one year later, the UN Environmental Program Finance Initiative's Freshfields Report (UNEP-FI 2005) reinforced the move toward integrating ESG considerations into traditional financial analysis and management. It argued that while "conventional investment analysis focuses on *value*, in the sense of financial performance," the integration of ESG considerations into these analyses can "more reliably predict financial performance" (UNEP-FI 2005: 13). The crucial claim made in the report was that considering social "values" should be perceived not as additional to traditional financial analysis but as integral to more holistically evaluating future financial performance (UNEP-FI 2005: 11).[2] While the institutionalization of nonfinancial data into financial analysis under the banner of ESG was established in the mid-2000s, Stefan Leins (2020) observes that it was not until the onset of the global financial crisis in 2008 that ESG began to move from niche to mainstream acceptance. By contrast with the adoption of "responsible investing" objectives, Leins (2020) shows that ESG became the subject of financial speculation and investment narratives. While hardened financial analysts were skeptical of the integration of ESG into fundamental economic analyses, he shows that it was enthusiastically adopted by the advisors of institutional investors at the Swiss bank where he worked as a means by which to take an analytical approach to addressing responsible investing. It was adopted, he observes, as a means "to anticipate what non-financial information could eventually materialize in the markets or hurt the company's reputation" (Leins 2020: 80).

ESG being a purportedly quantitative way of assessing the financial risk of companies' environmental, social, and governance practices, rating agencies emerged to satisfy demand for data measuring ESG performance, including Sustainalytics, Bloomberg ESG, S&P Global ESG, and Moody's. To do this, ratings agencies take self-reported data obtained from companies, combine this data with secondary data, then quantify this information into a weighted unitary index quantifying firms' ethical performance, which they can then use to satisfy and woo investors and other financial stakeholders.

As Matthew Archer (2022) and Ainur Begim (in-press) note, however, one of the problems with ESG data is that it often conveys contradictory findings. Rating agencies construct their ESG assessments differently, and they build differing categorized weightings into their ESG indices, by which firms can purportedly be compared. Often analysts are tasked with "cleaning" this data and even collecting additional primary data by which to triangulate information from ratings agencies. Translated into the language of finance, ESG data is ultimately communicated to investors in terms of "risk"—legal risks, climate risks, reputational risks—that can affect not only the returns investors might expect but also investors' public-facing reputations (Archer 2022; Begim in-press; Leins 2020). While there is no universal standard for measuring and calculating organizations' ESG scores, investor enthusiasm for

TABLE 5.1: Example ESG Framework and List of Underlying Factors That May Be Included.

Environmental	Social	Governance
Greenhouse Gas Emissions	Health & Safety	Board Composition & Diversity
Air & Water Pollution	Labor Conditions & Practices	Compensation Schemes
Biodiversity Impact	Employee Satisfaction	Financial Compliance
Waste Treatment & Disposal	Community Engagement	Auditing
Water Usage & Treatment	Human Rights	Data Security
Energy Efficiency		Intellectual Property Protection

Sources: CFA 2024; Leins 2020; PWC 2024; S&P Global 2019.

ESG has been astounding in recent years. In 2019, nearly 25 percent, or $21 billion, of US investor capital globally was funneled into funds that apply ESG principles, and this grew to $51.1 billion of net new money from investors in 2020, and to $120 billion in 2021 (McClimon 2020; Quinson 2021). This may be interpreted as guarding shareholder value from the risk of being eroded by unknown or distant factors, what economists call "externalities." It may also be interpreted as investors extending their considerations of corporate responsibility beyond three to eight years or to a broader group of cobeneficiaries who extend beyond financial stakeholders.

In my fieldwork, only a few large financial firms had a stated commitment to SRI in the first half of 2019, while most firms had some form of public-facing CSR policy, suggesting that CSR had more moral currency than SRI within these circles at the time of field research. By early 2020, nearly every hydrocarbon finance firm I encountered had an investor or public-facing ESG policy. I came to understand ESG in my fieldwork not so much as a quantitative index that interlocutors I know came to fret over but as a general call to review and "clean up" the operations of firms and portfolio companies, in order to demonstrate that they are ethically viable investment vehicles for existing and prospective investors. In this context, ESG's replacement of "corporate" and "responsible"—which feature in CSR and SRI—with "environmental" and "governance" signaled a shift in ethical focus from corporate responsibility, broadly defined, to financial accountability for the social and environmental impact of corporate activities on investors. While the purported object of both CSR and ESG is to expand the responsibility of firms beyond profit generation, the subtle shift in target stakeholders from local communities and laborers to investors signals, I believe, what might be described as the financialization of what Jamie Cross calls the "corporate gift." Following Marilyn Strathern's (1996) critical reinterpretation of gifting and exchange, Cross (2011, 2014) challenges scholars to destabilize notions of corporate gifting to explore how it creates knowledges, persons, and relations in ways that do more than bolster notions of reciprocity among the "exploited." By contrast with CSR, which Cross identifies as succumbing to classic capitalist-gift analyses, ESG, I suggest, opens up a new range of relations. Whereas CSR gifting activities—from sponsoring schools to building clinics—shares with ESG an interest in the corporate "bottom line," ESG initiatives are different because the target audience they are intended to woo is investors, not laborers and local communities. While laborers and communities may benefit from ESG activities, I suggest that this is secondary to attracting and retaining investment capital. In this vein, the inclusion of "environment" in ESG appears to signal a broadening of what corporations are accountable for to explicitly include flora, fauna, and nonhuman entities. The E, moreover, signals a shift in scale from exclusive concerns for localized environments and corporate waste and contamination practices, for example, to a more global concern for the anthropogenic impact of the industry. While what constitutes environmental action is vague and variously defined (which is also the case for what constitutes "social" and "governance"), the adoption of ESG by oil and gas financiers has moved in lock-step with growing investor interest and ESG's mainstream adoption across the broader US financial sector.

By 2021, over 80 percent of privately owned, medium-sized US exploration and production companies were found to have implemented ESG programs (Haynes Boone & Enercom 2021). Many of these firms promote their new methane-monitoring technologies, waste water programs, the electrification of field equipment, and the integration of renewable energy generation to supply electricity to their production sites as key elements of their public-facing ESG strategies (Haynes Boone & Enercom 2021). This same year, S&P Global (2021) launched its rating system on the impact of environmental, social, and governance issues, which it said would "inform future corporate credit ratings." While many hydrocarbon companies were found to have a neutral credit risk rating arising from their social and governance activities, S&P found that "environmental factors weigh[ed] negatively on the credit ratings of nearly all North American oil and gas companies." Assessments of firms' carbon emissions, efforts to minimize these emissions, and the possibility that regulations could restrict firms' ability to operate S&P found that "environmental risk is the most relevant ESG category for the upstream oil and gas and refining sectors due to issuers' exposure to climate transition risk and the potential loss of market share to product substitution and renewables. . . . Pollution and spillages can also give rise to severe credit consequences" (S&P Global 2021). Companies included in its ESG scorecard included supermajors such as ExxonMobil and Chevron, as

TABLE 5.2: S&P Global Ratings ESG Credit Indicators. ESG Credit Indicators: 1 indicates a positive consideration; 2 indicates a neutral consideration; 3 indicates a moderately negative consideration; 4 indicates a negative consideration; and 5 indicates a very negative consideration.

Firm	Credit Indicator			Market Capitalization & ESG	
	Environmental	Social	Governance	$ Billion	ESG Credit Factors
Exxon Mobil Corp.	4	2	2	260.41	Climate transition risks
Chevron Corp.	4	2	2	219.58	Climate transition risks
Conoco Phillips	4	2	2	94.82	Climate transition risks
EOG Resources	4	2	1	50.73	Climate transition risks; risk management, culture & oversight
Pioneer Natural Res.	4	2	2	44.06	Climate transition risks
Occidental Petroleum	4	2	2	28.03	Climate transition risks
Devon Energy Corp.	4	2	2	27.84	Climate transition risks
Diamondback Energy	4	2	2	19.11	Climate transition risks
Continental Resources	4	2	2	16.44	Climate transition risks
Marathon Oil Corp.	4	2	2	12.19	Climate transition risks
Chesapeake Energy	4	2	5	7.17	Climate transition risks; risk management; culture, and oversight; other governance factors

Data Source: S&P Global (2021). Note: Assessment dated November 23, 2021.

well as large independent producers such as EOG Resources, Occidental Petroleum, and Chesapeake (see table 5.2).[3]

ESG factors were already being integrated into S&P's credit ratings prior to the release of its indicators system, however. In 2019, for example, the credit "outlook" for the energy firm Duke Energy was revised from A- and "stable" to A- and "negative" because of the financial risks associated with the potential environmental and health outcomes of managing coal ash waste from energy generation (S&P Global 2019).

Other agencies, such as MSCI (2024), have used and continue to use similar ranking systems, which grade companies from "industry leaders" (AAA, AA) to industry "laggards" (B, CCC) according to their reported "exposure to ESG risks." For many interlocutors, the rapid move of ESG from the margin to the mainstream and its integration with mainstay economic forecasts and financial analyses were causes for anxiety. Framed in terms of risk to future value creation, as measured by the metrics explored in chapter 3, these measures of future-facing risk suggested that ESG factors *could* influence firms' capacity to meet their financial commitments and marked the first time that climate change concerns had seriously entered the world of financial calculus, even if in contested ways (S&P Global 2019, 2020, 2021).

The New Tobacco

By the autumn of 2019, the acronym "ESG" featured in nearly every firm presentation I attended, and it was a topic of conversation among industry participants. At the monthly breakfast meeting of the Houston Oil Finance Association that I attended in October 2019, for example, the CFO of an exploration and production company declared to the audience that "ESG" and "energy transition" is "very real." Suit-clad and staring confidently into the crowd against a backdrop of polished, prepared corporate slides, he suggested that ESG was no longer hypothetical or a potential threat of unknown quantities lurking on the horizon with an uncertain time of arrival. It had arrived. His investors were asking about it, and investors at other firms were asking about it too. With this declaration, there were a few muted gasps from the crowd and a moment of nervous whispering.

Preempting the speaker that same morning, as association members gathered to drink coffee and swap stories, Charlie asked me what I had been hearing about ESG from my interlocutors. Questions were swirling within the association, and indeed the industry, about what ESG meant and what implications it would have. Anxiety about the uncertainties of ESG had been punctuated a week earlier by a high-profile speaker at a closed-door Independent Petroleum Association of America (IPAA) meeting, who asserted that the oil and gas industry was now "more hated than tobacco." Experiencing a mixture of shock and exasperation at this assertion, Julia,[4] a respected corporate industry veteran, told me that the declaration that oil was the new tobacco had prompted her and others in the industry to experience a collective "heart attack."

Confirming these sentiments, a well-known financier whose advice many interlocutors follow, Alvin, explained to me that ESG and associated anti-oil arguments had to be understood within a long history of "social movements" that have swept through the financial sector. "The ESG argument and the tobacco arguments are similar," he explained. Mainstream "moral" finance started with the "anti-apartheid" divestment movement, he said, and then there was the "anti-tobacco investment strategy." Now, he said, socially motivated investors had come for the hydrocarbon industry. After a moment of pause as we talked, he said, "In fact, my next phone call is with our general counsel to talk about what we're going to say about ESG in our upcoming financial report." "I'm not denigrating anything about ESG," he explained, but he understood it within a traditional financial framework of risks, fiduciary responsibilities, and returns. Comparing antihydrocarbon ESG arguments to the antitobacco divestment movement, he explained,

> CalPERS, the California pension fund, had a consultant do an assessment of their antitobacco investment strategy in the past and they lost a huge amount of potential returns, which in effect penalizes their pensioners. I think that's something that's nagging in the back of their minds as they look at the new social issue of ESG. . . . I'm just saying you need to be careful. . . . Yes, if you want to be socially oriented and motivated and you want to invest on this basis, recognize you're going to have an inferior performance. Have you reconciled that against your fiduciary responsibility?

What is significant about Alvin's account is how he directly contests arguments that ESG should be associated with higher financial returns. He also invokes the notion of responsibility, suggesting that a conflict of interest associated with fiduciary duty arises when ESG does not lead to higher investor returns, echoing Milton Friedman's (1970) doctrine of doing good by making profit. This argument that exclusionary investment policies hurt investors' financial returns is a claim I heard reiterated by others. By late 2019, this was not a concern for investors considering excluding hydrocarbon investments from their portfolios, however, because relatively low oil and gas prices had rendered many of these investments as underperforming, so there was nothing to be lost from divesting from fossil fuels.

Shane echoed Alvin's observations. Shane is a founding partner at a successful boutique investment bank. I agreed to meet him at his office, located downtown, where many of my interlocutors' offices were located. As I rode the elevator up to the twenty-eighth floor, a screen inside the elevator flashed current news briefs, including a story about how climate protests were shutting down city streets around the world. I stepped out of the elevator into the largely nondescript hallway with grey carpets and white walls. There were only two firms with large offices located on this floor. Looking through the glass door of the office, I could see that there was no receptionist at the front desk of the brightly lit, modern-looking office with a white, grey, and black décor. As I was about to reach for the door handle, a man who appeared to be in his forties, wearing a white shirt, tie, and slacks, had come from down the corridor and tried to pull the door open. It was locked. He was slightly surprised and sheepishly turned to me and said he had forgotten his security card and that the receptionist was not in that day. He introduced himself, we shook hands, and he knocked on the glass door until a man appeared from somewhere inside the office to let us in, whereupon I waited in the reception area.

While I waited for Shane, I could hear the voices of men joking and teasing each other around the curved corridor. There was a geode on the coffee table alongside a stack of oil and gas industry magazines. On the adjacent wall there were several glass shelves lined with what appeared to be nearly identical glass trophies celebrating transactions and deals that the firm had been involved in—inscribed with the transaction and the amount: $82,000,000; $25,000,000; and $18,800,000 for example.

A few minutes later, Shane came to meet me and walked me back to a small conference room with a white marble table and four seats behind a frosted-glass partition wall. Wearing a beige suit and striped shirt, he seemed at ease and casually described the situation that oil and gas finance was facing as "serious." "One element," he explained, is that the "institutional [investment] world" is "really fed up with inadequate returns." The "other one that is just as powerful, and may end up being more powerful, is green-thinking, ESG, whatever you want to call it." He continued, "Apparently oil and gas is now the number one most banned industry among financial investors. . . . Number two is alcohol." The implication, he explained, was that ESG had helped usher in a "boycott of fossil fuels. . . . Pensions and others have taken the stance that they will divest and not own any investments in fossil fuels." Expanding on these implications, he said, "Limited partner investors in private equity firms, who are also the same people who drive the stock market, namely, pension funds primarily and endowments, foundations, whatever. . . . Their investment committees and boards of directors are taking that kind of stance."

Other interlocutors echoed these sentiments. Citing his anxiety about ESG, one private equity interlocutor explained, "I'm just worried with the ESG and let's call it a tidal wave. I just really worry about it on that front because clearly we, as an industry, have had a red problem in terms of losing money and the like, but we have a real green problem and it's not just, 'Oh, ESG, roll your eyes at it.' There are institutions today that are fundamentally saying we will not invest in hydrocarbons anymore and it just feels realer than it ever has." The industry was used to, even if it was made uneasy by, capital ebbing and flowing into the industry with booms and busts, he suggested. The withdrawal of investor capital based on ESG and "green" commitments signaled, however, something new and unforeseen. It was not as though climate change and environmental concerns were novel; these concerns had existed for decades. The cause for anxiety was that this time period marked the first notable instance when investors were withdrawing capital on this basis, marking a shift on climate change concerns from the general social zeitgeist into the professional worlds of financiers. In this vein, another person similarly explained to me, "There is some pressure on investors, especially large institutional investors, that they don't want to be associated with what they consider dirty assets or dirty fuel. Another thing I found interesting is . . . that there's a push from banks, especially large national and international banks . . . because they don't want to be associated with the money."

By 2019, oil and gas firms and their financiers were finding it more difficult to access capital and the basic financial services needed to manage that capital. For hydrocarbon financiers and industry experts, the implication that they were "dirty" constituted a moral judgment about the ethics of their practice—not because they were poor stewards of capital per se, nor because they lacked technical sophistication; many hydrocarbon private equity financiers had successfully combined the allure of high finance with the "cowboy" sensibilities associated with oilmen to forge a revered financial niche. Instead, this judgment had to do with the object of their trade—oil and gas—and investors' ethical appraisal of it. The private equity firm he used to work for, he said, raised what was likely to be its last oil and gas fund. "On their last fundraiser they did, they were able to meet their fundraising goal, but they have a feeling that will be the last one they're able to meet, just because there is so much pressure from student groups, faculty, all that, especially on the endowment side, then pension funds from education, that kind of stuff from the states, there's pressure on them to not do that."

An analyst at a large European bank, meanwhile, explained to me that his firm was getting pressure not from institutional investors but from wealthy individuals. Chatting with me in late 2019, he said that this pressure had begun a "few years ago" when he started at the bank. "A lot of ABS clients are high net worth individuals. If you look at their core clientele, their accounts are $25 million and up. They are demanding more bespoke investments and really want to know where their money is going. Especially when the younger generations are taking over. . . . They really have this interest in seeing that it's going to be put to good use." The challenge with these clients demanding that money be invested in ESG funds, he said, is that "no one really knows what it means because there are no criteria for everybody to follow." For example, he said, there are "a lot of ESG funds still investing in oil and gas . . . because they score well on governance issues," the G in ESG. There is a "disconnect," he said, between the way ESG is branded and what it "actually means." He was concerned, as an analyst, about the genuineness of ESG investment options and whether they were really meeting the expectations of the bank's wealthy clients. He was uncertain about how to interpret ESG data, how it was being communicated to investors, and whether the way investors understood it aligned with representations and claims made using the underlying data. For many, ESG had instigated anxiety and introspection not only because the negative implications were uncertain but also because it had dragged conversations about climate change, formerly confined to living rooms and bedrooms among those in hydrocarbon finance, into the public arena, giving cause for people in the industry to engage with climate change in public-facing ways that they had not before. If the time came to show that ESG compliance did equate to relatively higher shareholder returns, especially in regard to climate change concerns, moreover, what would it mean for the US hydrocarbon industry and allegories about shareholder value creation and material provisioning? Many seemed to wonder.

For institutional investors, ESG manifests both as an internal moral pressure and as a set of investment risks to be managed, as Mike explained. I took two elevators to get to Mike's office on the sixty-eighth floor. When I arrived at the suite, I pushed the doorbell button to the left of the locked glass door. A moment later, a man who appeared to be in his late thirties emerged from the office corridor to let me in and showed me into the large boardroom to wait for Mike. High above the streets, the boardroom windows looked northwest over the humid, sun-washed city. There was a large, flat screen on the wall at one end of the room and a glass wall separating the boardroom from the corridor. Eight black leather rolling chairs surrounded the long wooden board table, a picture of a frack operation leaned against the wall under the flat screen, and a book on Texas oil sat on the ledge near the window. Mike's firm, which he had cofounded a few years earlier with another veteran of hydrocarbon finance, operates in the niche alternative banking part of the sector. He raises funds from institutional investors and uses this capital to loan money to upstream and midstream companies, as well as provide hydrocarbon firms with "blended" mezzanine financial solutions. Mike arrived a few minutes later, and we sat down at the table, as we had the time before, and chatted. When I asked him about what impact ESG was having on the sector he explained, "We've been out raising money for the last two years. We've talked to a couple of big state pension plans, and yes, [ESG]'s high on their list. These were a couple of West Coast pension plans and they want to know about ESG. . . . One of them was saying, 'We got a question from one of our board members saying, when fossil fuels are phased out, what are we going to do next?'" He continued, "We have a big investor, who's looking at investing in us, and who's on the other side of the world. They asked a similar question: 'What happens if Elizabeth Warren is elected, and she kills the fossil fuel industry?'. . . . There's a lot of those questions being asked, no question about it." By the end of 2019, nearly every firm included ESG in its investor presentations. ESG was a way of addressing—or at least appearing to address—the financial risks posed by climate change and the regulations aimed at curbing hydrocarbons. While questions about ESG were met with skepticism in early 2019, by September skepticism had turned to anxiety, and by December anxiety had been palliated by adoption. What it meant to adopt a public-facing ESG strategy remained unclear. Did firms have to perform equally well on the E, the S, and the G? How was ESG being negotiated within institutional investors between boards of directors and investment committees? Was this another box-checking exercise or a genuine tidal change in investor preferences? The answers to these questions remained, at that time, uncertain.

ESG and the "Argument for Oil"

Since ESG became mainstream, the way it is integrated into investment practices has shifted and become more nuanced. If it began for some, as SRI did, in the spirit of avoiding "sin" investments, it has since evolved to include, as well as exclude, particular companies and sectors. Indeed, in the last couple of years large, influential firms such as Carlyle—a multinational private equity and asset management firm that invests in oil and gas—has shifted its approach from ESG exclusion to ESG inclusion (see table 5.3). In a 2022 report, for example, Carlyle (2022: 3) argued that "for too long, climate impact strategies have focused primarily on divestment." Drawing on "prior experiences with tobacco stocks," Carlyle shows that divestment strategies have aimed to curtail the growth of the hydrocarbon industries around the world by increasing energy companies' cost of capital by restricting "their access to equity and credit

TABLE 5.3: ESG Typology.

ESG Type	Description
ESG Inclusion	Integrating ESG criteria into financial evaluations of companies and sectors.
ESG Exclusion	Excluding companies and sectors that do not meet ESG criteria.
ESG Performance	Seeking companies and sectors ranked highly according to ESG criteria.
ESG Impact	Investing in highly rated ESG companies that also have measurable positive social and environment impact.

Sources: Goldman Sachs 2024; NTI 2024; OECD 2020; Vanguard 2021.

markets," forcing firms to resort to more expensive sources of money (Carlyle 2022: 3). This strategy, however, has "failed" to curb oil and gas production and hydrocarbon demand overall (Carlyle 2022: 7). Thus, Carlyle's analysis suggests that "energy transition may come to depend on investors' willingness to engage with those businesses likely to score worst on many ESG scorecards" by investing in and lending to these firms and changing them from the inside (Carlyle 2022: 10). Appealing to "traditional" investors and analysts, Carlyle argues that working internally to bring companies into ESG compliance can yield not only environmental benefits for the planet but also financial benefits for investors because "companies that disclose progress towards meeting clearly-defined GHG reduction goals are valued at twice the level of those of companies that make no such disclosures" (Carlyle 2022: 9).

This shift in approach to ESG has coincided with several high-profile dissenting voices from within the financial sector, particularly in the United States. The departure and confessional exposé of BlackRock's chief investment officer for sustainable investing, Tariq Fancy, is one such example. Charged with integrating ESG criteria into BlackRock's massive investment portfolio between 2018 and 2019,[5] Fancy argued after his departure that "my work at BlackRock only made matters worse by leading the world into a dangerous mirage" that ESG was exacting systemic changes across companies and sectors when it was not (Fancy 2021; also see, for example, Richie 2022). These critiques have dovetailed with other critiques from within the industry that the climate risks to firms' financial performance have been exaggerated (Kirk 2022). They have also coincided with evidence that the firms most highly rated by ESG indices tend to be service and financial firms with few material outputs, and evidence that financial firms can artificially boost their ESG ratings by excluding the emissions of their hydrocarbon investments (Davey 2022; Sustainalytics 2024d). The implication is that the way ESG is understood and utilized has quickly shifted since becoming "mainstream" in 2019. Not only has ESG's currency as a new standard for moral corporate behavior been eroded by critiques from within the global financial sector, but the way it is measured and by whom have increasingly been met with skepticism (Masters and Temple-West 2023). Yet, it remains an important generally accepted measure of corporate accountability and, more importantly, I suggest, a means by which firms can craft moral narratives about themselves and their investments.

An investment banker turned CFO of a major independent US oil and gas company explained that he was skeptical of new ESG standards because "if you don't like your score, you can pay [the rating agency] to tell you how to improve your score." He said he understood why firms like BlackRock and State Street care about ESG, however; it was a way to "differentiate themselves" in a crowded market where firms were competing to attract investors. Regardless of what he thought of ESG personally, he said, "I think it behooves the industry to get all over it, and to do the best we can." The industry long scored well on the S and was getting better at the G, he and others told me—hydrocarbon firms and hydrocarbon financiers had long sponsored local Little League teams and community initiatives, and they were working to diversify their corporate boards and workforces. The E was much harder for hydrocarbon firms and financiers to address because hydrocarbons are molecularly carbon dense—this density is what makes hydrocarbons such powerful fuels. For the CFO, ESG was an invitation to improve the industry by eliminating venting, flaring, and leaks. He explained, "We've got enough opposition as it is, why give them some real material to work with? . . . I think that we as an industry have to embrace it, because, at some point we're going to go away from hydrocarbons, it's going to happen, right? It will lengthen the runway for which hydrocarbons are relevant and economic, and that's a good thing in my mind, particularly natural gas." This account is suggestive of the CFO himself grappling with climate change demands. He was not convinced that ESG would generate financial value, reduce financial risk, or make most oil and gas companies more responsible than they already were, according to him. It was a means by which to confront the industry's critics while speaking directly to investors and, in doing so, achieving sustained hydrocarbon production, the longevity of hydrocarbon firms, and the profits they produce.

For Arthur, ESG manifested differently. As we talked, Arthur consumed the chicken satay that he ordered for lunch. We were sitting at a booth table in a British-style pub just west of Houston's downtown core, not far from his office. It is one of his favorite places to meet, and we had met there for lunch before. It was chilly outside by Texas standards, even for mid-November, and Arthur was wearing a crisply ironed white-collared shirt, sleeves rolled, with a dark fleece vest embroidered with the name of one of his portfolio companies on the left breast. By this time in 2019, a groundswell of student-led climate-change and anti–fossil fuel activism in the United States and around the world, inspired by Greta Thunberg's "Fridays for Future" protests, was eroding interest in hydrocarbon investments. There had even been a student-led climate protest in Houston, which was rare in a city that had been built by oil (Field 2023). Considering the rapidly changing social and economic environment as he gazed at his skewer of satay in this cozy pub booth, Arthur reflected on the growing importance of ESG. He explained, "ESG is of growing importance especially over the last twelve months. In fact, at our annual meeting in May we had a couple of ESG slides and my advice to my internal managing partner of our firm was, I said, 'Hey, we should probably put those ESG slides at the front of the presentation to say this is a top priority.' We did, and we got specific positive feedback talking about ESG at the very beginning." He continued, "I think our investor base has a healthy realism there, but what they need is our help in defending their decision to invest with us as opposed to some other options that they may have, whether it's real estate or clean energy, a wind power investment fund or whatever. They need our help to defend their decision to invest."

Echoing the CFO, for Arthur ESG was the impetus to capture natural gas and to stop flaring because "it's good for the environment, makes good financial sense to capture, then sell it and earn additional revenue." He tells me that his firm's commitment to ESG is "not just lip service." Crucially, he needed to make sure his "investors are educated about it, so then they can go defend their decisions." He explained, "We have made an effort to assist them in the case for oil and gas, the argument for oil. That's how it's manifested itself for us, ESG." Speaking with me twenty-four months later, Arthur impressed upon me that ESG has not faded away but was a prerequisite for participating in oil and gas private equity.

> If you don't have a plan, a story, messaging, a path . . . to address your phase one and phase two . . . to be carbon neutral by a certain date, then you're potentially uninvestable. But, if you do, it opens you up to just a much broader set of public equity investors, the big institutional investors, and that improves your value. . . . It's on our minds in terms of

raising new funds from investors and being able to tell them, "Hey, we have a plan for that. Here's our plan for that, therefore, we're investable for you, Mr. Endowment Investment Officer."

I was struck by the way Arthur talked about ESG, moving from general description to delving into the specifics of "scopes" over this time period,[6] indicating that his firm's approach to ESG had become more focused, in lockstep with the more sophisticated ESG demands of investors. I was also struck by his suggestion that ESG had, over this time, become not just a requirement of investor presentations that his firm delivered but integral to *their story* and the stories of their portfolio companies. It was integral to their future-gazing allegories about value, risk, and responsibility. ESG increased the future financial value of their portfolio investments by reducing their financial exposure to regulatory and environmental risks and indicated his firm's commitment to addressing climate change. Arthur's personal views on climate change had not shifted, so far as I could tell. Indeed, his invocation of "realism" was a nod toward the material-provisioning and American-way-of-life arguments explored in chapter 4. Couched in the allegories about shareholder value, as indicated by references to "financial sense" and "revenue," these ESG measures enabled him to translate what concerns he had about climate change into familiar morally laden financial narratives.

At a monthly breakfast meeting of Houston oil financiers in early 2022, the CEO of a medium-sized oil company explained how and why his company was diversifying into carbon capture and storage (CCS), echoing Arthur's sentiments. He emphasized that his firm was still an oil company, but he explained that they had to "adapt to where money is flowing." He explained to the audience of fellow financiers and oilmen, "The transition is happening. There are going to be investments in low carbon–type businesses. Are they going to be wind or are they going to be solar? Is there going to be anything else that could be a low-carbon business technology? Could a company like ours participate in any of that?" He explained that "the journey on this started with ESG reporting." As a publicly traded company, his firm, he said, needed to be able to communicate to the public about their greenhouse gas emissions, about how they were addressing corporate responsibility, and about how they were involved in their communities. "We're always involved in our community," he explained, and his firm had robust governance structures. Communicating the E in ESG in ways that resonated with concerns about climate change was more challenging. Then, he explained, "We realized, no, we actually can play in some of this. We can play in carbon capture. If we can show ourselves as a participant in this low carbon business we can maintain investor interest while we grow the oil and gas side of the house and, ultimately, build a company that can play both in the traditional oil and gas space and in the transition space in a meaningful way. That's the evolution of what we're trying to do." Selling this business diversification to a somewhat skeptical audience of oil and gas financiers staring back at him, he argued that "the principles of what makes us good oil and gas operators shifts itself into CCS." Under the rubric of ESG, he explained, carbon capture and storage technology offered "a chance for us to reintroduce ourselves to investors." He continued, "It actually opens up some of the funds that are now willing to take the meeting that maybe they wouldn't take three years ago. We want not only to be in front of those funds, but we want to be in front of those funds with a story . . . which is an ESG topic. That's where CCS comes in."

As the ethnographic data provided above shows, ESG defines risk in ways that are congruent with mainstay future-gazing economic models and financial metrics in hydrocarbon finance. Framed in terms of risk to the future financial value of firms, I suggest, ESG reinforces the centrality of these mainstay metrics and places investors and creditors at the center of responsibility concerns. First ignored, then met with skepticism and anxiety, many hydrocarbon financiers and independent oil and gas firms were quick not only to adopt ESG but to integrate it into their forward-gazing narration of the future and their place in this future. Integrated with net-discounted cash flow projections, the value of hydrocarbon reserves, barrels of production per day, and EBITDA, ESG has become another means by which firms can measure their "goodness" and by which they can craft allegorical narratives about themselves for investors and creditors. ESG performance has become "an expectation" that complements but does not supplement "operational performance and strong financials" (Haynes Boone & Enercom, 2021: 11). As such, ESG has forced hydrocarbon financiers to address issues of climate change in their professional lives in ways they did not have to previously, but it has not ushered in the moral-financial reckoning some have claimed. In many ways, ESG has come to allow hydrocarbon firms and financiers to counter their environmental critics in ways that CSR allowed corporations to become purveyors of corporate best practice in response to criticisms by NGOs and local activists. It has, in this vein, given them a new tool with which to build allegories about the industry, the firms in their portfolio companies, and themselves that do not just rely on material-provisioning arguments. My interpretation is that, couched in the language of risk to "value creation," ESG and allegories constructed with it have allowed financiers to "derisk" their firms by presenting to prospective investors and lenders climate change risk to capital as knowable, evaluated, and addressed. It remains, however, a point of internal contention and skepticism within industry circles.

"Bullshit"

Julia invited me over for afternoon coffee. It was autumn 2023. I parked on the street of the quaint neighborhood, walked up the private driveway, and rang the doorbell of the unassuming brick house in the cozy but upscale suburban enclave. Opening the door just a moment later, Julia warmly greeted me and invited me in. Smartly dressed in a power suit, as always, she led me through her lavishly decorated home of worldly-looking artifacts into the kitchen, where she offered me an americano and where we sat at the steel-topped island to chat. We talked about her recent trip to Europe and her love of travel before our conversation turned to the industry and what she was observing at its highest echelons. I asked her about ESG. Reflecting on what she had observed within the industry's innermost circles over the previous few years, she said that "nutty behavior . . . is happening in boardrooms all over." People at the highest echelons of the industry are "trying to say the right thing" and "do the right thing," but she lamented that the US hydrocarbon industry as a whole is "pissing away billions of dollars on bullshit that is going to accomplish nothing." Exasperated, she was disgruntled with "the hoops we jump through, the bullshit we write, and the people we employ to put together these glossy things that are useless," by which she was referring to public-facing ESG and sustainability reports meant to woo both shareholders and publics. There were, she admitted, some good examples of "new initiatives being started by clever people," but a lot of public-facing ESG activity was "superficial." It was not, according to her, ushering in the systemic global changes she thought were needed, and it was costing firms consultancy fees paid to ratings agencies for advice on how they could improve their ESG score. Her critique was a mixture of shareholder-oriented market fundamentalism infused with her own libertarian political leanings, and a geopolitical critique that the money being spent on ESG in the US hydrocarbon industry would be more impactful for people and would reduce the world's "carbon footprint" if it was spent on "leveling up" the world's poorest. "People are doing stupid things behind closed doors" in the name of ESG, she said, noting the disjunction between public-facing performances of "doing good" and, according to her, actually "doing good."

Speaking with me a few weeks later, a managing partner at an oil and gas private equity firm, Kyle (whom I introduced in chapter 2), told me that investors' ESG demands were "still there" but had "died down." By contrast with just a few years earlier, instead of having to address ESG within the "first two slides in a presentation," now ESG "has to be a slide somewhere in your presentation," he said, suggesting that it had become less important. ESG entered investors' "criteria in 2019–2020 and it's not something that's going to go away," but his firm just needed to have a plan to address it, especially the E. He explained, "It's like okay, yes, check the box. Okay, here's what we're doing." His contention was that his investors were less concerned with the S and the G than the E.

What these and the other ethnographic data show is how perceptions and responses to ESG have changed over the span of a few years. For publicly traded companies described by Julia and the oil CEO, public-facing ESG performances take a different form than the ESG performances presented by private equity financiers behind the closed doors of investor meetings. Out of the public eye, private equity firms can address ESG concerns, and indeed negotiate, directly with their limited partners. In public companies, ESG negotiations happen behind the closed doors of boards of directors' meetings but are performed publicly to the scrutiny of shareholders and publics alike. Moreover, these data reveal a division along the axes of regions and company size. Large integrated and independent oil and gas companies, whose shares are traded on stock exchanges, have led the adoption of ESG. European supermajors such as BP, Shell, and Total were among the first to announce ESG policies and a commitment to reaching net zero emissions by midcentury in a public acknowledgment of the contribution of hydrocarbons to anthropogenic climate change (BP 2019; Butler 2020). Occidental Petroleum was the first major US hydrocarbon company to set a net zero target by 2040, in November 2020. Other US hydrocarbon companies subsequently announced "green" and environmental sustainability plans (WBD 2021). Many small independent companies, by contrast, are unable to afford the expensive, public-facing ESG campaigns or afford the programs and technologies to support them, my interlocutors told me. Divisions along these axes give pause to consider whether futures that integrate ESG necessarily favor big oil companies over small ones, and what these futures will mean for anthropogenic climate change if European oil majors adopt ESG but other and state-run oil companies are slow to adopt ESG or do not adopt it at all.

Beyond these considerations, debates on the efficacy of ESG and how hydrocarbon firms and financiers should address it are by no means settled. For traditional financial analysts and investors examining return on investment (ROI), there is some evidence that ESG portfolios underperform by contrast with non-ESG portfolios (Hodgson 2021; Sargis and Wang 2024). There is also a temporal friction at the intersection of immediate-term energy needs, short-term shareholder demands, and medium- to long-term concerns about curbing climate change. Higher oil and gas prices sparked by the post-COVID recovery and Russia's invasion of Ukraine highlighted this friction, for example, by precipitating the first major energy crisis across Europe in nearly half a century and by giving investors around the world cause to reconsider whether they should invest in oil and gas as commodity prices rise and as hydrocarbon firms posted record profits (Flood 2022). Indeed, despite receiving negative ESG scores from firms such as Sustainalytics—ExxonMobil received a "Severe Risk" (41.6) ESG score, for example—nearly all have reported record quarterly profits in recent years, driven by higher commodity prices (Crace 2023; ExxonMobil 2023; Sustainalytics 2024a, 2024b, 2024c).

The Financializatsion of the Corporate Gift?

How might the rapid adoption and subsequent desedimentation of ESG discourses within the industry be understood? What might they tell us about the dynamics of this time period, the industry, and the constitution of corporate ethical performances? The collective anxiety that ESG initially prompted is, in part, an example of Knightian uncertainty turned to risk, when ESG went from being relatively unknown to a clear and present threat to hydrocarbon private equity financiers and their hydrocarbon firms accessing sources of capital. Once ESG became an investment criterion for institutional investors, it was quickly integrated into the allegorical narratives woven by private equity financiers and exploration and production companies alike. In the process, ESG became a means by which financiers could communicate how they were considering broader threats to shareholder value and future profit generation, as well as gesture toward climate-change considerations and responsibility for consequences that extended beyond the temporal limits of investing and lending. The subsequent authoritative erosion of ESG in these narratives may, on the one hand, be attributed to ESG moving from niche to mainstream practice, where it is just one more means by which investors assess "long-term value" (Edmans 2022: 5). On the other, this erosion may be attributed to mixed evidence that taking ESG seriously is correlated with shareholder value gains and profits (Chen et al. 2023; Liu et al. 2022; Rao et al. 2023). While narratives of "good" financial performance may be woven seamlessly with narratives of "good" ESG performance in allegories about investment portfolios or firms, seamlessly weaving the measures that underpin them remains elusive. This elusiveness stems, in part, from the empirical difficulty of testing the conceptual link supporting the positive coincidence of ESG and profit. This link assumes that embracing ESG will lead to some combination of lower regulatory and legal costs; lower the cost of capital by attracting ethically minded investors and lenders; and increase revenues by attracting ESG-minded buyers. While there is burgeoning literature on this link, it remains difficult to empirically measure because of the relative lack of time by which to have observed this coincidence to date and because it requires robust consumer and firm data across companies and sectors (see for example Lee and Koh 2024). The authoritative erosion of ESG also raises questions about the integration of ESG and financial metrics. Attention to environmental, social, and governance issues can, ESG has shown, be framed in terms of financial values and risk to future shareholder value and profit. Even if this framing is reductive and inaccurate, to *whom* this value should accrue is where, I suggest, ESG and financial metrics remain incommensurable. The metrics and models of the industry place investors and lenders at the center of their financial calculus. ESG narratives, by contrast, espouse that firms can generate forms of value for a wide range of cobeneficiaries that extend beyond investors and creditors, overlapping with material-provisioning arguments. My observation is that ESG very narrowly and incompletely enters the monetary accounting of the mainstay metrics of the industry—as costs and revenues—thereby privileging the interests of investors and creditors to the exclusion of a wider group of cobeneficiaries.[7]

The rise and decline of ESG as a new corporate moral code, however, is suggestive of a yearning to reconcile financial *value* and a broader set of *social values* within the prevailing political economy of the United States, within which this ethnographic data is situated. It should be understood as indicative of a period in time when the world of corporate finance began to grapple with considerations of climate change, and when climate change concerns began to be seriously considered, rather than ignored, by financial expert practitioners. It should be understood as moving conversations about anthropogenic climate change and who is responsible for it out of the living rooms and into the boardrooms of interlocutors working in hydrocarbon finance. It did not herald a moral reckoning in the US hydrocarbon sector, however, because it has not, as of yet, fundamentally caused an upheaval in prevailing notions of financial value or how these values are measured. One interpretation that can be gleaned from this time period is that prevailing shareholder value–centric ideologies and the moral underpinnings of these ideologies are resilient in the face of broader societal pressures to extend notions of value to include cobeneficiaries who are not financial stakeholders. Another interpretation is that ESG constitutes the financialization of the "corporate gift," creating knowledges and circuits of reciprocity that primarily serve financial stakeholders—not under the guise of community projects, as in the case of CSR, but by taking financial stakeholders as the forward-facing subject of primary concern (Cross 2011, 2014). The knowledges it creates regarding climate change are framed in the language of risk to capital and shareholder value. The target audience of ESG knowledge is financial stakeholders, and the objective of this knowledge for many, as demonstrated in this chapter, is to advance prevailing modes of financial capitalism in the US hydrocarbon sector and beyond. Thus, ESG can be interpreted as integrating traditional shareholder value–centric evaluations of value with broader concerns about social values, but not in the way some might have thought. ESG has, I suggest, been used to frame what might be termed broader social values—or ethics, especially in regard to climate change—in terms of financial values, rather than reckoning these financial valuations within the rubrics of broader social value concerns.

As a corporate moral code, it is yet another register by which my interlocutors must orient their ethical sensibilities alongside historical imaginaries, Christian capitalist cosmologies, future-gazing financial metrics, and feelings of fiduciary and material responsibility. Not all moral registers intervene equally in my interlocutors' ethical sensibilities; indeed, I have suggested that this milieu of registers and the influence these registers have are idiosyncratic. Some tend to have greater moral weight, while other registers tend to be met with skepticism and reluctance. For Arthur, for example, the emergence of ESG left his cosmological and material-provisioning moral commitments relatively unaltered because ESG's articulation and his private equity firm's adoption of it, I observe, have not challenged these commitments as of yet. ESG has, however, prompted him to ethically negotiate with climate change and how he should respond to it in ways that extend beyond his close kinship and social circles and into his professional world, through his relationships with pension funds and endowments. These institutional investors are the limited partners in his firm's "funds," and Arthur is responsible for managing their investment capital in oil and gas. In his professional world, he must now negotiate with climate change in ways that engage with mainstay industry measures of financial value, consider financial and ESG risks, conciliate financial and ESG time horizons, and reconcile his fiduciary, personal, and cosmological feelings of responsibility.

In the energetic era, time, and place in which this ethnography is situated, my argument throughout this book is that this array of moral registers matters to the ethical sensibilities of people working at the intersection of the finance and hydrocarbon industries who make decisions that affect people around the planet. With the ethnographic data in this chapter in mind, ESG should be understood as the subject of corporate moral performance but also as an ethical register that is negotiated by those within the expert hierarchies of hydrocarbon finance and the broader financial sector. To understand our present energetic era, scholars must pay analytical attention to these registers and how they are negotiated if they wish to understand what the next energetic era might hold, what a post-ESG planet might look like, and whether new moral industry standards should be cast in the mold of CSR, SRI, and ESG.

Conclusion

Boom, Bust, . . . Echo?

I left Houston in late January 2020 after what felt like a whirlwind fourteen months of multisited ethnographic fieldwork. Before I left, I had an opportunity to present at the monthly Oil Finance breakfast meeting, which many of my interlocutors attend and through which I had come to know many within the industry. Charlie had asked me months earlier to present at January's meeting, to which I had agreed. I was terrified. What could I possibly tell the audience that they did not already know? My ethnographic research centered on them; plus, I had been so busy collecting observational data and meeting people for interviews that I had not had any time to analyze the hundreds of pages of notes, documents, and interview transcripts I had collected. I could, I thought, present an economics-oriented analysis, but they had likely heard much of this before and, according to Charlie, people wanted to hear what I had been observing. Moreover, this was not going to be like a university lecture because members of the audience were experts in the subject matter. After weeks of contemplating what I would present, punctuated by a few moments of panic, I titled my presentation "Pride and Precipice," reflecting two of my overarching observations at the time. Most, if not all, were proud of their work at the intersection of the finance and hydrocarbon industries, and the hydrocarbon sector, as a whole, seemed to be at a point of inflection, if not a cliff edge. There was a growing consensus that the shale revolution had entered into a new phase as investor enthusiasm for hydrocarbons waned and a major contraction in private equity–funded independent firms seemed imminent. There also was anxiety about what ESG would mean for the industry as student-led climate protests reached record levels around the world and addressing climate change concerns became a key demand of institutional investors. There was, moreover, the looming 2020 presidential election that many feared would usher in new climate change and environmental regulations that would curtail the US oil and gas industry's ambitions for future growth. Some took solace in their faith, and some were reassured that Texas's oil and gas industry had survived "bust" cycles before. Most assured me that the world would depend on hydrocarbons for years to come and the Texas oil and gas industry would have a place in this future. In January 2020, however, most admittedly worried about the months ahead. No one knew, at that time, that the precipice would be much more profound than anyone had expected.

The unprecedented fall in oil prices in April 2020, prompted by a global economic slowdown due to the COVID-19 pandemic, caused oil and gas producers to curtail production and expedited a consolidation in the US oil and gas industry. For the first time in history, a barrel of West Texas Intermediate (WTI) crude oil for delivery in May fell 306 percent from its Friday close of $18.27 to -$37.63 by the close of trading on the following Monday (High and Field 2020). In what is a textbook example of economic geography, the shale revolution had unlocked previously unthinkable quantities of oil and gas, challenging the United States' landlocked infrastructure of pipelines, storage tanks, and refineries to keep pace. When US refineries reduced production in response to falling demand for refined products, storage facilities quickly filled up, and then eventually there was nowhere for the oil to go. Some producers "shut in" oil wells, ceasing production altogether (Ferman 2020; Osborne 2020b; Sherman 2020). Some hailed the slowdown in fossil fuel production and refining during lockdowns as a "win" for the planet (Crace 2020; Le Quéré et al. 2020; UNEP 2020) and the beginning of a new era defined by renewable energy production. By January 2021, however, US crude oil prices had returned to pre-crash levels, and both US crude oil and natural gas prices began to rise, peaking in mid-2022 following Russia's invasion of Ukraine. While regions the world over were experiencing an energy price crisis as a consequence, some regions (including the UK and parts of Europe) were facing potential shortfalls of energy supplies. While 2020 revealed how quickly a sudden drop in energy demand could prompt a contraction in the hydrocarbon industry, 2022 revealed countries and regions to be stubbornly dependent on fossil fuels and the global hydrocarbon sector to meet their energy needs. It also revealed how places such as the United Kingdom had not facilitated the delivery of non–fossil fuel infrastructures despite repeated COP pledges and a governmental commitment to "build back greener."

During this time and in the many months that followed, I kept in touch with my interlocutors. With government-mandated lockdowns, much of the world working from home, and Zoom meetings becoming a new norm, it was actually easier to stay in touch and continue to participate in industry circles than I had anticipated. Some I lost touch with, however. Some email addresses started bouncing back because they no longer existed while others fell silent. I later reconnected with a couple of my interlocutors, discovering that they had changed firms or left the company they had been working for to start their own business. I had planned to reconnect with my interlocutors in person in 2021, and then in 2022, but travel restrictions made subsequent trips during this time period difficult.

When I returned to Houston in the autumn of 2023, the industry and the city had noticeably changed. One large, successful hydrocarbon private equity firm that I knew had laid off over one hundred staff after one of its funds suffered major losses. Another large oil and gas private equity firm, EnCap, had moved its office out of the downtown, and smaller private equity firms had followed suit. Tony told me that with everyone working from home, a lot of firms judged that it no longer made sense to pay high office rents. It made sense, he and others told me, to have offices located downtown when the shale revolution was in full swing because that is where people would bump into one another and informally share information on emergent "deals" and prospects. With the US hydrocarbon industry entering a new phase following a feverish two decades of growth and far fewer "deals" to be had, it also no longer made sense to be downtown.

My observations paid credence to these claims. Whereas in 2019 the streets and tunnels that connected the large office towers were bustling at the noon hour and late afternoon, in the autumn of 2023 the streets and the tunnels were mostly vacant. There were still a few hip coffee shops where office workers congregated, but the city seemed to be a shadow of its bustling self. This was also true of the monthly Oil Finance breakfast meeting. Excited to attend the meeting in person and to connect with many people I knew, I was surprised to find that many of the people I used to see there were not in attendance. The gathering was noticeably smaller, and there were several new faces. Association memberships expectedly change and meeting attendance fluctuates with the seasons, but where were many of the regular pillars of the association that I had come to know? I wondered. Moreover, some of the new attendees seemed strangely out of step with the crowd. For example, while suits and ties were standard attire in 2019, ties had gone out of fashion for all but a few senior members of this community. The closed-door industry gathering was considerably more casual, and the rectangular engraved name tags for seasoned members of the association, which I had pridefully received by late 2019, had been replaced with printed sticker name tags. In this more casual context one of the new attendees who was rapidly "working" the room, whom I had also seen at the Houston Petroleum Club the day before, was sporting a vintage tuxedo that appeared to be from the 1980s. Another new member, meanwhile, was wearing a bright purple suit and was adorned with large gold jewelry. In the context of the association's relatively conservative crowd mostly wearing muted-blue and grey suits, these professional performances and embodied representations were unusual. Who were these people?

When I asked Julia about the association over afternoon coffee in her kitchen, she agreed that it had changed. "They don't get such good speakers anymore," she said, and the CEOs and CFOs rarely attend now, which means the bankers and lawyers do not attend either. She said that the association is now largely composed of "old men who like to drink coffee and have drifted down the food chain" and a "lot of hangers on," a catchment term she used to describe these newer, out-of-step members who were eager to be a part of the hydrocarbon finance industry but had seemingly little to offer it at a time of contraction. Her reflections suggested that the association's status and influence, which coincided with the changing demographic and the empowerment of its participating members, had eroded. It was not clear whether this erosion was temporary, but changes in the association's membership seemed emblematic of trends in the expert hierarchies of hydrocarbon finance. Capital was no longer flowing through the US hydrocarbon finance sector as it once had, there were fewer private equity firms funding independent exploration and production companies, and the excitement that had enchanted nearly two decades of growth had dissipated.

I had met with Jacob for breakfast the day before at a popular Texan-style diner northwest of the downtown. The first time I met up with Jacob was in the private members dining room of the Houston Petroleum Club, where he was a member. Sitting at a table in the luxurious dining room beside the floor-to-ceiling windows overlooking the city, he had been sharply dressed in a tailored blue suit. This time, he was casually dressed in running shoes, sporting vest, and collared shirt, and he had grown a beard since we had last met in late 2019. Jacob is a managing director of oil and gas lending for a large multinational firm that works with PE firms, but he told me that he did not know what the future held for him. Despite having built a successful oil and gas lending portfolio in 2021, he said that questions started to be asked at the firm's European head office about his "portfolio . . . and all-around carbon accounting." With long pauses in his explanation of what had transpired over the last few years while he seemingly searched for the right words, he said that the hydrocarbon-focused unit he had built at the firm's Houston office had suffered a "death by a thousand cuts." At first, the size of his oil and gas lending portfolio was capped, meaning he could not grow the number of oil and gas loans he was making. In response, his unit diversified into energy transition, but the problem was that there were "very few opportunities" in the renewable energy sector that fit the risk-and-return profile of his firm. His unit did pursue a few energy transition opportunities that involved decommissioning oil wells and carbon capture and storage, but his head office said that his unit was no longer allowed to enter into new contracts with hydrocarbon firms. It has been "super frustrating" he said, looking somewhat downtrodden, and his unit was in the final stages of shutting down. My 2023 visit provided ethnographic evidence that a systemic shift had, indeed, taken place in Houston's hydrocarbon finance sector since I had left.

One interpretation of this shift is that the present phase of the US shale revolution requires fewer exploration and production firms and, thus, fewer financiers than it did a decade ago, characterizing a contractive cycle in the century-old industry. Another, related interpretation is that the heyday of private equity hydrocarbon finance that spurred a flurry of exploration and production activity has now passed and sectors of the US oil industry are consolidating back to a pre–unconventional extraction configuration of firms and financiers. Yet another interpretation is that the US oil industry and its hydrocarbon finance sector are the bellwether for changes in the global hydrocarbon economy and that what we are witnessing is the precipice of a global energy transition that has yet to unfold on the heels of the last US oil boom. While time will reveal what elements of these interpretations are correct, history has demonstrated that the US oil industry and the financial subsector that has capitalized it are more resilient than sometimes thought. One financier recalled to me, for example, that when he decided to specialize in reservoir engineering in college in the late 1970s, his aunt told him that he should pick another specialization because the oil industry was going to be extinct in a decade when global oil reserves ran out. Forty years later, through boom and bust, the US and global hydrocarbon industries are producing more oil and gas than ever before, expanding with new technological innovations and responding to new social demands for ethical corporate behavior (Enerdata 2023; Statista 2024; USEIA 2021c). While the shale revolution will yield material gains and ecological consequences for decades to come in ways that have yet to be seen, history suggests that it will also have social-cultural reverberations that echo on for generations to come in the form of petrocultural norms, new historical imaginaries, and stratifications carved along the cleavages of social and regional axes. These echoes, in turn, will shape future energy extraction practices, the way these practices are perceived, and allegories about these practices by those inside and outside the energy industries.

Carbon Capital

The overarching argument I have made in this book is that by understanding how energy financiers ethically and financially value energy—oil and gas in particular—we can understand how experts shape flows of capital, and how capital, in turn, shapes the worlds we find ourselves in. Hydrocarbon finance is vitally important to understand because the US oil and gas industry fundamentally turns on capital. To understand hydrocarbon finance, you have to understand the people who perform this work, and profit seeking alone does not explain the motivations, ambitions, decisions, and moral conclusions of the industry insiders whom I have described. Offering a window into the lives of people who work at the intersection of the US hydrocarbon and finance industries, I have suggested that there is something else that draws them to oil and gas finance and keeps them there.

I began by exploring how historical representations and romantic historical imaginaries of Texas's settler-colonial past and twentieth-century oilmen come to bear on my interlocutors' perceptions of risk, value, and responsibility. I showed that my interlocutors draw on the past and representations thereof to orient themselves in the present and their visions of the future. From historical imaginaries of the cowboy arising from settler-colonial narratives of the frontier to iconic twentieth-century oilmen such as Roy Cullen, these temporal moral registers, I argued, continue to be drawn on by my interlocutors today and are a formative part of what might be described as the culture of US hydrocarbon finance in Houston, Texas.

Then, I turned attention to how a combination of technology and finance at a particular junction in time led to the revitalization and revaluation of previously inaccessible or exhausted conventional hydrocarbon reserves, and why hydrocarbon private equity firms were vital to this process. Without private equity financiers, the US shale revolution could not have unfolded as it did because they provided the vital capital that small to medium-sized exploration and production companies needed, funding a twenty-first-century US oil boom that transformed the energy landscape of the United States and the world. Many of these financiers had investment and commercial banking experience. Engaging with the concepts of value, risk, time, and responsibility in their professional practice, they came to define a subsector of private equity akin to venture capital and distinct from the generalist US private equity sector. I also expounded the mainstay metrics and models interlocutors use in practices of hydrocarbon finance and how these practices evolved during the twentieth century to gaze into the future and define value in new ways. Through this expounding, I explored how the notions of value, time, and risk entered into the calculative tools of US hydrocarbon finance. I argued that these tools make moral prescriptions about how value, time, and risk should be defined and that these prescriptive norms have far-reaching implications for evaluating the worldly importance of hydrocarbon forms of energy.

I then explored how my interlocutors' perceptions of time, risk, responsibility, and value came to be entangled with their understandings of climate change, and how they drew on cosmology to extend their temporal gaze to uncertain futures. Present-leaning implicit social discount rates adopted by my interlocutors parallel the presentist time horizons of contemporary oil and gas finance. These presentist leanings were exemplified by material-provisioning arguments. Beyond these relatively short time horizons, my interlocutors tended to invoke the limits of their own agency and placed faith in their Christian cosmology to guide them through uncertain futures.

Finally, I examined the emergence of ESG as a new moral framework for corporate ethical behavior that emphasized attention to climate change and how it was widely adopted within the industry. I argued that the "mainstreaming" of ESG marked the first time that climate change had been taken seriously by the US financial industry, including its hydrocarbon finance sector. It may be understood as the financialization of the corporate gift, but also as the catalyst for forcing conversations about climate change among my interlocutors and their families out of their homes and into the corporate and public domains. It has not, however, fundamentally intervened in the ethical frameworks of my interlocutors.

In making my arguments, I have suggested throughout that it is worth paying attention to the allegories that people in the industry craft for themselves and others, as well as the components of these narratives, because they can tell us something about my interlocutors' ethical registers and how they are dealing with new registers coming to bear on them. In doing all of this, I have shown that energy financiers are moral agents who apply ethical frameworks to evaluate energy and what worldly futures should be imagined and materialized.

To facilitate my analytical investigation, I have adopted an "ordinary" ethics approach to energy, by taking seriously my interlocutors' own ethical persuasions, motivations, and yearnings, without endorsing their moral views. Taking this approach gives one license to explore a diversity of ethical worlds, *analytically* evaluating them without *morally* evaluating them. Some might consider this as indulging in a kind of moral relativism. I have made the case, however, that drawing themes, commonalities, and distinctions among these worlds and viewpoints and the contradictions therein guards against such relativisms, especially when these comparisons reveal insights into the workings of a community or network of people. This approach could be a productive basis for new understandings of the notion of culture—not as an emic concept, such as the "cowboy culture" referred to by my interlocutors but as an analytical concept that describes shared ethical sensibilities informed by knowledges, modes of expertise, and tools that draw people together and connect personal and professional practices. Indeed, by contrast with reinforcing colonial power dynamics, generalizing communities of people, and ignoring diversities, it could be used to describe complex intersections of shared understandings, practices, and ethical orientations. In this analytical vein, social anthropologists are well positioned to do this work by paying attention to the way people themselves understand their worlds, by unsettling taken-for-granted emic concepts, and by making the familiar unfamiliar (Tett 2022).

Focusing on a specific group of hydrocarbon finance experts during a unique period in time, I have illustrated what might be described as a distinct cultural moment whereby an array of time- and place-specific ethical registers came to bear on evaluations of energy in profound ways. While this group is by no means homogeneous, many shared a set of evaluative tools, historical imaginaries, experiences, and cosmologies that oriented them toward similar moral conclusions about energy, the climate, society, and the political economy of the United States. I have explored these intersections using the concepts of value, time, risk, and responsibility because these concepts can tell us something about what people think is important, to whom they feel obligated, where they understand their agency to begin and end, and how the past, present, and future figure into their evaluations. The insights revealed in the preceding chapters not only contribute to scholarly explorations of these concepts and social-science inquiries into the practice of finance but also emphasize how ethnographic attention to people and communities can yield vital insights into the making of our shared worlds.

While all times are arguably transitional, my sense is that the United States is indeed on the precipice of a social, political, and technological energy transition, but it is not clear what it is transitioning toward. A new hydrocarbon era? A renewable energy era? Or something in between? And, what will the political economy of what comes next look like? Transitional times can be exciting as well as anxiety provoking. This book has developed against the backdrop of a fundamental change in the way the United States produces energy and documents the financial modalities and people who have facilitated that change. Contributing to studies at the intersections of finance, energy, and expertise, it contributes novel empirical and conceptual insights into the professional performances and lives of people who are empowered to make evaluations about energy that, collectively, have far-reaching implications. Whatever energy future awaits the United States and the world at large, it will not be set by governmental agendas and pledges alone. It will be shaped by flows of capital into high and low sources of carbonous energy, where carbon is an indicative measure of anthropogenic emissions. It will be shaped by carbon capital and the people who direct this capital.

ACKNOWLEDGMENTS

Many thanks are due to a huge number of people, without whom this book would not have happened. First, I wish to thank my family, who have endured me through researching and writing this book, which has entailed many months of travel, adventure, living in separate countries, late nights, missed birthdays, missed funerals, and numerous deadlines that have collided with planned family holidays. Special thanks are due to Meagan Crane, who has read, considered, and commented on nearly every word of this book manuscript and draft versions of the chapters. Special thanks are also due to Megan Field.

I owe my deepest thanks to Mette High for her thoughtful encouragement, kind support, and mentorship since this book project's conception in early 2018. This research would have never started without her support and the support of the European Research Council (ERC) Horizon 2020–funded Energy Ethics project (grant agreement no. 715146) led by her. She has profoundly shaped the analytical lens that I apply in this book.

I am very grateful to Jennifer Hammer, senior editor at New York University Press, for supporting this book project, for her guidance, and for her patience with me throughout the writing process. Thanks are also due to the two anonymous reviewers for their very thoughtful comments and suggestions, which made the book manuscript much better. Further thanks are due to editorial assistant Brianna Jean, senior production editor Alexia Traganas, and copyeditor Emily Wright for help and assistance in seeing this manuscript through the copyediting process.

Thanks are due to friends and interlocutors in Houston, Texas, for sharing their work and their lives with me. I am not permitted to thank them by name for research-ethics reasons, but without them this book would not exist in its present form, if at all. I owe many thanks to Bernard (Buddy) Clark for sharing with me his archive of documents on oil and gas finance, for sharing his book *Oil Capital* with me, and for his encouragement and advice throughout the research process. He significantly contributed to my understanding of hydrocarbon finance and fundamentally shaped this book.

Finally, through the process of drafting, revising, and presenting chapters of this book and the ideas therein, a great number of colleagues have provided feedback, advice, guidance, support, and encouragement, including Ainur (Aina) Begim, Aneil Tripathy, Anna Seager, Anna-Sophie Hobi, Bridget Bradley, Caitlin Zaloom, Caura Wood, Chelsie Yount-Andre, Cymene Howe, Daniel Knight, Daniel Souleles, Dominic Boyer, Doug Holmes, Doug Rogers, Ewan Gibbs, Gavin Bridge, Hirokazu Miyazaki, Lorenzo Sapochetti, Mark Brightman, Mark Harris, Matthew Archer, Patrick O'Hare, Pauline Destree, Richard Irvine, Sarah O'Brien, Sayde Randle, Simon Abram, and Stefan Liens.

NOTES

INTRODUCTION

1. The word "our" can be ambiguous or tend to generalize whole groups of people in unreflexive and unwanted ways. Where I use "our" in this book, I intend to speak directly to readers and the human conditions we share in common rather than assume homogeneity or consensus.
2. I had contemplated titling the book "Oil Capital" as well, but this is the title Bernard Clark's (2016) book that I draw on throughout this book.
3. Within the philosophy of ethics, scholars have been known to study meta-ethics, which deals with questions related to the nature and the origin of ethics. They have also been known to study normative ethics, which deals with the judgment of right and wrong, and applied ethics, which examines particular topics. These fields can be further subdivided. For example, within the field of normative ethics, scholars have examined virtue ethics, which emphasizes the expression of moral character; deontology, which emphasizes duties and rules; and consequentialism, which emphasizes the consequences of actions.
4. The United States has been the largest producer of oil and gas in the world since 2012 (UAEIA 2018, 2021c).
5. Karl Marx (1990 [1867]), too, wrote about the role of hydrocarbons in the making of lives and the shaping of industry, although focused on the dismal and dangerous conditions faced by coal miners and the abhorrent use of child labor, pining for transition away from the labor practices on which industry was founded.
6. See Rosa et al. (1988) for a sociological review of some other early scholars who reflected on energy.
7. White's universalist thinking about energy, his desire to closely tie thermodynamics to culture, and his evolutionist theory did not resonate within anthropological circles in the mid-twentieth century. He, however, provides an inspiring bridge between the early and contemporary anthropological scholarship on energy, in particular the continuity between energy harnessed from humans and hydrocarbons, as explored by David Hughes (2017) and Miles Lennon (2017).
8. I invoke the term "empowerment" to refer to "power" in the sociocultural sense, that is, the ability to control and influence the conduct of others with or without their consent within the shifting hierarchical social structures, institutions, and norms of the United States.

9   Building on Boyer's (2005, 2008) work on experts and expertise, Mason (2019) shows how financial expertise involves combining ways of "knowing"—signaled by the deployment of economic theory, financial modeling, and industry "know-how"—with embodied performances that define what it means to be an expert, as well as the quality of expertise on offer.
10 Wood (2019) also provides brilliant insights into the financial moralities of "orphaned oil wells" and the financial maneuvering used to move these assets-turned-liabilities on and off firms' balance sheets.
11 Risieri Frondizi (1971) argues that both Thomas Hobbes's and David Hume's philosophical contributions on the subjects of ethics and virtue were a precursor to Smith's articulations on what would be called "value."
12 Anthropologist Clyde Kluckhohn (1951: 395) also famously took up the question of value, defining it as a "conception, explicit or implicit, distinctive of an individual or characteristic of a group, of the desirable which influences the selection from available modes, means and ends of action." Anthropological inquiries into value and values have been since taken up by Louis Dumont (1980, 2013 [1980]), and later by Nancy Munn (1986) and Terence Turner (2003, 2008).
13 Social theorists of various stripes have been interested in risk in the context of social change and stability. See, for example, Ulrich Beck (1992), Anthony Giddens (1999), Francis Fukuyama (1995), and Elinor Ostrom (1990).
14 Risk is more closely associated with the cognate disciplines of psychology and sociology.
15 I explore some aspects of these performances in Field (2021b).

CHAPTER 1. THE LONE STAR STATE

1   This is where famed frontiersman Davy Crockett was reportedly killed.
2   Production was interrupted by the US Civil War, 1861–1865, and by pests such as the boll weevil, which began devastating crops in the late 1800s. After the Civil War, cotton farming largely took the form of a crop-lien system whereby tenant farmers paid landowners for inputs plus a portion of their harvest. This left many nonwhite (as well as white) farmers impoverished and reproduced the racial and class hierarchies that existed before the Civil War (Britton et al. 1976). Tomlinson (2014) notes that increasing cotton production in India and Egypt put pressure on US producers.
3   Moore (2012: 23) notes that not all African Americans were slaves and that some were landowners. She explains that alongside Mexican landowners, many were forced off their land following Texas's independence: "Mexicans who owned land grants were intimidated into leaving or selling their land to the Anglo ranchers in the region after the Texas revolution. Others were forced out later when Anglo ranchers such as Richard King and Mifflin Kenedy fenced in their land and blocked access to water sources, some of which did not actually belong to them. On the Gulf Coast, intimidation also displaced a number of black landowners. Aaron Ashworth owned over 3,000 head of cattle in Jefferson County in 1850 but was driven off by envious Anglos."

4 The front page of this article depicts a picture of H. L. Hunt with the caption "Is this the richest man in the US?" The following page juxtaposes images of oil-carrying rail cars, cattle, and the mansion of Henry Russell in conjunction with the text "Oil + Cattle = Rolls-Royce." A digital copy of this issue and the associated article can be sourced through Google Books.

5 The connection among the Bush family, Texas cattle "culture," and the state's oil industry is well documented (Burrough 2009; Harvey 2003; Huber 2013). At an annual industry conference I attended a few weeks after meeting John, the luncheon keynote speaker was former president George W. Bush, whose appearance was received with much enthusiasm.

6 Notions of the cowboy were not homogenous across places and over time. As Moore (2012: 7, 14) notes, in some places cowboys were known for "drinking, fighting, and swearing" and in parts of the United States (such as Arizona) they were associated with "lawless" gangs that plagued the countryside.

7 The disappearance of the "frontier" was chronicled in the 1891 US Census Bulletin, which stated, "Up to and including 1880 the country had a frontier of settlement, but at present the unsettled area has been so broken into by isolated bodies of settlement that there can hardly be said to be a frontier line. In the discussion of its extent, its westward movement, etc., it cannot, therefore, any longer have a place in the census reports" (US Census 1891: 4).

8 In his 1920 volume, Turner powerfully draws on the 1895 Census report that declared the frontier to be lost and to no "longer have a place in the census reports" (Porter et al. 1895: xxxiv; also see Nash 1980).

9 In this vein, the president of Princeton College, John Witherspoon, argued in 1781, for example, that he preferred the term "frontier" to "back settlements" to describe inland American towns because "the settlements in America were begun to be made near the ocean, and were gradually advanced into the country" (Mood 1948: 79, citing Witherspoon).

10 Houston is located on the lands of the Sana, Atakapa-Ishak, Coahuiltecan, Karankawa, and Akokisa indigenous peoples (Denetclaw 2021; Harris County 2020).

11 Turner revised some of the text between the 1893 version and the 1920 version.

12 Historical-imaginary cowboys are often symbolic of rugged masculinity, possessing few "emasculated milk-and-water moralities" (quoting US president Theodore Roosevelt) and are "wise, not through formal education, but because he was close to nature" (Moore 2012: 13–14).

13 High (2022) discusses how these producers are commemorated at annual gala events across oil-producing states, where the industry bestows an annual wildcatter award to a successful independent producer in the industry. I did not attend one of these while on fieldwork, but my interlocutors also mentioned that Texas held a similar wildcatters ball once per year.

14 Schumpeter contrasted this with profits gleaned from monopoly or landlord powers that enabled the extraction of excess profits through higher prices.

Anthropologist Richard Pfeilstetter (2021: 4) shows, however, that the etymological root of the concept, the German term "*Unternehmer*," "literally means something similar to 'someone who is undertaking.'"

CHAPTER 2. FINANCING THE US SHALE REVOLUTION

1. As Karen Ho (2009: 85) explains, analysts' primary job is to "do the financials" for prospective financial transactions, and these calculations become part of "pitch books" that are presented to prospective clients. After two years, analysts typically leave investment banking to pursue an MBA and seek out other career opportunities. Some reenter investment banking after competing an MBA as an associate, while a few are promoted from analyst to associate directly.
2. Wells can also be "pumped" using a pumping jack, if pressure is low and oil will not migrate to the surface on its own.
3. Proppants are solid materials such as sand that are intended hold the cracked rock open so oil and gas can migrate (or "drain") from their trapped position to the horizontal well. Fracking fluids, meanwhile, can be water mixtures, gels, and foams.
4. "Major" and "super-major" oil companies are not only publicly traded, meaning their shares can be bought and sold on stock exchanges; they are also "integrated," meaning they have operations along the supply chain—from production to refining, distribution, and retail. Independents typically focus on one or two segments of the supply chain.
5. Loans given to E&P companies were typically for less than twelve months and based on the net worth of the borrower, including the value of oil in storage and in transit (Clark 2016).
6. They can also issue other forms of short- and longer-term debt, such as corporate credit cards, lines of credit, and term-based loans.
7. According to Clark (2016), a few generalist PE firms became involved in the US hydrocarbon sector in the mid-twentieth century, but it was not their sole focus.
8. This partnership is formalized in a legal document called Private Placement Memorandum (PPM) or Offering Memorandum.
9. My interlocutors confirmed these fee ranges, but none were willing to disclose the precise fee structure for any of their funds. One PE managing partner remarked that he worried that I might go tell his competitors if he told me the specifics of their fee structure.
10. A leverage buyout has been a tool used by venture capitalists since the 1950s, and refers to a large proportion of debt to equity used to purchase firms (Wilson 1985). In the 1980s, however, it was popularized by Wall Street private equity firms that used high-yield, otherwise known as "junk," bonds to raise capital to purchase companies. See Burrough and Helyar (2008 [1989]), Wilson (1985), Souleles (2019), and Ho (2009) for examples.
11. To sell the company as a whole, the firm could find a private buyer or take the firm "public" by selling shares on a stock market through an initial public offering (IPO).

12 Kohlberg, Kravis, and Roberts (KKR), which was founded in 1976, is perhaps the most well-known example of a private equity firm that utilized the leveraged buyout strategy in the 1980s (Burrough and Helyar 2008 [1989]; Ho 2009: 139; Souleles 2019: 64).
13 These regulations could influence the portfolio companies of private equity firms, however, if they planned to "go public" by selling shares to be traded on the stock market.
14 This includes the required financial soundness that firm managers need to maintain, the duration of the loan, collateral securing the loan, the capital structure of the firm, the repayment schedule, and recourses should these covenants be broken.
15 "Btu" is the abbreviation for "British thermal units." It is a standard unit of measurement for natural gas and is equivalent to the heat needed to raise the temperature of one pound of water by one degree Fahrenheit when that water temperature is about thirty-nine degrees. (USEIA 2022b).
16 The Nasdaq composite index that indexes stocks listed on the Nasdaq stock exchange peaked in March 2000.
17 Fifty-two of these ninety PE firms collectively fund-raised $68.7 billion dollars between 2003 and 2013 (Haines 2013a).
18 EnCap's first upstream fund raised $20 million in 1988.
19 This type of risk could be split into production risk, where the pipeline infrastructure does not exist to transport oil and gas from the place of production to buyers, and market structure risks associated with changes in the "food chain," as described above.

CHAPTER 3. ETHICAL CALCULATIONS

1 This is a pseudonym.
2 The Black-Scholes model was developed in 1973 and is used to estimate the value of options contracts (derivatives).
3 These historical documents were given to me by an interlocutor.
4 Alternately, the discount rate can be interpreted as the return from investing elsewhere (Chiapello 2015).
5 "Internal" refers to the omission of the cost of borrowing and inflation, "external" factors, from the IRR (Wright and Gallun 2008: 301).
6 NPV is expressed as a monetary value, IRR as a percentage.
7 ROI = [(Value of Investment − Cost of Investment)/(Initial Cost of Investment)].
8 ROR = [(Value of Investment − Initial Value of Investment)/(Initial Value of Investment)] x 100.
9 TEV = market capitalization + market value of debt + preferred stock − excess cash and equivalents.
10 PV10 disclosure requirements for public companies were formalized, effective, on December 15, 1982. Before then, some undiscounted disclosures of future net revenues were required but did not include PV10. Source: email exchange between author and associate chief accountant of the SEC, dated June 24, 2021.

11   Reserves are depleted and production declines over time as hydrocarbons are extracted.
12   These calculations are usually done by engineers from independent firms and cross-checked by "in-house" engineers in investment firms, banks, and E&P companies.
13   An interlocutor confirmed the accuracy of this representation and the correctness of these calculations. IRR was calculated in MS Excel using the "IR" function.
14   The banks surveyed in figure 3.1 each use a proprietary algorithm for forecasting prices (Haynes & Boone LLP 2019).
15   The indicator for time—"t"—often represents years but can also represent quarters, entering the equations as consecutive sequences of numbers (1, 2, 3, 4 . . .) giving time a linear characteristic.
16   Companies with little or no current profitability but a portfolio of hydrocarbon wells that are anticipated to produce profit in the future are likely to use NPVs with longer time horizons (e.g., five years).
17   "Fidelity" refers to Fidelity Investments Inc.
18   This is a pseudonym.

CHAPTER 4. NOT A DICHOTOMY

1   Through my interlocutors I understood that some firms had arranged private book signings with Epstein and that he had private speaking events in cities located in other US oil-producing regions, like Colorado.
2   Both images are purportedly sourced from the Center for the Study of Carbon Dioxide and Global Change.
3   Epstein points to computers, MRI machines, agricultural equipment, fertilizers, pharmaceuticals, and transportation technologies that would not be possible without fossil fuels.
4   Calls for limiting hydrocarbon exploration, production, and consumption, Epstein says, curb individuals' creative freedoms, makes people less safe, and endangers the world's poorest (Epstein 2012: 76). Accordingly, he labels "climate catastrophists" as "major sinners" and posits that "mankind's use of fossil fuels is supremely virtuous" (Epstein 2012: 136, 209). Roy Spencer makes many similar arguments in his bestselling *Climate Confusion* (2009), written from the perspective of an atmospheric scientist that was formally a senior scientist for climate studies with NASA. Spencer says that his research "has only strengthened my belief that mother Nature . . . is largely responsible for any climate change we happen to experience" (2009: x). The suggestion by "global warming alarmists" that climate change is a threat to humanity, he argues, "represents a leap of faith from what science tells us is theoretically possible, to a belief in worst case scenarios in which Mother Earth punishes us for our sins against her" (2009: xiii). Like Epstein, he claims his intervention is not just to shed light on how he interprets climate science but is a political and economic one. "Access to abundant, affordable energy is necessary for the world's poor to be lifted out of poverty," he says, and

regulations curbing fossil fuels and carbon dioxide emissions in response to the claims of climate alarmists are having "devastating effects" and "enabling the genocide of the world's poor" (Spencer 2009: x–xi). Many of the arguments made by Spencer are echoed by Epstein.

5 White (1967) was among the first to highlight this connection.
6 It had not worked correctly for some time, but it was not really a necessity until the heat of the Houston summer began to set in and it became difficult to drive very far without getting symptoms of heat stroke or sweating through my suit on the way to meet my interlocutors. For these initial couple of weeks of June, I drove to appointments wearing a T-shirt with ice-packs tied around me, and would then quickly put my shirt and tie on when I arrived.
7 Evidence indicates that Hurricane Harvey was made more severe by climate change (Nielsen-Gammon et al. 2021). Signs of Harvey were visible all over the city. Debris was still wedged in the bearings of bridges over the city's bayous, and a number of houses south of where we lived were either condemned or severely damaged due to flooding.
8 According to the president of Dallas Federal Reserve, "[Hurricane Harvey] disproportionately impacted low-income families by wiping out their savings, impacting their ability to safely domicile their families and increasing their need for health care and related services" (Kaplan 2019).
9 Relatedly, Houston is well known for its lack of zoning bylaws, which allows industrial and residential land uses to be colocated or located in close proximity. The impact has been that poor and racialized residents are more likely to be exposed to hazardous air pollutants (Hernandez et al. 2015).
10 At the time of writing.
11 The Memorial Day Flood in May 2015 (twelve inches of rain in ten hours), the Tax Day Flood in April 2016 (fourteen inches of rain in twelve hours), and Hurricane Harvey, August 2017 (fifty-one inches of rain over six days) (Boyer and Vardy 2022).
12 He too recommended that I read Epstein's book, although he conceded that his scholarly orientation left him wanting "more" out of it, by which he explained that he wished Epstein had engaged more deeply with the history of the US oil industry and the people who had shaped it.

CHAPTER 5. "WHAT THE HELL IS ESG?" AND THE MORAL CASE FOR OIL

1 This is a pseudonym for this organization. Martin is a managing partner of a well-known private equity firm that invests in a range of industries from oil and gas to real estate.
2 The combination of these two reports is reported to have led to the foundation of the UN-backed Principles for Responsible Investment organization, whose purpose is to advance ESG integration into financial practice (see www.unpri.org).
3 Interestingly, S&P Global (2021) also found that the physical effects of climate change, such as risks posed by floods and rising sea levels, posed a credit risk to

individual firms' infrastructures but, overall, the sector's credit risk in this category was "lower than the collective risk for all corporate entities."
4 Julia was one of a handful of women interlocutors.
5 At the time BlackRock was the world's largest asset manager.
6 "Scopes" refers to accounting for greenhouse gas emissions (see for example, "Zero in on . . . Scope 1, 2, and 3 Emissions," Deloitte UK, May 12, 2021 (www2.deloitte.com/uk).
7 Framed in terms of a misalignment of incentives, a similar observation has been made by Mark Kramer and Marc Pfitzer (2022), suggesting ESG and financial performance measures are often mismatched.

REFERENCES

Ahmed, Tarek, and D. Nathan Meehan. 2012 [2004]. *Advanced Reservoir Management and Engineering*. London: Elsevier.

Appadurai, Arjun. 2011. "The Ghost in the Financial Machine." *Public Culture* 23(3): 517–39.

———. 2016. *Banking on Words: The Failure of Language in the Age of Derivative Finance*. Chicago: University of Chicago Press.

Appel, Hannah. 2012a. "Offshore Work: Oil, Modularity, and the How of Capitalism in Equatorial Guinea." *American Ethnologist* 39(4): 692–709.

———. 2012b. "Walls and White Elephants: Oil Extraction, Responsibility, and Infrastructural Violence in Equatorial Guinea." *Ethnography* 13(4): 439–65.

———. 2019. *The Licit Life of Capitalism: US Oil in Equatorial Guinea*. Durham, NC: Duke University Press.

Appel, Hannah, Arthur Mason, and Michael Watts (eds.). 2015. *Subterranean Estates: Life Worlds of Oil and Gas*. New Haven, CT: Cornell University Press.

Archer, Matthew. 2022. "The Ethics of ESG: Sustainable Finance and the Emergence of the Market as an Ethical Subject." *Focaal* 93(1): 18–31.

Arrighi, Giovanni. 1994. *The Long Twentieth Century: Money, Power, and the Origins of Our Times*. London: Verso.

Bainbridge, John. 1961. *The Super-Americans: A Picture of Life in the United States, as Brought into Focus, Bigger Than Life, in the Land of the Millionaires—Texas*. Garden City, NY: Doubleday.

Baptist, Edward E. 2014. *The Half Has Never Been Told: Slavery and the Making of American Capitalism*. New York: Basic Books.

Barney, Darin. 2017. "Who We Are and What We Do: Canada as a Pipeline Nation." In: *Petrocultures: Oil, Politics, Culture*, S. Wilson, A. Carlson, and I. Szeman (eds.). London: McGill-Queen's University Press. 78–119.

BBC. 2014. "Oil Prices Plunge after OPEC Meeting." November 28. www.bbc.co.uk.

Bear, Laura. 2015. "Capitalist Divination: Popularist Speculators and Technologies of Imagination on the Hooghly River." *Comparative Studies of South Asia, Africa, and the Middle East* 35(3): 408–23.

———. 2020. "Speculation: A Political Economy of Technologies of Imagination." *Economy and Society* 49(1): 1–15.

Beck, Ulrich. 1992. *Risk Society: Towards a New Modernity*. London: Sage Publications.

Begim, Ainur. In-press. "From Words to Numbers and Back Again: ESG Data and Sustainable Investing in the Age of Sustainability." *Journal of Cultural Economy*.

Bhandari, Shyam B., and Mollie T. Adams. 2017. "On the Definition, Measurement, and Use of the Free Cash Flow Concept in Financial Reporting and Analysis: A Review and Recommendations." *Journal of Accounting and Finance* 17(1): 11–19.

Biondi, Yuri. 2006. "The Double Emergence of the Modified Internal Rate of Return: The Neglected Financial Work of Duvillard (1755–1832)." *European Journal of the History of Economic Thought* 13(3): 311–35.

Birch, Kean. 2017. "Rethinking Value in the Bio-economy: Finance, Assetization, and the Management of Value." *Science, Technology, & Human Values* 42(3): 460–90.

Blackburn, Jim, and Philip Bedient. 2018. "Houston a Year after Harvey: Where We Are and Where We Need to Be." Baker Institute for Public Policy and SSPEED Centre, August 10. www.bakerinstitute.org.

Blum, Jordan. 2016. "The March from Humble Oil to Exxon Dates Back More Than a Century: From the Spindletop Gusher of 1901 Sprang Exxon Mobil's Tale of Success." *Houston Chronicle*, March 25. www.chron.com.

Boone, Michael M. 1980. "Structuring and Documenting the Oil and Gas Loan." Paper presented at the Third Annual Banking Law Institute, Austin, TX, March.

Botson, Michael R. Jr. 2005. *Labour, Civil Rights, and the Hughes Tool Company*. College Station: Texas A&M University Press.

Boyer, Dominic. 2005. "The Corporeality of Expertise." *Ethnos* 70(2): 243–66.

———. 2008. "Thinking through the Anthropology of Experts." *Anthropology in Action* 15(2): 38–46.

———. 2014. "Energopower: An Introduction." *Anthropological Quarterly* 87(2): 309–33.

Boyer, Dominic, and Mark Vardy. 2022. "Flooded City: Affects of (Slow) Catastrophe in Post-Harvey Houston." *Current Anthropology* 63(6). https://doi.org/10.1086/722270.

BP. 2019. "Energy with Purpose". *BP Sustainability Report*. www.bp.com.

Brand, Donald D. 1961. "The Early History of the Range Cattle Industry in Northern Mexico." *Agricultural History* 35(3): 132–39.

Brands, Henry W. 2005. *Lone Star Nation: The Epic Story of the Battle for Texas Independence*. New York: Anchor Books.

Braudel, Fernand. 1992. *Civilization and Capitalism, 15th–18th Century: The Perspective of the World*. Translated by S. Reynolds. Berkeley: University of California Press.

Britton, Karen G., Fred C. Elliott, and E. A. Miller. 1976. "Cotton Culture." Paper delivered at Texas State Historical Association, October 7. www.tshaonline.org.

Broome, John. 1992. *Counting the Cost of Global Warming*. Isle of Harris, Scotland: White House Press.

———. 2008. "The Ethics of Climate Change." *Scientific American* 298(6): 96–100.

Bryant, Rebecca, and Daniel Knight. 2019. *The Anthropology of the Future*. Cambridge: Cambridge University Press.

Burrough, Brian. 2009. *The Big Rich: The Rise and Fall of the Greatest Texas Oil Fortunes*. London: Penguin.

Burrough, Brian, and John Helyar. 2008 [1989]. *Barbarians at the Gate: The Fall of RJR Nabisco*. London: Collins Business.

Burrough, Brian, Chris Tomlinson, and Jason Stanford. 2021. *Forget the Alamo: The Rise and Fall of an American Myth*. New York: Penguin Press.
Butler, Nick. 2020. "How Oil Majors Bought into Green Energy." *Financial Times*, July 15. www.ft.com.
Çalışkan, Koray, and Michel Callon. 2009. "Economization, Part 1: Shifting Attention from the Economy towards Processes of Economization." *Economy and Society* 38(3): 369–98.
Campbell, Randolph B. 1993. *Sam Houston and the American Southwest*. New York: Harper Collins.
Canavan, Gerry. 2014. "Retrofutures and Petrofutures: Oil, Scarcity, Limit." In: *Oil Culture*, R Barrett and D. Worden (eds.). Minneapolis: University of Minnesota Press. 331–49.
Capps, Kriston. 2018. "Why Are These Tiny Towns Getting So Much Hurricane Harvey Aid?" *Bloomberg*, October 3. www.bloomberg.com.
Carlyle. 2022. "Global Insights: The Inclusive Approach to Energy Transition," May 25. www.carlyle.com.
Carney, Mark. 2021. *Value(s): Climate, Credit, COVID, and How We Focus on What Matters*. London: William Collins.
CFA. 2024. "What Is ESG Investing and Analysis?" CFA Institute. www.cfainstitute.org.
Chen Simin, Yu Song, and Peng Gao. 2023. "Environmental, Social, and Governance (ESG) Performance and Financial Outcomes: Analyzing the Impact of ESG on Financial Performance." *Journal of Environmental Management* 345(1).
Chiapello, Eve. 2015. "Financialisation of Valuation." *Human Studies* 38(1): 13–35.
Chidester, David. 1996. *Savage Systems: Colonialism and Comparative Religion in Southern Africa*. Charlottesville: University Press of Virginia.
Clark, Bernard. 2016. *Oil Capital: The History of American Oil, Wildcatters, Independents, and Their Bankers*. San Francisco: IngramSpark.
CNNMoney. 2001. "Oil and Gold Prices Spike." *CNN*, September 11. https://money.cnn.com.
Crace, John. 2020. "On the Horizon: The End of Oil and the Beginnings of a Low-Carbon Planet." *The Guardian*, November 1. www.theguardian.com.
———. 2023. "Oil and Gas Giants ExxonMobil and Chevron Post Record First-Quarter Profits." *The Guardian*, April 28. https://www.theguardian.com.
Cross, Jamie. 2011. "Detachment as a Corporate Ethic: Materializing CSR in the Diamond Supply Chain." *Focaal* 60(2011): 34–46.
———. 2014. "The Coming of the Corporate Gift." *Theory, Culture & Society* 31(2–3): 121–45.
———. 2020. "Capturing Crisis: Solar Power and Humanitarian Energy Markets in Africa." *Cambridge Journal of Anthropology* 38(2): 105–24.
Cullen Foundation. 2023. "The Founders." www.cullenfdn.org.
Davey, Edward. 2022. "Emissions Declarations by Equity Firm Carlyle under Question." *Associated Press*, September 26. https://apnews.com.
Denetclaw, Pauly. 2021. "Mapping Indigenous Communities of Texas: Atakapa Ishak." *Texas Observer*, September 3. www.texasobserver.org.

Dobroski, Sonja. 2022. "'This Stuff Speaks to Me': Settler Materiality, Identity, and Nationalism among Collectors of Native American Material Culture." *History and Anthropology* 35(2): 271–91. https://doi.org/10.1080/02757206.2022.2037583.

Drakeman, Donald, and Nektarios Oraiopoulos. 2020. "The Risk of De-Risking Innovation: Optimal R&D Strategies in Ambiguous Environments." *California Management Review* 62(3): 42–63.

Duff & Phelps. 2017. "Oil and Gas Intelligence Report: Price Forecasting Methodologies." www.duffandphelps.com.

Dumont, Louis. 1980. *Homo Hierarchicus: The Caste System and Its Implications*. Chicago: Chicago University Press.

———. 2013 [1980]. "On Value: The Radcliffe-Brown Lecture in Social Anthropology." *HAU: Journal of Ethnographic Theory* 3(1): 287–315.

Eccles, Robert G., Linda-Eling Lee, and Judith C. Stroehle. 2020. "The Social Origins of ESG: An Analysis of Innovest and KLD." *Organization and Environment* 33(4): 575–96.

Edmans, Alex. 2022. "The End of ESG." *Financial Management* 52(1): 3–17.

EnCap Investments LP. 2023. "History." www.encapinvestments.com.

Enerdata. 2023. "World Energy and Climate Statistics." https://yearbook.enerdata.net.

Epstein, Alex. 2012. *The Moral Case for Fossil Fuels*. New York: Penguin.

Ernst & Young. 2018. *Guide to Going Public: Strategic Considerations before, during, and post IPO*.

Everett, Bob, Godfrey Boyle, Stephen Peake, and Janet Ramage. 2012. *Energy Systems and Sustainability: Power for a Sustainable Future*. Oxford: Oxford University Press.

ExxonMobil. 2023. "ExxonMobil Announces Third-Quarter 2023 Results." https://corporate.exxonmobil.com.

Fancy, Tariq. 2021. "The Secret Diary of a 'Sustainable Investor'—Part 1." *Medium*, August 20. https://medium.com.

Ferman, Mitchell. 2020. "As Oil Price Crisis Grips the Globe, Small Texas Producers Feel the Ripple Effects." *Texas Tribune*, April 6. www.texastribune.org.

Field, Sean. 2021a. "Natural Gas in the UK, Part 1: Infrastructures and Geopolitics." *Energy Blog*, https://energyethics.st-andrews.ac.uk/blog.

———. 2021b. "Power and Precariousness in the Expert Hierarchies of the US Hydrocarbon Industry." *Critique of Anthropology* 41(3): 303–19.

———. 2022a. "Carbon Capital: The Financial Lexicon and Allegories of the US Oil and Gas Sector." *Economy and Society* 52(1): 235–58.

———. 2022b. "Risk and Responsibility: Private Equity Financiers and the US Shale Revolution." *Economic Anthropology* 9(1): 47–59.

———. 2023. "Value as Ethics: Climate Change, Crisis, and the Struggle for the Future." *Economic Anthropology* 10(2): 177–85.

———. 2024. "Carbonous Concealment: Governing 'Wild' Substances and Subterranean Storage in an Era of Climate Change." *Antipode*. (online first: https://doi.org/10.1111/anti.13026).

Fisher, Irving. 1930. *The Theory of Interest: As Determined by Impatience to Spend Income and Opportunity to Invest It*. New York: Macmillan.
Fiske, Amelia. 2017. "Bounded Impacts, Boundless Promise: Environment Impact Assessment of Oil Production in the Ecuadorian Amazon." In: *ExtrACTION: Impact, Engagements, and Alternative Future63s*, K. Jalbert, A. Willow, D. Casagrande, and S. Paladino (eds.). London: Routledge. 63–76.
Flood, Chris. 2022. "Energy Crisis Prompts ESG Rethink on Oil and Gas." *Financial Times*, July 17. www.ft.com.
Flowers, Simon. 2019. "Private Equity Assesses Its Options for Exiting Oil and Gas." *Forbes*, November 13. www.forbes.com.
Forbes. 2003. "The Ebitda Folly." *Forbes*, March 17. www.forbes.com.
Foucault, Michel. 1994. *Ethics: Subjectivity and Truth*, edited by P. Rainbow. New York: New Press.
Foxhall, Emily, and Rebecca A. Schuetz. 2022. "Years after Harvey, Houston-Area Homes Remain in Disrepair: Federal Watchdogs Want to Know Why." *Houston Chronicle*, January 10. www.houstonchronicle.com.
Friedman, Milton. 1970. "A Friedman Doctrine: The Social Responsibility of Business Is to Increase Its Profits." *New York Times*, September 13. www.nytimes.com.
Frigo, Giovanni. 2017. "Energy Ethics, Homogenization, and Hegemony: A Reflection on the Traditional Energy Paradigm." *Energy Research and Social Science* 30(1): 7–17.
Frondizi, Risieri. 1971. *What Is Value?* La Salle, IL: Open Court.
Fukuyama, Francis. 1995. *Trust: The Social Virtues and the Creation of Prosperity*. London: Hamish Hamilton.
Fulgate, Francis L. 1961. "Origins of the Range Cattle Era in South Texas." *Agricultural History* 35(3): 155–58.
Gardiner, Stephen M. 2004. "The Ethics of Global Climate Change." *Ethics* 114(3): 555–600.
———. 2011. *A Perfect Moral Storm: The Ethical Tragedy of Climate Change*. Oxford: Oxford University Press.
Gardner, Katy, Zahir Ahmed, Fatema Bashir, and Masud Rana. 2012. "Elusive Partnerships: Gas Extraction and CSR in Bangladesh." *Resources Policy* 37(1): 168–74.
Gibbs, Ewan. 2021. *Coal Country: The Meaning and Memory of Deindustrialization in Postwar Scotland*. London: University of London Press.
Giddens, Anthony. 1999. "Risk and Responsibility." *Modern Law Review* 62(1): 1–10.
Gluckman, Max (ed). 1972. The Allocation of Responsibility. Manchester: Manchester University Press.
Goldberg, Robert. 2008. "The Western Hero in Politics: Barry Goldwater, Ronald Reagan, and the Rise of the American Conservative Movement." In: *Political Culture of the New West*, J. Roche (ed.). Lawrence: University Press of Kansas. 13–50.
Goldman, Michael, and Rachel A. Schurman. 2000. "Closing the 'Great Divide': New Social Theory on Society and Nature." *Annual Review of Sociology* 26(1): 563–84.
Goldman Sachs. 2024. "ESG and Impact Investing."

Graczyk, Michael. 2013. "The Big Story: George P. Mitchell, Billionaire Texas Oilman, Developer, and Philanthropist, Dead at 94." *Associated Press*, July 26. https://apnews.com.

Graeber, David. 2001. *Toward an Anthropological Theory of Value: The False Coin of Our Dreams*. New York: Palgrave MacMillan.

———. 2012. *Debt: The First 5,000 Years*. London: Melville House Publishing.

———. 2013. "It Is Value That Brings Universes into Being." *HAU: Journal of Ethnographic Theory* 3(2): 219–43.

Greater Houston Partnership. 2020. "Energy." www.houston.org.

Gulf. 2022. "Our History." www.gulfoilltd.com.

Guyer, Jane I. 2007. "Prophecy and the Near Future: Thoughts on Macroeconomic, Evangelical, and Punctuated Time." *American Ethnologist* 34(3): 409–21.

Haines, Leslie. 2013a. "Gentlemen: Start Your Engines." In: *Oil and Gas Investor*, L. Haines (ed.). Houston, TX: Hart Energy. 6–11.

———. 2013b. "Superstars in Private Equity." In: *Oil and Gas Investor*, L. Haines (ed.). Houston, TX: Hart Energy. 4

Hämäläinen, Nora. 2016. *Descriptive Ethics: What Does Moral Philosophy Know about Morality?* New York: Palgrave Macmillan.

Hann, Chris, and Don Kalb. 2020. *Financialization: Relational Approaches*. Oxford: Berghahn.

Harris County. 2020. "Acknowledging Native Land." Robert W. Hainsworth Law Library. www.harriscountylawlibrary.org.

Hart, Keith. 2001. *Money in an Unequal World: Keith Hart and His Memory Bank*. New York: Texere.

Harvey, David. 2003. *The New Imperialism*. Oxford: Oxford University Press.

———. 2006 [1982]. *The Limits to Capital*. New York: Verso Books.

Hawley, Frederick B. 1893. "The Risk Theory of Profit." *Quarterly Journal of Economics* 7(4): 459–79.

Haynes & Boone LLP. 2019. "Energy Bank Price Deck Survey: Fall 2019," October 3. www.haynesboone.com.

Haynes Boone & Enercom. 2021. "Oil and Gas Tracker." Haynes & Boone LLP and EnerCom Inc., August.

Hayward, Tim. 2012. "Climate Change and Ethics." *Nature Climate Change* 2: 843–48.

Hernandez, Maricarmen, Timothy W. Collins, and Sara E. Grineski. 2015. "Immigration, Mobility, and Environmental Injustice: A Comparative Study of Hispanic People's Residential Decision-Making and Exposure to Hazardous Air Pollutants in Greater Houston, Texas." *Geoforum* 60(1): 83–94.

High, Mette M. 2019. "Projects of Devotion: Energy Exploration and Moral Ambition in the Cosmoeconomy of Oil and Gas in the Western United States." *Journal of the Royal Anthropological Institute* 25(1): 29–46.

———. 2022. "Utopias of Oil: Energy Finance and Entrepreneurial Ambition in the US Oil and Gas Industry." *Cultural Anthropology* 37(4): 738–63.

High, Mette M., and Sean Field. 2020. "Oil, Oil, Who Wants Some Oil? Part 2: Pipelines and Oil Prices." *Energy Blog*, July 21, 2020. https://energyethics.st-andrews.ac.uk/blog.

High, Mette M., and Jessica M. Smith. 2019. "Introduction: The Ethical Constitution of Energy Dilemmas." *Journal of the Royal Anthropological Institute* 25(1): 9–28.

Hitchens, Christopher. 2003. "'Cowboy': Bush Challenged by Bovines." *Slate*, January 27. https://slate.com.

Ho, Karen. 2009. *Liquidated: An Ethnography of Wall Street*. Durham, NC: Duke University Press.

Hodgson, Camilla. 2021. "BlackRock's Fink Says Climate Pressure on Public Companies Is 'Biggest Arbitrage in My Lifetime.'" *Financial Times*, November 3. www.ft.com.

Holmes, Doug. 2014. *Economy of Words: Communicative Imperatives in Central Banks*. London: University of Chicago Press.

Howe, Cymene. 2019. "Greater Goods: Ethics, Energy, and Other-Than-Human Speech." *Journal of the Royal Anthropological Institute* 25(2): 160–76.

Huber, Matthew T. 2013. *Lifeblood: Oil, Freedom, and the Forces of Capital*. London: University of Minnesota Press.

Hughes, David. 2017. *Energy without Conscience: Oil, Climate Change, and Complicity*. Durham, NC: Duke University Press.

Hulme, Mike. 2009. *Why We Disagree about Climate Change: Understanding Controversy, Inaction, and Opportunity*. Cambridge: Cambridge University Press.

Hunt Oil Company. 2022. "Eight Decades of Excellence." www.huntoil.co.uk.

IPCC. 2022. "Climate Change 2022: Mitigation of Climate Change." Intergovernmental Panel on Climate Change. www.ipcc.ch.

Irvine, Richard. 2019. *An Anthropology of Deep Time: Geological Temporality and Social Life*. Cambridge: Cambridge University Press.

Jalbert, Kirk, Anna Willow, David Casagrande, and Stephanie Paladino (eds). 2017. *Extraction: Impacts, Engagements, and Alternative Futures*. London: Routledge.

Jenkins, Kirsten, Darren McCauley, Raphael Heffron, Hannes Stephan, and Robert Rehner. 2016. "Energy Justice: A Conceptual Review." *Energy Research & Social Science* 11(1): 174–82.

Jenkins, Kirsten, Benjamin K. Sovacool, Niek Mouter, Nick Hacking, Mary-Kate Burns, and Darren McCauley. 2021. "The Methodologies, Geographies, and Technologies of Energy Justice: A Systematic and Comprehensive Review." *Environmental Research Letters* 16(4): 1–25.

Jensen, Michael C. 1986. "Agency Costs of Free Cash Flow, Corporate Finance, and Takeovers." *American Economic Review* 76(2): 323–29.

Johnson, Rebecca O. 2019. "A Lot like War: Petrocapitalism, 'Slow Violence,' and the Struggle for Environmental Justice." *Social Justice* 46(1): 105–18.

Jordan, Terry G. 1969. "The Origin of Anglo-American Cattle Ranching in Texas: A Documentation of Diffusion from the Lower South." *Economic Geography* 45(1): 63–87.

Kaplan, Robert S. 2019. "Economic Conditions and the Stance of Monetary Policy." Federal Reserve Bank of Dallas, June 24. www.dallasfed.org.

Kati, Efe. 2022. "What Are Private Equity General Partners?" Legal Vision. https://legalvision.co.uk.

Keane, Webb. 2015. *Ethical Life: Its Natural and Social Histories.* Princeton, NJ: Princeton University Press.

Kirk, Stuart. 2022. "Why Investors Need Not Worry about Climate Risk." Paper delivered at Moral Money Summit, London, May 19. www.youtube.com/watch?v=bfNamRmje-s.

Klamer, Arjo, and Donald McCloskey. 1992. "Accounting as the Master Metaphor of Economics." *European Accounting Review* 1(1): 145–60.

Kluckhohn, Clyde. 1951. "Values and Value-Orientations in the Theory of Action." In: *Towards a General Theory of Action*, T. Parsons and E. Shils (eds.). Cambridge, MA: Harvard University Press. 388–433.

Knight, Daniel. 2017. "Energy Talk, Temporality, and Belonging in Austerity Greece." *Anthropological Quarterly* 90(1): 167–92.

Knight, Daniel, and Charles Stewart. 2016. "Ethnographies of Austerity: Temporality, Crisis, and Affect in Southern Europe." *History and Anthropology* 27(1): 1–18.

Knight, Frank. 1964 [1921]. *Risk, Uncertainty, and Profit.* New York: A. M. Kelley.

Kottasova, Ivana. 2014. OPEC: "No Cut in Oil Production and Prices Keep Falling." *CNN Money*, https://money.cnn.com.

Kramer, Mark R., and Marc W. Pfitzer. 2022. "The Essential Link between ESG Targets and Financial Performance: It's Key to Building a Sustainable Business Model." *Harvard Business Review*, September–October. 128–37.

Kruse, Jack, Judith Kleinfeld, and Robert Travis. 1982. "Energy Development on Alaska's North Slope: Effects on the Inupiat Population." *Human Organization* 41(2): 95–106.

Kumar, Kanchan. 2015. "Growing Opportunities for Private Equity in Oil and Gas." Global Resources Partnership, April 1. www.globalresourcespartnership.com.

Labban, Mazen. 2008. *Space, Oil, and Capital.* Oxon: Routledge.

———. 2010. "Oil in Parallax: Scarcity, Markets, and the Financialization of Accumulation." *Geoforum* 41(4): 541–52.

———. 2014. "Against Shareholder Value: Accumulation in the Oil Industry and the Biopolitics of Labour under Finance." *Antipode* 46(2): 477–96.

Laidlaw, James. 2014. *The Subject of Virtue: An Anthropology of Ethics and Freedom.* Cambridge: Cambridge University Press.

Lambek, Michael. 2008. "Value and Virtue." *Anthropological Theory* 8(2): 133–57.

———. 2010. "Toward an Ethics of the Act." In: *Ordinary Ethics: Anthropology, Language, and Action*, M. Lambek (ed.). New York: Fordham University Press. 39–63.

Langley, Paul, Gavin Bridge, Harriet Bulkeley, and Bregje van Veelen. 2021. "Decarbonizing Capital: Investment, Divestment, and the Qualification of Carbon Assets." *Economy and Society* 50(3): 494–516.

Lee, Jooh, and Kyungyeon Koh. 2024. "ESG Performance and Firm Risk in the U.S. Financial Firms." *Review of Financial Economics* 42(3): 328–44, https://doi.org/10.1002/rfe.1208.

Leins, Stefan. 2018. *Stories of Capitalism: Inside the Role of Financial Analysts.* London: University of Chicago Press.

———. 2020. "'Responsible Investment': ESG and the Post-Crisis Ethical Order." *Economy and Society* 49(1): 71–91.
Leins, Stefan, and Cheslie Yount-André. In-press. "Economic Moralities: Value Claims on the Future." *Journal of Cultural Economy*.
Lennon, Myles. 2017. "Decolonizing Energy: Black Lives Matter and Technoscientific Expertise amid Solar Transitions." *Energy and Social Science Research* 30(1): 18–27.
Le Quéré, Corinne, Robert B. Jackson, Matthew W. Jones, Adam J. P. Smith, Sam Abernethy, Robbie M. Andrew, Anthony J. De-Gol, et al. 2020. "Temporary Reduction in Daily Global CO2 Emissions during the COVID-19 Forced Confinement." *Nature Climate Change* 10(1): 647–53.
Life. 1948. "Southwest Has a New Crop of Super Rich." *Life* 24(14): 23–27.
Lin, John. 2018. "Hurricane Harvey." *Voices in Bioethics* 4: n.p. https://doi.org/10.7916/vib.v4i.6019.
Liu, P., B. Zhu, M. Yang, and X. Chu. 2022. "ESG and Financial Performance: A Qualitative Comparative Analysis in China's New Energy Companies." *Journal of Cleaner Production* 379(1).
Lotze, Rudolph Hermann. 1841. *Metaphysik*. Leipzig: Weidmann.
Love, Clara M. 1916. "History of the Cattle Industry in the Southwest." *Southwestern Historical Quarterly* 19(4): 370–99.
MacKenzie, Donald. 2001. "Physics and Finance: S-Terms and Modern Finance as a Topic for Science Studies." *Science, Technology, & Human Values* 26(2): 115–44.
———. 2004. "The Big, Bad Wolf and the Rational Market: Portfolio Insurance, the 1987 Crash, and the Performativity of Economics." *Economy and Society* 33(3): 303–34.
Malinowski, Bronislaw. 2010 [1922]. *Argonauts of the Western Pacific*. Oxford: Benedicton Classics.
Marx, Karl. 1990 [1867]. *Capital*, vol. 1. London: Penguin.
Mason, Arthur. 2007. "The Rise of Consultant Forecasting in Liberalized Natural Gas Markets." *Public Culture* 19(2): 367–79.
———. 2012. "Corporeality of Consultant Expertise in Arctic Natural Gas Development." *Journal of Northern Studies* 6(2): 83–96.
———. 2019. "Consulting Virtue: From Judgement to Decision-Making in the Natural Gas Industry." *Journal of the Royal Anthropological Institute* 25(1): 124–39.
Mason, Arthur, and Maria Stoilkova. 2012. "Corporeality of Consultant Expertise in Arctic Natural Gas Development." *Journal of Northern Studies* 6(2): 83–96.
Massey, Sara R. (ed.). 2000. *Black Cowboys of Texas*. College Station: Texas A&M University Press.
Masters, Brooke, and Patrick Temple-West. 2023. "The Real Impact of the ESG Backlash." *Financial Times*, December 4, www.ft.com.
Maurer, Bill. 2002. "Repressed Futures: Financial Derivatives' Theological Unconscious." *Economy and Society* 31(2): 15–36.
———. 2010. "Debate: Religion and the 'Credit Crunch.'" *Religion and Society: Advances in Research* 1(1): 146–55.

McClimon, Timothy J. 2020. "The Impact of Environmental, Social, and Governance (ESG) Issues on Companies Today." *Forbes*, June 29. www.forbes.com.

McCloskey, Deirdre N. 1998. *The Rhetoric of Economics*. Madison: University of Wisconsin Press.

McCloskey, Donald N. 1995. "Metaphors Economists Live By." *Social Research* 62(2): 215–37.

McLean, Bethany. 2018. *Saudi America: The Truth about Fracking and How It's Changing the World*. New York: Columbia Global Reports.

McLean, Bethany, and Peter Elkind. 2004. *The Smartest Guys in the Room: The Amazing Rise and Scandalous Fall of Enron*. London: Penguin.

Merrill, Karen R. 2012. "Texas Metropole: Oil, the American West, and US Power in the Postwar Years." *Journal of American History* 99(1): 197–207.

Mitchell, Timothy. 2009. "Carbon Democracy." *Economy and Society* 38(3): 399–432.

———. 2011. *Carbon Democracy: Political Power in the Age of Oil*. London: Verso.

Miyazaki, Hirokazu. 2000. "Faith and Its Fulfillment: Agency, Exchange, and the Fijian Aesthetics of Completion." *American Ethnologist* 27(1): 31–51.

———. 2007. "Between Arbitrage and Speculation: An Economy of Belief and Doubt." *Economy and Society* 36(3): 396–415.

———. 2013. *Arbitraging Japan: Dreams at the End of Finance*. Berkeley: University of California Press.

Mood, Fulmer. 1945. "The Concept of the Frontier, 1871–1898: Comments on a Select List of Source Documents." *Agricultural History* 19(1): 24–30.

———. 1948. "Notes on the History of the Word 'Frontier.'" *Agricultural History* 22(2): 78–83.

Moore, Jacqueline M. 2012. *Cow Boys and Cattle Men: Class and Masculinities on the Texas Frontier, 1865–1900*. New York: NYU Press.

———. 2014. "'Them's Fighting Words: Violence, Masculinity, and the Texas Cowboy in the Late Nineteenth Century." *Journal of the Gilded Age and Progressive Era* 13(1): 28–55.

Morse, Edward L., and Amy M. Jaffe. 2001. "Strategic Energy Policy Update." Council on Foreign Relations. www.jstor.com/stable/resrep00276.

MSCI. 2024. "ESG Ratings: Measuring a Company's Resilience to Long-Term, Financially Relevant ESG Risks." MSCI. www.msci.com/.

Muniesa, Fabian. 2017. "On the Political Vernaculars of Value Creation." *Science as Culture* 26(4): 445–54.

Munn, Nancy D. 1986. *The Fame of Gawa: A Symbolic Study of Value Transformation in a Massim (Papua New Guinea) Society*. Durham, NC: Duke University Press.

Nader, Laura. 1964. "Perspectives Gained from Field Work." In: *Horizons of Anthropology*, S. Tax (ed.). Chicago: Aldine Press. 148–59.

———. 1972. "Up the Anthropologist: Perspectives Gained from Studying Up." In: *Reinventing Anthropology*, D. Hymes (ed.). New York: Pantheon Books. 284–311.

———. 1980. *Energy Choices in a Democratic Society: The Report of the Consumption, Location, and Occupational Patterns Resource Group, Synthesis Panel of the*

Committee on Nuclear and Alternative Energy Systems. National Research Council. Washington, DC: National Academies Press.

Nader, Laura, and Stephen Beckerman. 1978. "Energy as It Relates to the Quality and Style of Life." *Annual Review of Energy* 3(1): 1–28.

Nash, Gerald D. 1980. The Census of 1890 and the Closing of the Frontier. *The Pacific Northwest Quarterly* 71(3): 98-100.

NEPDG (National Energy Policy Development Group). 2001. *Reliable, Affordable, and Environmentally Sound Energy for America's Future: Report of the National Energy Policy Development Group.* www.nrc.gov.

Nielsen-Gammon, John, Sara Holman, Austin Buley, and Savannah Jorgensen. 2021. "Assessment of Historic and Future Trends of Extreme Weather in Texas, 1900–2036." Texas A&M University and Office of the Texas State Climatologist. https://climatexas.tamu.edu.

Nordhaus, William D. 2007. "A Review of the Stern Review on the Economics of Climate Change." *Journal of Economic Literature* 55(3): 686–702.

Nordstrom, Jean, James P. Boggs, N. J. Owens, and JoAnn Sootkis. 1977. *The Northern Cheyenne Tribe and Energy Developments in Southeastern Montana.* Vol. 1, *Social and Cultural Investigations.* Lame Deer, MT: Northern Cheyenne Research Project.

NTI. 2024. "ESG Integration and Exclusion Explained." The Northern Trust Institute. www.northerntrust.com.

O'Brien, Sarah G. P. 2023. "'Jobbos' and the 'Wageless Life': Exploring Work and Responsibility in the Anti-Fracking Movement in Lancashire, United Kingdom." *Economic Anthropology* 10(1): 55–64.

OECD. 2020. "OECD Business and Finance Outlook 2020: Sustainable and Resilient Finance," September 29. www.oecd-ilibrary.org.

Ortiz, Horacio. 2013. "Financial Value: Economic, Moral, Political, Global." *HAU: Journal of Ethnographic Theory* 3(1): 64–79.

———. 2014. "The Limits of Financial Imagination: Free Investors, Efficient Markets, and Crisis." *American Anthropologist* 116(1): 38–50.

———. 2021a. *The Everyday Practice of Valuation and Investment: Political Imaginaries of Shareholder Value.* New York: Columbia University Press.

———. 2021b. "A Political Anthropology of Finance: Studying the Distribution of Money in the Financial Industry as a Political Process." *Anthropological Theory* 21(1): 3–27.

Osborne, James. 2020a. "Can the Oil Sector Get Work?" *Houston Chronicle*, June 15. www.houstonchronicle.com.

———. 2020b. "The Great Texas Oil Shutdown Has Begun." *Houston Chronicle*, April 28. www.houstonchronicle.com.

Ostrom, Elinor. 1990. *Governing the Commons: The Evolution of Institutions for Collective Action.* Cambridge: Cambridge University Press.

Otto, Ton, and Rane Willerslev. 2013a. "Introduction: Value as Theory; Comparison, Cultural Critique, and Guerrilla Ethnographic Theory." *HAU: Journal of Ethnographic Theory* 3(1): 1–20.

———. 2013b. "Prologue: Value as Theory; Value, Action, and Critique." *HAU: Journal of Ethnographic Theory* 3(2): 1–10.
Ouma, Stefan. 2020. "This Can('t) Be an Asset Class: The World of Money Management, 'Society,' and the Contested Morality of Farmland Investments." *Environment and Planning A: Economy and Space* 52(1): 66–87.
Özden-Schilling, Canay. 2021. *The Current Economy: Electricity Markets and Techno-Economics*. Stanford, CA: Stanford University Press.
Parker, R. H. 1968. "Discounted Cash Flow in Historical Perspective." *Journal of Accounting Research* 6(1): 58–71.
Petacoff, Marc. 2016. "On EBITDA: Buffett versus Malone." *Seeking Alpha*, September 16. https://seekingalpha.com.
Pfeilstetter, Richard. 2021. *The Anthropology of Entrepreneurship: Cultural History, Global Ethnographies, Theorizing Agency*. London: Routledge.
Porter, Robert P., Henry Gannett, and William C. Hunt. *Progress of the Nation, 1790 to 1890, Part 1*. N.d. Last modified February 24, 2015. United States Census Bureau, https://www2.census.gov.
Powell, Dana. 2017. *Landscapes of Power: Politics of Energy in the Navajo Nation*. Durham, NC: Duke University Press.
PWC. 2024. "Environmental Social Governance." PWC. https://www.pwc.com.
Quinson, Tim. 2021. "The ESG Market Is Controlled by a Few Big Investors." *Bloomberg*, December 1. www.bloomberg.com.
Quintana Resources. 2023. "Our History." www.quintanaresources.com.
Raffoul, François. 2018. "The History of Responsibility." In: *Moral Engines: Exploring the Ethical Drives in Human Life*, C. Mattingly, R. Dyring, M. Louw, and T. S. Wentzer (eds.). Oxford: Berghahn Books. 271–92.
Rajak, Dinah. 2011. *In Good Company: An Anatomy of Corporate Social Responsibility*. Stanford, CA: Stanford University Press.
Rao, Amar, Vishal Dagar, Kazi Sohag, Leila Dagher, and Tauhidul I. Tanin. 2023. "Good for the Planet, Good for the Wallet: The ESG Impact on Financial Performance in India." *Finance Research Letters* 56(1).
Ricardo, David. 2004 [1817]. *The Principles of Political Economy and Taxation*. Mineola, NY: Dover Publications.
Richie, Greg. 2022. "Ex-Citi Banker Warns of Bond Vigilantes' Lopsided ESG Tactics." *Bloomberg*, August 9. www.bloomberg.com.
Robbins, Joel. 2015. "Ritual, Value, and Example: On the Perfection of Cultural Representations." *Journal of the Royal Anthropological Institute* 21(S1): 18–29.
Robbins, Lynn A. 1980. *The Socioeconomic Impacts of the Proposed Skagit Nuclear Power Plant on the Skagit System Cooperative Tribes*. Bellingham WA: Lord and Associates.
———. 1984. "Energy Developments and the Navajo Nation: An Update." In *Native Americans and Energy Development*. Cambridge MA: Anthropology Resource Centre. 35–48.

Rogers, Douglas. 2015a. *The Depths of Russia: Oil, Power, and Culture after Socialism.* Ithaca, NY: Cornell University Press.

———. 2015b. "Oil and Anthropology." *Annual Review of Anthropology* 44(1): 365–80.

Rosa, Eugene A., Gary E. Machlis, and Kenneth M. Keating. 1988. "Economy and Society." *Annual Review of Sociology* 14(1): 149–72.

S&P Global. 2019. "The Role of Environmental, Social, and Governance Credit Factors in Our Ratings Analysis." S&P Global Ratings. www.spglobal.com.

———. 2020. "ESG Industry Report Card: Oil and Gas." S&P Global Ratings. www.spglobal.com.

———. 2021. "S&P Rolls Out New ESG Credit Indicators for Oil and Gas Companies." S&P Global Market Intelligence, November 24. www.spglobal.com.

Sandberg, Joakim, Carmen Juravle, Ted M. Hedesström, and Ian Hamilton. 2009. "The Heterogeneity of Socially Responsible Investment." *Journal of Business Ethics* 87(4): 519–33.

Sargis, Madison, and Patrick Wang. 2024. "How Does Investing in ESG Companies Affect Returns?" Morningstar. www.morningstar.com.

Sawyer, Suzana. 2010. "Human Energy." *Dialectical Anthropology* 34(1): 67–75.

———. 2015. "Crude Contamination: Law, Science, and Indeterminacy in Ecuador and Beyond." In: *Subterranean Estates: Life Worlds of Oil and Gas*, H. Appel, A. Mason, and M. Watts (eds.). Ithaca, NY: Cornell University Press. 126–46.

———. 2022. *The Small Matter of Suing Chevron.* Durham, NC: Duke University Press.

Schnädelbach, Herbert. 1984. *Philosophy in Germany, 1831–1933.* Cambridge: Cambridge University Press.

Schumpeter, Joseph A. 2008 [1942]. *Capitalism, Socialism, and Democracy.* London: Harper Perennial.

———. 2017 [1912]. *Theory of Economic Development.* New York: Routledge.

Scudder, Charles. 2018. "Who Wore It Best? Cowboy Hat Photo Ops Are a Presidential Tradition." *Dallas Morning News*, February 19. www.dallasnews.com.

Shearer, R. C. 2000. "Oil and Gas Lending: The Borrower's Perspective." Paper presented at 26th Annual Earnest E. Smith Oil, Gas, and Mineral Law Institute, University of Texas School of Law, Austin, TX, March.

Sherman, Natalie. 2020. "Oil Collapse: 'Right Now Everything I Have Is Shut Down.'" *BBC*, May 19. www.bbc.co.uk.

Sherrod, Gerald E. 1968. "What Makes Those Bank Engineers So Conservative?" Paper presented at Sixth Annual Meeting of the Society of Petroleum Evaluation Engineers, Houston, TX, November.

Shever, Elana. 2012. *Resources for Reform: Oil and Neoliberalism in Argentina.* Stanford, CA: Stanford University Press.

Simpson, Michael. 2019. "The Annihilation of Time by Space: Pluri-Temporal Strategies of Capitalist Circulation." *Environment and Planning E: Nature and Space* 2(1): 110–28.

Smiley, Kevin T., Ilan Noy, Michael F. Wehner, Dave Frame, Christopher C. Sampson, and Oliver E. J. Wing. 2022. "Social Inequalities in Climate Change–Attributed Impacts of Hurricane Harvey." *Nature Communications* 13. https://doi.org/10.1038/s41467-022-31056-2.

Smith, Adam. 1999a [1776]. *The Wealth of Nations Books IV–V*. New York: Penguin.

———. 1999b [1776]. *The Wealth of Nations Books I–III*. New York: Penguin.

Smith, Jessica M., and Mette M. High. 2017. "Exploring the Anthropology of Energy: Ethnography, Energy, and Ethics." *Energy Research and Social Science* 30(1): 1–6.

Sneath, David, Martin Holbraad, and Morten A. Pedersen. 2009. "Technologies of the Imagination: An Introduction." *Ethnos* 74(1): 5–30.

Sosa, Luis A., and Daniel J. Desnyder. 2003. "Energy Markets, US Energy Policy, and the Terrorist Attacks of 11 September 2001." *Minerals and Energy: Raw Materials Report* 18(3): 14–24.

Souleles, Daniel. 2019. *Songs of Profit, Songs of Loss: Private Equity, Wealth, and Inequality*. Lincoln: University of Nebraska Press.

Sovacool, Benjamin K. 2013. *Energy and Ethics: Justice and the Global Energy Challenge*. Basingstoke, UK: Palgrave Macmillan.

Sovacool, Benjamin K., and Michael H. Dworkin. 2014. *Global Energy Justice: Problems, Principles, and Practices*. Cambridge: Cambridge University Press.

Sovacool, Benjamin K., Raphael J. Heffron, Darren McCauley, and Andreas Goldthau. 2016. "Energy Decisions Reframed as Justice and Ethical Concerns." *Nature: Energy* 1: 16024. https://doi.org/10.1038/nenergy.2016.24.

Spencer, Roy W. 2009. *Climate Confusion: How Global Warming Hysteria Leads to Bad Science, Pandering Politicians, and Misguided Policies That Hurt the Poor*. London: Encounter Books.

St. Louis Federal Reserve. 2023. "Effective Federal Funds Rate." https://fred.stlouisfed.org.

Statista. 2024. "Oil Production Worldwide from 1998 to 2022." July 9. www.statista.com.

Stern, Nicholas. 2007. *The Economics of Climate Change: The Stern Review*. Cambridge: Cambridge University Press.

Stiles, Jo, Judith W. Linsley, and Ellen W. Rienstra. 2002. *Giant under the Hill: A History of the Spindletop Oil Discovery at Beaumont, Texas, in 1901*. Austin: Texas State Historical Association.

Strathern, Marilyn. 1996. "Cutting the Network." *Journal of the Royal Anthropological Institute* 2(3): 517–35.

Strauss, Sarah, Stephanie Rupp, and Thomas Love (eds.). 2016. *Cultures of Energy: Power, Practices, Technologies*. London: Routledge.

Sustainalytics. 2024a. "Company ESG Risk Ratings: Chevron Corp." Morningstar Sustainalytics. www.sustainalytics.com.

———. 2024b. "Company ESG Risk Ratings: Exxon Mobil Corp." Morningstar Sustainalytics. www.sustainalytics.com.

———. 2024c. "Company ESG Risk Ratings: Marathon Oil Corp." Morningstar Sustainalytics. www.sustainalytics.com.

———. 2024d. "2024 ESG Top-Rated Companies: Sustainalytics' List of Companies with the Best ESG Risk Rating Scores." Morningstar Sustainalytics. www.sustainalytics.com.

Svetlova, Ekaterina. 2012. "On the Performative Power of Financial Models." *Economy and Society* 41(3): 418–34.

Taymans, Adrien C. 1951. "Marx's Theory of the Entrepreneur." *American Journal of Economics and Sociology* 11(1): 75–90.

Terry, Lyon F., and Kenneth E. Hill. 1953. "Valuation of Oil and Gas Producing Properties for Loans Purposes." Presented at annual meeting of the petroleum branch, America Institute of Mining and Metallurgical Engineers. Los Angeles, CA, February.

Tett, Gillian. 2022. *Anthro-Vision: How Anthropology Can Explain Business and Life*. London: Penguin.

Texaco. 2022. "About the Company." www.texaco.com.

Texas Almanac. 2022. "History of Oil Discoveries in Texas." www.texasalmanac.com.

TGLO (Texas General Land Office). 2015. "History of Texas Public Lands." www.glo.texas.gov.

Thygesen, Tine. 2019. "Everyone Is Talking about ESG: What Is It and Why Should It Matter to You?" *Forbes*, November 8. www.forbes.com.

Tomlinson, Chris. 2014. *Tomlinson Hill: The Remarkable Story of Two Families Who Share the Tomlinson Name—One White, One Black*. New York: St Martin's Press.

Tripathy, Aneil. 2017. "Translating to Risk: The Legibility of Climate Change and Nature in the Green Bond Market." *Economic Anthropology* 4(2): 239–50.

Turner, Frederick J. 1893. "The Significance of the Frontier in American History." *Annual Report of the American Historical Association* 1(1): 199–227.

———. 1928 [1920]. *The Frontier in American History*. New York: Henry Holt.

Turner, Terence. 2003. "The Beautiful and the Common Inequalities of Value and Revolving Hierarchy among the Kayapo." *Tipiti: Journal of the Society for the Anthropology of Lowland South America* 1(1). https://digitalcommons.trinity.edu.

———. 2008. "Marxian Value Theory: An Anthropological Perspective." *Anthropological Theory* 8(1): 43–56.

UN. 2004. *Who Cares Wins: Connecting Financial Markets to a Changing World*. United Nations & Swiss Federal Department of Foreign Affairs. https://documents.worldbank.org.

UNEP. 2020. *Transforming the Energy System: A Post-COVID-19 Win-Win for People and Planet*. United Nations Environment Programme. www.unep.org.

UNEP-FI. 2005. *A Legal Framework for the Integration of Environmental, Social, and Governance Issues into Institutional Investment*. United Nations Environment Programme Finance Initiative. www.unepfi.org.

US Census. 1891. *Extra Census Bulletin, No. 2*. Washington, DC, April 20. https://archive.org.

USEIA (US Energy Information Administration). 2016. "United States Remains Largest Producer of Petroleum and Natural Gas Hydrocarbons." www.eia.gov.

———. 2018. "United States Remains the World's Top Producer of Petroleum and Natural Gas Hydrocarbons." www.eia.gov.
———. 2021a. "International Energy Outlook." www.eia.gov.
———. 2021b. "Natural Gas Explained: Where Our Natural Gas Comes From." www.eia.gov.
———. 2021c. "What Countries Are the Top Producers and Consumers of Oil?" www.eia.gov.
———. 2022a. "Oil and Petroleum Products Explained: Oil Imports and Exports." www.eia.gov.
———. 2022b. "Units and Calculators Explained: British Thermal Units (Btu)." www.eia.gov.
———. 2023a. "Petroleum and Other Liquids: Cushing, OK WTI Spot Price FOB." www.eia.gov.
———. 2023b. "Natural Gas: Henry Hub Natural Gas Spot Price." www.eia.gov.
———. 2024. "Petroleum and Other Liquids: US Field Production of Crude Oil." www.eia.gov.
Vanguard. 2021. "ESG Screening Approaches: A Primer." https://www.vanguard.co.uk.
Watkins, Katie. 2022. "Nearly 5 Years after Hurricane Harvey, Thousands of Houston Homeowners Are Still Waiting for Assistance—and Might Not Get It." *Houston Public Media*, February 3. www.houstonpublicmedia.org.
WBD. 2021. "ESG: How It Applies to the Oil & Gas Industry and Why It Matters." Womble Bond Dickinson, September 22. www.womblebonddickinson.com.
Weber, Max. 1958 [1905]. *The Protestant Ethic and the Spirit of Capitalism*. Translated by T. Parson. New York: Charles Scribner's Sons.
Weszkalnys, Gisa. 2011. "Cursed Resources, or Articulations of Economic Theory in the Gulf of Guinea." *Economy and Society* 40(3): 345–72.
———. 2015. "Geology, Potentiality, Speculation: On the Indeterminacy of First Oil." *Cultural Anthropology* 30(4): 611–39.
White, Leslie. 1943. "Energy and the Evolution of Culture." *American Anthropologist* 45(3): 335–56.
———. 1967. "The Historical Roots of Our Ecological Crisis." *Science* 155(3767): 1203–7.
Widdershoven, Guy, and Lieke van der Scheer. 2008. "Theory and Methodology of Empirical Ethics: A Pragmatic Hermeneutic Perspective." In: *Empirical Ethics in Psychiatry, International Perspectives in Philosophy and Psychiatry*, G. Widdershoven et al. (eds.). Oxford: Oxford University Press. 23–36.
Wilson, John W. 1985. *The New Venturers: Inside the High-Stakes World of Venture Capital*. Boston: Addison-Wesley.
Wilson, Sheena, Adam Carlson, and Imre Szeman (eds.). 2017. *Petrocultures: Oil, Politics, Culture*. London: McGill-Queen's University Press.
Wilson, Wallace W. 1966 [1962]. *Bank Financing of Oil and Gas Production Payments*. Continental Illinois National Bank and Trust Company of Chicago.
Wood, Caura. 2016. "Inside the Halo Zone: Geology, Finance, and the Corporate Performance of Profit in a Deep Tight Oil Formation." *Economic Anthropology* 3(1): 43–56.

———. 2019. "Orphaned Wells, Oil Assets, and Debt: The Competing Ethics of Value Creation and Care within Petrocapitalist Projects of Return." *Journal of the Royal Anthropological Institute* 25(1): 67–90.

World Bank. 2016. "De-risking in the Financial Sector." www.worldbank.org.

Wright, Charlotte J., and Rebecca A. Gallun. 2008. *Fundamentals of Oil and Gas Accounting*. Tulsa, OK: PennWell.

Wrightstone, Gregory. 2017. *Inconvenient Facts: The Science That Al Gore Doesn't Want You to Know*. Allegheny, PA: Silver Crown Productions.

Wylie, Sara A. 2015. "Securing the Natural Gas Boom: Oil Field Service Companies and Hydraulic Fracturing's Regulatory Exemptions." In: *Subterranean Estates: Life Worlds of Oil and Gas*, H. Appel, A. Mason, and M. Watts (eds.). Ithaca, NY: Cornell University Press. 108–25.

———. 2018. *Fractivism: Corporate Bodies and Chemical Bonds*. London: Duke University Press.

Yanosek, Kassia, Sana Ahmad, and Dionne Abramson. 2019. "How Women Can Help Fill the Oil and Gas Industry's Talent Gap." McKinsey & Company. www.mckinsey.com.

Yearly, Steve. 2006. "How Many 'Ends' of Nature: Making Sociological and Phenomenological Sense of the End of Nature." *Nature and Culture* 1(1). https://doi.org/10.3167/155860706780272006.

Yergin, Daniel. 2009. *The Prize: The Epic Quest for Oil, Money, and Power*. London: Free Press.

Zalik, Anna. 2015. "Vicious Transparency: Contesting Canada's Hydrocarbon Future." In: *Subterranean Estates: Life Worlds of Oil and Gas*, H. Appel, A. Mason, and M. Watts (eds.). Ithaca, NY: Cornell University Press. 354–70.

Zaloom, Caitlin. 2003. "Ambiguous Numbers: Trading Technologies and Interpretation in Financial Markets." *American Ethnologist* 30(2): 258–72.

———. 2004. "The Productive Life of Risk." *Cultural Anthropology* 19(3): 365–91.

———. 2006. *Out of the Pits: Traders and Technology from Chicago to London*. London: University of Chicago Press.

———. 2009. "How to Read the Future: The Yield Curve, Affect, and Financial Prediction." *Public Culture* 21(2): 245–68.

Zuckerman, Gregory. 2014. *The Frackers: The Outrageous Inside Story of the New Billionaire Wildcatters*. London: Penguin.

INDEX

Page numbers in italics indicate figures

abundance, of hydrocarbons, 15
Adventists, 125
affordances, ethical, 48
African Americans, 28, 121, 172n3
agency, human, 125–26
agential capacity, 118
agential independence, 52
agential responsibility, 82
the Alamo, 40, 43, 49
The Alamo (film), 43
Alaska, 16
allegory, 17–18, 32, 37, 88, 103–5, 129; about climate change, 118; energy, 89–92; ESG and, 132, 144, 151, 154; future-gazing, 3, 25, 30, 149; for private equity, 85; time horizons of, 23; value and, 22
American exceptionalism, 45
American masculinity, 43
American Revolution, 46
American-way-of-life, 25, 55, 110, 113, 149
American West, 44
AnaOil, 86
Anglo-American migration, 42
Anthropocene, 120
anthropogenic climate change, 13, 23, 88, 108, 129, 153
anthropology: of ethics, 5; of risk, 23
antihydrocarbon ESG arguments, 140
antitobacco divestment movement, 140
Appadurai, Arjun, 77–78
Appel, Hannah, 103
arbitrage, 22

Archer, Matthew, 135
argument for oil, *145,* 145–51
Arizona, 38
Ashworth, Aaron, 172n3
assetization, of hydrocarbons, 96
Austin, Stephen, 39

Babel, myth of, 114
banking, 79
Banking on Words, 90
banks: Bank of England, 20; Chase National Bank, 93; commercial, 62; First National Bank, 93; state, 41
Baptist, Edward E., 39
Barnett Shale, 10
Bear, Laura, 91
Begim, Ainur, 135
Black and Scholes (B&S), 87, 91, 175n2
BlackRock, 146, 147, 178n5
Black-Scholes-Merton options pricing theory, 92
Blackstone, 75
Bloomberg ESG, 135
BNP Paribus, 134
booms, 99, 127, 142; cotton, 40; in hydrocarbon production, 12; oil, 31, 46, 60, 83, 164–65; postwar, 44; shale revolution and, 102
Boyer, Dominic, 14, 120, 122, 172n9
BP, 61, 152
Britain, 13
British thermal units (Btu), 175n15

197

Broome, John, 116
Bryant, Rebecca, 24
B&S. *See* Black and Scholes
Btu. *See* British thermal units
"build back greener," 161
Burrough, Bryan, 39, 43, 44, 49
Bush, George H. W., 45
Bush, George W., 45, 173n5
busts, 77, 99–100, 102, 127, 142, 160

California, 38
capital, 22, 33, 73, 154, 162; carbon, 164–68; debt, 40, 63; decarbonization of, 88, 104; flows of, 90; hydrocarbon, 103–5; investment, 60; investor, 142; unconventional time in oil, 9–12, 12. *See also* venture capital
Capital Fund XI, 76
capitalism, 22, 79–80, 82, 88, 114, 156; evolutionary process of, 53; global corporate, 133; hydrocarbon, 25; industrial, 14; Marx on, 19; petrocapitalism, 14; Texas and, 36
capital value creation, 23
Capital X, 67
carbon, 5, 168; emissions, 137; high- and low- investments, 104
carbon capital, 164–68
carbon capture and storage (CCS), 149–50
Carbon Democracy (Mitchell, T.), 3
carbon dioxide (CO2), 107, 111, 119
carbon footprint, 152
Carlson, Adam, 15
Carlyle, 145–46
Carney, Mark, 20
carried interest, 63
cattle, 38–43, 173n5
cattlemen, 45
causal responsibility, 117
CCS. *See* carbon capture and storage
Census Bulletin, US (1891), 173n6
Chase National Bank, 93
Chesapeake, 138

Chevron, 51, 61, 137
Christianity, 123–28; cosmology, 4; Judeo-Christianity, 108, 114, 129
circular temporality, of investment, 99
civilization, 47
Civil War, US (1861–1865), 42, 49, 172n2
Clark, Bernard, 9, 93, 171n2, 174n7
class mobility, 47
climate alarmists, 176n4
climate change, 2–3, 8, 25, 31–32, 105–6, 110–23, 147, 150; anthropogenic, 13, 23, 88, 108, 129, 153; climate alarmists and, 176n4; as crisis of the future, 128–30; faith in God and, 123–28; institutional investors and, 159; as intergenerational conflict, 107; mitigation, 104. *See also specific topics*
Climate Confusion (Spencer), 176n4
climate control, 115
climate protests, 159
CO2. *See* carbon dioxide
coal, 13
coal ash waste, 138
Colorado, 66, 84
commercial banks, 62
commodity traders, 24
Compromise of 1850, 41
Congress, US, 41
Conoco Phillips, 72
"conquering," 114
Continental, 70
conventional extraction, 12
conventional wells, 61
corporate gifting, 136, 153–57
corporate raiders, 63
corporate social responsibility (CSR), 132, 134, 136
cosmology, 4
cotton, 38–43, 172n2
COVID-19 pandemic, 32, 153, 160–61
"cowboy phase," 74
cowboys, 37, 43, 53, 55, 173n6, 173n12; culture, 42, 45, 167; financial, 83–85;

frontiers and, 45–48; oilmen and, 48–51; sensibilities, 143
creative destruction, 53
credit, 22, 90
Crockett, Davy, 35, 172n1
Cross, Jamie, 136
crude oil, 12, 42, 82
CSR. *See* corporate social responsibility
Cullen, Ezekiel Wimberly, 49, 50, 51
Cullen, Hugh Roy, 36–37, 44, 48–49, 165
culture, 38; cowboy, 42, 45, 167; evolution of, 14; independence, 51; oil, 43; petrocultural norms, 164; petrocultures, 14; Texas, 54–56; thermodynamics and, 171n7

Dallas, Texas, 9
Davey Crockett (television series), 43
DCF. *See* discounted cash flow
Dean, James, 44
debt capital, 40, 63
decarbonization, of capital, 88, 104
democracy, 46
derisking, 75–76, 77–80
descriptive analytical approach, 8
Devon Energy, 10, 69, 70
discounted cash flow (DCF), 89, 93–94, 97
discounting, 93
Disney, Walt, 43
distilled life, 100–101
divine intervention, 127–28
Dobroski, Sonja, 46
Don Draper (fictional character, *Mad Men*), 1
dot.com bubble, 72
Drakeman, Donald, 79
Duke Energy, 138
Duke University, 111
Dumont, Louis, 172n12

EBITDTA, 32, 92, 95, 99, 100, 150
Eccles, Robert, 133
economic analysis, 86

economic growth, 112
Economy of Words, 90
empowerment, 171n8
EnCap, 62, 76, 161, 175n18
"energopower," 120
energy allegories, 89–92
energy demand, 3
energy ethics, 5, 29
energy financialization, 10
energy justice, 8
energy shortages, 33
energy transition, 107, 110, 139, 146
Enlightenment, 114
Enron, 10, 11, 58, 70, 72, 127
"entrepreneurial spirit," 51–54, 59
entrepreneurship, 52, 59
environment, 14, 120, 137
Environmental, Social, and Governance (ESG), 4, 32, 130, 131, 152, 166; allegory and, 132, 144, 151, 154; argument for oil and, 145, 145–51; corporate gifting and, 153–57; institutional investors and, 132, 135, 144–45, 154; new corporate ethical registers of, 133–39, 135, 138; tobacco and, 139–45
EOG Resources, 70, 138
E&P. *See* exploration and production
Epstein, Alex, 107–8, 111–15, 120, 126, 176n4
equity, 64. *See also* private equity
Ernst & Young, 64
ESG. *See* Environmental, Social, and Governance
Esso, 113
ethical affordances, 48
ethics: energy, 5, 29; meta-ethics, 171n3; Protestant, 125; research, 27; value and, 21. *See also specific topics*
European immigration, 45
European Union (EU), 29
evaluation, 21
evolution of culture, 14
exchange value, 19

experts, 17, 167, 172n9
exploration and production (E&P), 60–62, 75, 78, 103
exploration plays, 65
externalities, 136
ExxonMobil, 28, 51, 61, 69, 137, 153
Exxon Valdez, 2

Fancy, Tariq, 146
FCF. *See* free cash flow
Federal Reserve, 73
finance, as political, 7
financial cowboys, 83–85
financial imaginaries, 89–92
financialization, 22; of corporate gift, 153–57; energy, 10
First National Bank, 93
Fisher, Irving, 93
the flood, biblical story of, 128
Forbes (magazine), 132
forecasting, 16
Fortune (magazine), 44
fossil fuels, 32, 114; *The Moral Case for Fossil Fuels,* 107, 111, 120, 126; transition away from, 110
fracking. *See* unconventional extraction
free cash flow (FCF), 95, 99
freedom, 113; frontier, 51; oil and gas industry and, 2
"Fridays for Future" protests, 148
Friedman, Milton, 140
Frondizi, Risieri, 172n11
frontier, 173n6, 173n9; cowboys and, 45–48; freedoms, 51; settler-frontier, 35, 37, 43, 45–48, 54
The Frontier in American History (Turner, F.), 46
funds, 58–59
future, climate change as crisis of the, 128–30
future cash potential, 89
future energy imaginaries, 103
future-gazing allegories, 3, 25, 30, 149

future monetary value, 22
future-oriented practices, 23
future price forecasts, 97
future price risks, 16
future profitability, 102

Gardiner, Stephen, 117
general partner (GP), 63
Genesis, Book of, 114
GFC. *See* global financial crisis of 2008–2009
GHG. *See* greenhouse gas
Giant (film), 44
Gibbs, Ewan, 129
gifting, corporate, 136, 153–57
global corporate capitalism, 133
global financial crisis of 2008–2009 (GFC), 75, 102
God, 114, 123–28
Goldman Sachs, 20
GP. *See* general partner
Graeber, David, 19, 20
Graham, Lindsay, 106
"green" commitments, 142
greenhouse gas (GHG), 116
Gulf of Mexico, 86
Gulf Oil Company, 50
Guyer, Jane, 113

Haggard, Merle, 110
Hawley, Frederick, 77, 80
Hayward, Tim, 117
High, Mette, 5, 26, 65, 66, 143n13
high-carbon investments, 104
Ho, Karen, 7, 63, 174n1
Hobbes, Thomas, 172n11
Holbraad, Martin, 91
Holmes, Doug, 90, 91
homelessness, 124
hostile takeovers, 63
Houston, Sam, 38
Houston, Texas, 9–10, 11, 12, 26–27, 30
Houston Chronicle (newspaper), 121

INDEX | 201

Houston Country Club, 126
Houston Oil Finance Association, 101, 139
Houston Petroleum Club, 127, 162, 163
HSBC, 134
Huber, Matthew, 85, 112–13
Hughes, Howard, 48
Hulme, Mike, 114
human agency, 125–26
Humble Oil, 50, 51
Hume, David, 172n11
The Hunger Games (movies), 119, 129
Hunt, H. L., 44, 50, 173n4
Hunt Oil Company, 50
Hurricane Harvey, 121–22, 127, 177n7, 177n11
Hurricane Katrina, 9
hydrocarbon capital, 103–5
hydrocarbon capitalism, 25
hydrocarbon industry. *See specific topics*
hydrocarbon potentiality, 89
hydrocarbons, 5. *See also specific topics*
hydrogen, 5
hypocrisy, 124

imagination, 47, 89, 91, 101
immigration, European, 45
immorality, of hydrocarbon industry, 4
imperialism, Victorian, 114
Inconvenient Facts (app), 107, *109*, 111
Inconvenient Facts (Wrightstone), 111
independence culture, 51
Independent Petroleum Association of America (IPAA), 139
Independents Chesapeake, 70
indigenous peoples, 7
individualism, 46
industrial capitalism, 14
industrial development, 41
industrialization, 13, 42, 45
infant mortality, 4
initial public offering (IPO), 174n11
injustice: settler-colonial, 7; social, 132
institutional investors, 71, 81, 83, 143; climate change and, 159; dot.com bubble for, 72; ESG and, 132, 135, 144–45, 154; GFC and, 75, 102; private equity for, 58, 60, 73
interest, 65, 75; carried, 63; discounting and, 93; rates of, 72, 93
intergenerational conflict, climate change as, 107
Intergovernmental Panel on Climate Change (IPCC), 128
internal rate of return (IRR), 94, 97, 100
investment, 22; circular temporality of, 99; high-carbon, 104; low-carbon, 104; ROI, 95, 153; "sin," 145; SRI, 132, 134, 136. *See also* institutional investors
investment capital, 60
"investment-grade" exploration, 120
investor capital, 142
"the invisible hand," 117
IPAA. *See* Independent Petroleum Association of America
IPCC. *See* Intergovernmental Panel on Climate Change
IPO. *See* initial public offering
IRR. *See* internal rate of return
Irvine, Richard, 100

Japan, 24, 80
Jensen, Michael, 95
Judeo-Christianity, 108, 114, 129
junk bonds, 63, 174n10
justice, 117–18; energy, 8; injustice, 7, 132

Keane, Webb, 47–48
Kenedy, Mifflin, 172n3
King, Richard, 172n3
Kirby, John Henry, 48
KKR. *See* Kohlberg, Kravis, and Roberts
Kluckhohn, Clyde, 172n12
Knight, Daniel, 24, 129
Knight, Frank, 77–78
Kohlberg, Kravis, and Roberts (KKR), 175n12
Kramer, Mark, 178n7

labor theory of value, 18
Laidlaw, James, 5, 24, 82
Lambek, Michael, 19
land reform, 40
Langley, Paul, 4, 104
Leins, Stefan, 90, 134
lending, 22
leveraged buyouts, 63, 174n10
liability, 24
libertarianism, 54, 108
Life (magazine), 44
lifeblood metaphor, 85
limited partners (LP), 63
linear temporality, of investment, 99
loans: agreements, 64; reserve-based, 62, 93; short-term, 93
long-term value, 154
Lotze, Hermann, 19
Louisiana, 9, 40, 55, 84
Love, Clara, 42
low-carbon investments, 104
low interest rates, 72
LP. *See* limited partners

MacKenzie, Donald, 92
Mad Men (TV series), 1
mainstreaming, of ESG, 166
Malinowski, Bronislaw, 19
Malone, John, 95
management fees, 63
market fundamentalism, 152
Marx, Karl, 19, 171n5
masculinity, 45; American, 43; rugged, 173n12
Mason, Arthur, 16, 103, 172n9
mastery, of nature, 115
Maurer, Bill, 91
McClendon, Aubrey, 70
McCloskey, Deirdre, 91
McKibben, Bill, 111
Memorial Day Flood (2015), 177n11
meritocracy, 7
Merrill, Karen R., 44

meta-ethics, 171n3
Methodists, 125
Mexican landowners, 172n3
Mexico, 36, 38–39
MGM, 43
migration: Anglo-American, 42; settler, 39
mineral rights, 40
Mitchell, George, 69, 70
Mitchell, Timothy, 3, 129
Mitchell Energy and Development Corporation, 10, 69, 78, 79
Miyazaki, Hirokazu, 24, 80, 125
modernity, 129
Montana, 42
Mood, Fulmer, 46
Moody's, 135
Moore, Jacqueline, 42, 43, 172n3, 173n6
The Moral Case for Fossil Fuels (Epstein), 107, 111, 120, 126
moral claims, 22
moral relativism, 8, 166
Morgan Stanley, 134
MSCI, 139
multistage fracking, 70, 84
Muniesa, Fabian, 23, 89
Munn, Nancy, 172n12
Murchison, Clint, 44

Nader, Laura, 14–15, 16
Nasdaq composite index, 175n16
Native Americans, 47
natural gas, 12, 76, 148; prices, 72; shale rock and, 69
natural gas partners (NGP), 62
nature, 114–15
Nebraska, 42
net present value (NPV), 89, 93–94, 100, 116
net zero emissions, 153
New Mexico, 38
New Orleans, Louisiana, 9, 40
NGOs. *See* nongovernmental organizations
NGP. *See* natural gas partners
"nonfinancial information," 133

nongovernmental organizations (NGOs), 133, 151
nonwhite workers, 28
Nordhaus, William, 116
normative analytical approach, 8
norms: petrocultural, 164; well-established, 38
NPV. *See* net present value

Occidental Petroleum, 10, 138, 153
Offering Memorandum, 174n8
oil and gas industry. *See specific topics*
Oil and Gas Investor (magazine), 75
oil booms, 31, 46, 60, 83, 164–65
oil capital, unconventional time in, 9–12, *12*
oil culture, 43
oil demand, 110
oil deposits, quality of, 58
oilmen, 17, 31, 35, 43–44, 48–51, 69, 143
oil potentiality, 77–80
oil prices, 32, 72, 160
oil rush, 43
Oklahoma, 55
OPEC, 15, 44, 75
Oraiopoulos, Nektarios, 79
orphaned oil wells, 172n10
Ortiz, Horacio, 7, 21, 22
overdrilling, 77
Özden-Schilling, Canay, 54–55

Papua New Guinea, 20
PDPs. *See* percent developed and producing
Pedersen, Morten A., 91
pension plans, 144
percent developed and producing (PDPs), 68, 102
performance fees, 63
Perm Region, of Russia, 133
petrocapitalism, 14
petrocultural norms, 164
petrocultures, 14
petrofutures, 14
petroleum, 76

Pfitzer, Marc, 178n7
Pfizer, 79
pharmaceutical industry, 79
"political elites," 119
post-COVID recovery, 153
postwar boom, 44
potentiality, of oil, 77–80
poverty, 4
power, 2, 87, 110, 171n8
PPM. *See* Private Placement Memorandum
present value 10 (PV10), 96–98, *97, 98*
price decks, 96–98, *97, 98*
private equity, 64–67, 69, 76, 81, 83, 143, 162–63; allegory for, 85; exit strategy for, 62; funds for, 59; for institutional investors, 58, 60, 73; shale revolution and, 31, 60; Souleles on, 7, 20–21; venture capital and, 63, 84, 165
Private Placement Memorandum (PPM), 174n8
production risk, 175n19
profitability, 65, 104; future, 102
proppants, 174n1
Protestant ethics, 125
"proven but undeveloped" drilling prospects (PUDs), 10, 68, 74, 102
public lands, 36, 40
PUDs. *See* "proven but undeveloped" drilling prospects
Puritan asceticism, 14
PV10. *See* present value 10

Quintana Petroleum, 50

racism, 50
rags-to-riches, 44, 49–50
Rajak, Dinah, 133
Rand, Ayn, 54
rate of return (ROR), 95
Reagan, Ronald, 44–45
realism, 149
"redomaining," 78
renewable energy transition, 110

Republic of Texas, 36
research ethics, 27
reserve-based loans, 62, 93
responsibility, 18–26, 30, 118, 140, 165, 167; agential, 82; causal, 117; CSR, 132, 134, 136; risk taking and, 80–83; SRI, 132, 134, 136
return on investment (ROI), 95, 153
Ricardo, David, 19
Richardson, Sid, 44
"rightness," 5, 88, 91, 123
risk, 18–26, 30–31, 116, 132, 135, 165, 167, 172n14; anthropology of, 23; derisking, 75–76, 77–80; future-oriented practices and, 23; future price, 16; production, 175n19; taking, 60, 80–83
risk-return matrix, 66
Robbins, Joel, 19
Rogers, Douglas, 15, 133
ROI. *See* return on investment
Roman Catholicism, 123
Romney, Mitt, 106
ROR. *See* rate of return
rugged masculinity, 173n12
Russell, Henry, 173n4
Russia, 12, 32, 133, 153, 160

Saudi Arabia, 12
scarcity, of time, 15
Schumpeter, Joseph, 53–54, 143n14
SEC. *See* Security and Exchange Commission
Second World War, 44
Security and Exchange Commission (SEC), 64, 96
seismic mapping, 79
self-reliance, 54
settler-colonial injustices, against indigenous peoples, 7
settler-colonialism, 45, 46, 165
settler-frontier, 35, 37, 43, 45–48, 54
settler migration, to Texas, 39
shale revolution, 10, 57–59, 70–76, 88, 103, 159, 163–64; booms and, 102; derisking and, 77–80; financial cowboys and, 83–85; "golden ticket" of, 65–69, 66; "oxygen" of industry and, 60–65; private equity and, 31, 60; risk taking and, 80–83
shareholder value, 7, 149
Shell, 61, 113, 126, 152
short-term loans, 93
"sin" investments, 145
sin stocks, 133
slavery, 39–40, 172n3
"slick-water frack" method, 69
Smith, Adam, 13–14, 18–19, 22
Smith, Jessica, 5
Sneath, David, 91
social injustice, 132
socially responsible investing (SRI), 132, 134, 136
social movements, 140
social values, 18, 21, 134, 155, 156
Souleles, Daniel, 7, 20–21, 63, 83
Spain, 38–39, 42
Spencer, Roy, 176n4
S&P Global, 135, 137, 177n3
Spindletop gusher, 9, 42, 48, 50
SRI. *See* socially responsible investing
Stanford, Jason, 39, 43
state banks, 41
state flag, of Texas, 38
State Street, 147
Steinsberger, Nick, 69
stereotypes, 37
Stern, Nicholas, 116
Stories of Capitalism, 90
Strathern, Marilyn, 136
"studying up," 14–15
Sustainalytics, 135, 153
Szeman, Imre, 15

Tax Day Flood (2016), 177n11
techno-realism, 113
temporality, 99. *See also* time
TEV. *See* total enterprise value

Texaco. *See* Texas Fuel Company
Texas, 30, 35, 37; capitalism and, 36; cotton, war, and cattle in, 38–43; culture, 54–56; "entrepreneurial spirit" of, 51–54, 59; Houston, 9–10, *11*, 12, 26–27, 30; settler migration to, 39; Spindletop gusher, 9, 42, 48, 50; state flag of, 38; University of Texas, 36, 58; war of independence of, 38, 40, 43, 49; WTI, 160
Texas Fuel Company (Texaco), 50, 51
Texas Revolution (1835–1836), 38
thermodynamics, 171n7
Thunberg, Greta, 148
Thygesen, Tyne, 131
time, 19–26, 165, 167; in oil capital, 9–12, *12*; scarcity of, 15; transitional, 13–18; value and, 22
time horizons, 23, 99–100
time value of money, 94
tobacco, 139–45
Tomlinson, Chris, 39, 43, 172n2
Total, 153
total enterprise value (TEV), 95
transitional times, 13–18
tropical storms, 122
Trump, Donald, 27
Turner, Frederick Jackson, 45–46
Turner, Terence, 172n12

Ukraine, 32, 153, 160
uncertainty, 23, 116–17, 154
unconventional extraction (fracking), 9, 12, 30, 55, 67–68, 76; multistage fracking, 70, 84; "slick-water frack" method, 69
UN Environmental Program Finance Initiative's Freshfields Report (UNEP-FI 2005), 134
United Kingdom, 160
United Nations, 134
University of Texas, 36, 58
urban expansion, 45

valuation, 21
value, 18–26, 79, 88, 165, 167, 172n12; allegory and, 22; exchange, 19; future monetary, 22; labor theory of, 18; long-term, 154; NPV, 89, 93–94, 100, 116; PV10, 96–98, *97, 98*; shareholder, 149; TEV, 95; time and, 22; time value of money, 94
value creation, 18, 23, 60, 69, 89, 151
values, social, 18, 22, 134, 155, 156
Vardy, Mark, 122
venture capital: leverage buyout and, 174n10; private equity and, 63, 84, 165; real estate, 60, 74
Viagra, 79
Victorian imperialism, 114

war, 38–43
war of independence, of Texas, 38, 40, 43, 49
Warren, Elizabeth, 144
Wayne, John, 43
The Wealth of Nations (Smith, A.), 13, 18
Weber, Max, 13
West, Jim, 48
West Texas Intermediate (WTI), 160
Weszkalnys, Gisa, 78
White, Leslie, 14, 15, 171n7, 177n5
Who Cares Wins (2004 United Nations report), 134
wilderness, 46–47
Wilson, Sheena, 15
Witherspoon, John, 173n9
women, 28
Wood, Caura, 16, 23, 25, 78, 83, 89, 172n10
World War II, 44
Wrightstone, Gregory, 111
"wrongness," 5, 88, 91
WTI. *See* West Texas Intermediate

Zaloom, Caitlin, 24–25, 97
zoning bylaws, 177n7
Zuckerman, Gregory, 70

ABOUT THE AUTHOR

SEAN FIELD is Senior Research Fellow in the Department of Social Anthropology and the Director of Policy at the Centre for Energy Ethics at the University of St Andrews, Scotland. He leads the Financial Pathways theme of the multiyear Scottish Research Alliance for Energy, Homes and Livelihoods, funded by the Scottish Funding Council.

www.ingramcontent.com/pod-product-compliance
Lightning Source LLC
Chambersburg PA
CBHW031149020426
42333CB00013B/583